Making Animal Quilts:
Patterns and Projects

Making Animal Quilts:
Patterns and Projects

Willow Ann Soltow

Good Books

Intercourse, Pennsylvania 17534

Acknowledgments

Design by Craig Heisey

We wish to give special thanks to the Pennsylvania Farm Museum, Lancaster, Pennsylvania, whose artifacts appear in the opening section of this book.

The front and back cover projects were designed by the author: on the front—"The Animal Tree" (see page 26, Project 1); on the back—"Bear in the Woods" (see page 52, Project 9, Variation 1).

Photograph Credits

Cover photos: Jonathan Charles
Photos of artifacts: Kenneth Pellman

Making Animal Quilts: Patterns and Projects
Copyright © 1986 by Good Books, Intercourse, PA 17534
International Standard Book Number: 0-934672-39-3
Library of Congress Catalog Card Number: 86-81231

For my grandmother, Helen Winona Martin,
without whose advice,
my first quilt might have been my last.

Table of Contents

Animals in Folk Art		6
Discovering Designs		10
Getting Started		18
Project 1	**The Animal Tree**	26
Project 2	**The Folk Tree**	30
Project 3	**Animal Town**	34
Project 4	**Seal Mother and Baby**	37
Project 5	**Hummingbird and Flowers**	40
Project 6	**Gulls on the Water**	42
Project 7	**Wolves and the Rising Moon**	46
Project 8	**Down on the Farm**	49
Project 9	**Night in the Forest**	52
Project 10	**Noah's Ark**	54
Project 11	**Out of Africa**	57
Project 12	**Animals at Our House**	60
Project 13	**Animal Alphabet**	62
Project 14	**Fox and Geese**	64
Project 15	**Cats and Mice**	66
Project 16	**Flying Geese**	68
Project 17	**The Pond**	70
Project 18	**La Paloma**	74
Project 19	**The Shore**	76
Project 20	**Ideas and More Ideas**	78
Template Diagrams		81
Readings and Sources		189
Index		191

Animals in Folk Art

Have you ever had difficulty following directions? Well, welcome to **Making Animal Quilts**! Here you will constantly be encouraged NOT to follow the directions!

As you look through these pages, you'll find 20 basic projects each with up to five variations. You can follow the basic project directions if you like. Or you can follow the directions for one of the variations. Or you can combine ideas from several different variations to come up with a project that is uniquely your own creation. That's what is meant by NOT following the directions.

Making Animal Quilts is designed to allow your creative energy to flow, without leaving you high and dry when it comes to planning details.

The World of Animals

Animals share our world. For many of us, well-loved animals also share our lives and our homes. A few of the lucky ones even share our quilts, selecting, perhaps, a corner of a cozy, quilt-covered bed as their own private domain. For those of us who love animals and love quilting, it's only natural to want to combine our interests.

The desire to portray animals, as well as other elements from our daily lives, in our quilts is rooted in the American quilting tradition. For generations, pioneer women relied on creative needlework as one of the few socially acceptable outlets by which to express themselves.

Many of these women designed beautiful pieced and appliqued quilts. A few particularly ambitious ones created exquisite, one-of-a-kind quilts that were more than needlecraft; they were pictures executed in fabric. In these picture quilts, early American quilters portrayed that which was dearest to them—animals, people, flowers, a home, a church or a village. Many of these unique picture quilts featured animal motifs or elaborate scenes in which domestic and wild creatures played a part.

This book regards an animal quilt as any appliqued or pictorial quilt that emphasizes animal motifs. It is not necessarily a quilt that portrays animals to the exclusion of all else—it is the quilt about which we can say, when we come away from it, that we remember the animals best of all. Human animals have always been fascinated with the non-human co-habitants of our world. Likewise, many of us are drawn to quilts that portray the creatures with whom we share the earth.

Picture quilts and animal quilts were never more popular than during the 19th century. Some animal quilts were crib quilts. Others were crazy quilts, with animal shapes appliqued or embroidered onto random fabric patches. Still others were executed as more formal designs with calico animal motifs arranged on white muslin backgrounds.

Animals and People

Animal quilts are special not only because they are fun to make, but because they hint of a simpler way of life. They are reminiscent of a time when the daily lives of people and animals were more closely intertwined. Few children today (few adults, for that matter) have ever actually seen the cow that produced the milk they drink or the hen that laid their morning eggs. In contrast, animals played an important role in the day-to-day activities of most nineteenth-century Americans.

In Vermont, for instance, in the late 1800s, 75 percent of the land was used for farming and only 25 percent was wooded. Most of these farms were owned and run by one family. They included a complement of animals hand-raised by the people themselves. Today the above figures are reversed.[1]

The small, one-family farm has to struggle just to survive in a world of large agricultural conglomerates. With "factory farming" and intensive animal husbandry at an all-time high, there are not fewer animals—just fewer animals to be seen. But the lifestyle of most rural nineteenth-century Americans fairly revolved around animals they saw each day.

As a result, animals were popular subjects in folk art, the everyday art of everyday people. Animal shapes were incorporated into weather vanes, toys, tools and decorations of all kinds. Stencils of birds and butterflies decorated walls, floors and furniture. Carved animals adorned canes and walking sticks. In the kitchen, animal shapes formed pot lids and spoon handles, cookie cutters, candy molds and baking molds. In addition, countless animal designs were hand-drawn and sewn into quilts and coverlets of all types and sizes.

Today, country fashions and folk-art styles are enjoying an unparalleled revival. Many of the motifs used in creating contemporary country-style fashions and furnishings are animal motifs—stylized birds, cats or cows, among others. All these designs have their roots in the American folk art tradition.

Folk Art

Not long ago, primitive paintings, weathervanes, samplers, quilts, wood carvings, and other creative outpourings of folk culture were not regarded as art. At best they were looked upon as historically interesting artifacts; at worst, mere dust-catchers. Today, however, such pieces are highly prized by discriminating collectors.

There is a spirit embodied by American folk art which, according to many veteran collectors, is largely responsible for its popularity. American folk art objects are sturdy, unpretentious, simple, and original. They represent, in their humble way, many of the ideals on which this country was founded.

One of the appealing qualities of folk art lies in its blissful ignorance of the formal traditions of fine art. Folk art emphasizes pleasing designs, rather than optical tricks used to instill a sense of realism. As often as not, folk art is also utilitarian. Its decorative and functional aspects are frequently inseparable. It is as impossible to ignore the warmth-giving qualities of a treasured family quilt as it is to overlook its lovingly hand-sewn intricacies of color and design.

The creators of yesterday's quilts and other American folk art objects believed, for the most part, in a characteristic American spirit. Their belief was not just an abstract ideal. It was a way of life. This belief was eloquently expressed by Thomas Jefferson when he wrote to his daughter admonishing her to be diligent in studying her Latin:

It is a part of the American character to consider nothing as desperate; to surmount every difficulty. . . . In Europe there are shops for every want; its inhabitants, therefore, have no idea that their wants can be supplied otherwise. Remote from all other aid, we are obliged to invent and to execute; to find means within ourselves, and not lean on others. Consider, therefore, the conquering your Livy as an exercise in the habit of surmounting difficulties; a habit which will be necessary to you in the country where you are to live and without which you will be . . . less esteemed.[2]

In keeping with the need to "find means within" themselves, the creators of American folk art also created a unique style. The women who made original animal quilts overcame the difficulty of drawing and patterning their designs without the help of formal art training. Many of them would have protested that they "couldn't draw a straight line." But they did not let that stop them from executing their own personal fabric pictures. Today, we can create folk-art style quilts and crafts by drawing upon some of the same appealing animal motifs which they used. We can continue the tradition they began.

A Little History Lesson

There was a time when Americans bought and used factory-made goods as enthusiastically as we purchase and display handmade articles today. But from that time to this, quilts have always stood out as something special.

Making quilts with animal themes was not uncommon for our quilting ancestors. Even patchwork or "pieced work" patterns featured animal names or called to mind ideas relating to animals. The geometric perfection of such pieced designs as The Lobster, Duck's Foot in the Mud, or Flying Geese reflects a tribute not only to the women who made them, but to the beauty and intrinsic worth of the animals themselves. In addition, some adventuresome needle-craftswomen created unique appliqued picture quilts featuring nearly every creature imaginable.

In early America, quilts were a necessity. The discomfort of a New England colonial home in winter can scarcely be imagined today. Puritan forefather Cotton Mather observed "a great Fire, that the juices forced out at the end of short billets of wood by the heat of the flame in which they were laid, yet, froze into Ice on their coming out."[3] Layers of sturdy quilts afforded some protection against the frigid conditions.

Quilts were important enough to be named in wills and personal inventories and were often described in loving detail. But the round of daily chores left little time for fancy stitching and applique work. As far as we know, most quilts from this period were probably simply pieced from scraps.

As each generation moved farther west, rural pioneer life fostered indigenous styles of living and creating. Patches were shamelessly applied to worn clothes and worn quilts alike. In cities back East, however, increasing numbers of women found themselves with a little more leisure for fancy needlework. Some of the earliest examples of animal quilts took the form of a technique known as Broderie Perse. Animals, leaves, flowers and other motifs from printed fabrics were cut out and appliqued in a new design, often onto a white background. Removing the printed animals, birds, and flowers from their original background permitted the needleworker to open up and reorganize a printed design. In addition, the technique allowed frugal colonial women to make the most of small, expensive pieces of printed chintz. As printed cottons became cheaper and more readily available, Broderie Perse coverlets became more and more a thing of the past.

Gradually, in the mid-1700s, life in the American colonies began to attain a measure of stability and comfort. Although successive generations continued to push farther west, women in more settled areas were no longer necessarily obliged to "make do." There was sufficient time and availability of supplies for women to give free rein to their needle talents. Frugal, pieced work, which wasted nothing, gave way more and more often to intricate applique work, which was somewhat wasteful of fabric.

With improved availability of fabric and the leisure to create, came the impetus for more imaginative work, including the development of countless animal designs in all areas of needlework. Sometimes animal motifs represented real animals. At other times, animals became symbols of various virtues like patriotism, loyalty and strength.

The Revolution and events leading up to it inspired patriotic feelings and unprecedented pride in homemade articles. In revolt against England's restrictive trade acts, colonial merchants refused to purchase English goods. The result was that domestic goods became a fashionable symbol of patriotism. Animals of the New World became popular in all the needle arts.

Shaping the home environment held an importance for early American women which contemporary Americans can scarcely appreciate today. In an age in which a woman could not vote, could not own property, and in which childbirth and sudden death represented an ever-present threat, quilt-making held special significance. It provided a creative outlet, a chance to make unchallenged choices, and relaxation without guilt, for quilts were a necessity.

A move across country left many pioneer women alone in unfamiliar surroundings, cut off from other women and from their men, a long work day away in the fields. Small wonder that animals found their way into the quilts and needlework objects of so many wives and their daughters. Coping with day-to-day loneliness, many women must have appreciated the company provided by family pets and farm animals.

If the 19th century brought with it a flowering of American quilting, it heralded, as well, the heyday of the making of pictorial animal quilts. Quilts depicting animal motifs were never more popular than during this period. The animals that inspired their creation were a regular feature of typical family-run farms. "My very first memory," observed one Kansas pioneer, "is of chasing a pet duck about on a sunny hillside, the 'quack, quack' with which he would elude my outstretched hands when I pursued him, and then the happy way he would come and settle himself in my lap or by my side at other times. I have thought of that duck many times in later years. . . ."[4]

The fabric pictures of animals which many women sewed into their quilts during this time are a quiet tribute to the many different creatures they found all around them.

Some of the animal quilts from this period represent virtual catalogs of farm and forest activity. Every domestic animal made an appearance in the quilt art of the day, from dogs and cats, to horses, sheep, pigs, goats, cows, chickens, and ducks. Wild animals were also represented. Moose, deer, foxes, beavers, rabbits, bears, birds, mice, and insects were portrayed. Occasionally, exotic animals showed up in the needlework of the times. Such creatures as ostriches, giraffes, tropical birds, tigers, lions, and elephants appear in a number of heirloom quilts, indicating to modern observers that a circus may at one time have passed through the quilter's town.

For many women, quilts provided a means of expressing strong religious commitment. A number of religious themes inspired the creation of quilts and other forms of needlework depicting animal subjects like Noah's Ark, The Peaceable Kingdom, and The Garden of Eden.

The Noah's Ark theme, in particular, was the inspiration for many enchanting crib quilts. Traditionally animal quilts held a special appeal for children. Loving mothers and grandmothers sewed appealing animal crib quilts to delight their youngsters, and in some cases, to instruct them as well. Animal picture quilts encouraged young children to identify the animals and sometimes also to count them.

Gradually, the art of quilting changed as new fashions came into vogue. The Victorian age ushered in "crazy quilts," patched from swatches of costly fabrics and painstakingly decorated with lace and embroidery. Reliable fabrics—solid cottons and calicos, whose tight weave facilitated intricate applique work—were set aside in favor of fussier materials during this period of crazy quilt mania.

With the Victorian Era, too, came the dawning of social reform and the animal welfare movement, with advocates like Henry Bergh and George Angell protesting cruelty to animals and children.

Kindness to animals began to be seen more popularly as a moral issue. Needleworkers responded consciously or unconsciously by sewing numerous animal motifs into their quilts and coverlets. Crazy quilts were often decorated with various animals including birds, dogs, cats, horses and other creatures, domestic and wild. These were often appliqued and/or embroidered onto colorful, random scraps of rich velvet, satin and brocade. Amazingly popular in its day, the crazy quilt "craze" extended well into the turn of the century.

In time, the Depression brought a revival of old-time cotton fabric work in pieced and appliqued quilt designs. WPA craft-training projects aroused national interest in quilt-making and collecting. Applique animal quilts enjoyed a quiet revival although their popularity did not approach that of our own day.

Today, with the renewed emphasis on country styles, modern animal quilts are as fashionable and intriguing as ever. Interestingly, the arguments in favor of quilt-making too, are much the same as they were generations ago. Dwindling energy resources underline the practical aspect of quilt-making. Creative hand-sewing continues to give us needed time for reflection in a hectic modern world, while still making ourselves useful.

Contemporary quilt-makers have more resources at their fingertips than ever before. We can draw upon two centuries of creative animal quilts in making our own unique designs. We also have a wealth of traditional folk art motifs and modern graphic art styles to inspire us. We can take our choice of old or new designs and use them to create contemporary fabric pictures that express ourselves and the world we share with animals.

Discovering Designs

In Search of the Animals

Like "water, water, everywhere. . . ," the animals are all around us, yet may seem, at times, out of our grasp. Many of us have no difficulty visualizing the finished design we want to achieve in a quilt. But executing that design—drawing the animals from scratch and combining them successfully—is sometimes another story.

Some people might argue that you can't teach folk art or American country design styles. After all, it is that personal, untaught quality that makes

folk art and "country" what they are.

Like every folk art object, every quilt is also unique. Each quilt or quilted wall hanging in which you give something of yourself reflects a little bit of you—and that makes it one-of-a-kind. You can trace the animal designs that are provided in this book. You can even combine them in some of the ways suggested later, but your creation will be uniquely yours.

Begin with one of the projects outlined in this book. Or start by tracing some of the animal pat-

terns and combining them in your own personal way to make a quilt or a smaller project. The animal patterns are meant to provide you with a basis for designing your very own animal motifs.

As you make use of the projects and patterns, keep in mind that the project diagrams are approximate renditions only. The exact sizes of the animal patterns in relation to each other may differ slightly from what is portrayed. (Your own sewing habits may influence the sizes of the animals somewhat, but enough leeway has been built into the projects that this should not present a problem.) All yardage requirements given are for 44″ wide fabric.

You may find it helpful to start an animal picture collection of your own for ideas and inspiration. For instance, you may want to create a wall hanging that shows a particular breed of dog representing a loved pet. Or you might discover a need for an animal subject in a different position from that included in the pattern section. Don't be afraid to experiment! Try designing your own animals and the motifs needed to complement them in various picture scenes.

If you need help getting started, there are many sources for animal designs with an old-time feel to them. Folk art animals are waiting to be rediscovered by quilters in books at the local library, and in collections at museums, historical societies, antique

shops and flea markets. And they don't all reside in the form of quilts. The flat, unshaded animal motifs needed for quilting can be found in a variety of places other than needlework. You just have to know where to look.

Quilting and Two-Dimensional Folk Art

The following section offers different resources for designing, creating and combining your own animal patterns. You might want to experiment with some of the various mediums discussed to give yourself practice in working with the two-dimensional quilted image. Or take a look through some of the resources listed in the bibliography just to help build your appreciation of the wide variety of animal motifs that have made an appearance down through the years. Either way, you'll enjoy seeing the world through a quilter's eye.

For the most part, the animal designs which we have come to think of as folk art are two-dimensional. They have length and breadth but no depth. The flat quality of these designs makes them perfect for quilting. They can be represented in pure color, with no need to portray light and dark shadows.

We perceive our world three-dimensionally, as did our ancestors. In the days before photography, however, early Americans were more accustomed to seeing the two-dimensional motif than we are today. The women who created antique animal quilts had plenty of inspiration for making the flat, two-dimensional animal cutouts needed for quilting. It was easy for them to transform the real animals they saw into stylized quilting motifs.

Today our sense of imagery is dominated by the three-dimensional photographic image which we see in magazines, on television, in books and newspapers. These things define for us how designs are "supposed" to look. In order to learn how to transform what we see into the two-dimensional designs needed for quilting, we have to learn to "see" the world all over again. We have to learn to see it as our ancestors did—with an eye to two-dimensionality.

The old-time quilters had much to inspire them in creating flat quilting motifs. Many of them practiced the then popular pastimes of silhouette and papyrotamia or paper-cutting art. They found the two-dimensional folk art image all around them in various household objects. Nearly every barn was topped by a bold, black weather vane, often styled to represent an animal. Two-dimensional animal images were incorporated into carved signs, kitchen utensils, farm tools, grave markers, furniture and children's toys. Creative women copied these designs, cut them from fabric scraps and sewed them into one-of-a-kind animal quilts. The strong, stylized silhouette motifs that made their needlework so exciting are still with us today just waiting to be rediscovered.

Silhouettes

Reviving the decorative two-dimensional motif is really not a new idea. Commercial designers and graphic artists have been doing it for years. Business logos and international signs frequently feature silhouette images because of their incisive, message-carrying qualities. Artists like Matisse and Picasso experimented with silhouette and folk art images as a means of revitalizing their own expressive idioms.

Largely relegated to the specializing craftsperson today, silhouette art was once practiced by people from all walks of life.

Silhouettes received their name from an eighteenth-century French finance minister who made cut paper portraits as a hobby. They were, for early Americans, an art form, a practical memento of loved ones and an enjoyable pastime. Instead of taking a snapshot, Colonial housewives recorded the profiles of their children in a piece of unfolded cut paper. Many self-sufficient, American families were of limited means, and found the paper silhouette an attractive, inexpensive form of portraiture.

Professional silhouette cutters, along with their colleagues, the limners and portrait painters, took the place of the modern professional photographer in recording family likenesses. Traveling silhouettists found a ready market for their craft. Often they boarded with the family whose paper portraits they were hired to produce.

William Henry Brown was a famous American silhouettist of the early 19th century. While most silhouette artists supported themselves by cutting likenesses of people, he produced elaborate scenes of daily life as well. Brown was famous for his cuttings of ships, trains and village scenes—some of which included animals.

The designs of William Henry Brown and his contemporaries can still be enjoyed in books of silhouette art today. For a time, around the turn of the century, silhouettes were also a fairly common embellishment in children's literature. Old children's books may provide you with some unexpected animal shapes and designs as you collect animal motifs to inspire your own needle art.

Paper-cutting Arts

Closely related to silhouette-making was the craft of fancy paper-cutting. Among colonial New Englanders, it was known by the glamorous name of "papyrotamia" from the word for the earliest form of paper, Egyptian papyrus or reed paper. Elaborate cut-out scenes included various kinds of animals: wild, domestic and exotic, as well as people, flowers, trees and symbols. Papyrotamia was popular with professional and amateur artisans alike.

Paper was a treasured commodity in early America and was treated with deference. It was carefully folded in half, the design drawn and then cut with scissors, producing intricate mirror-image designs.

Similarly, "scissors cuttings" or Scherenschnitte was performed by the Pennsylvania Germans. This folk art was originally brought to this country by Swiss and German peoples fleeing religious persecution. Mennonites, Schwenkfelders and Moravians, among others, unconsciously disseminated their craft traditions in the new homeland. Scherenschnitte, like its New England counterpart, was the technique of cutting one piece of paper in an intricate design, although the paper itself was often folded up to three times.

During the 18th century, exquisite scissors cuttings with religious themes were popular. Many included animals as a matter of course. Hand-cut decorations adorned birth and marriage certificates as well as other legal documents. Carefully cut designs were often mounted, framed and hung in the home. Many were enhanced with earthy, muted wa-

tercolors: yellow ochre, brick red, teal blue, and warm, nut brown. Elaborate valentines were also cut and exchanged between friends and courting couples. Traditional valentine images included doves and other animals, as well as hearts, flowers and twining foliage.

Simpler Scherenschnitte designs were routinely used to decorate the home. In contrast to the more formal scissors cuttings, simple, lively cut-paper designs were used as doilies, and decorative shelf and mantle coverings. They were designed to be used, and as they became soiled, to be discarded and replaced.

Frugal housewives saved all papers of useful size including newspapers and shopkeepers' wrapping papers. Children could be entertained on a rainy day by cutting out whimsical animal shapes from their fathers' old ledgers or bits of newsprint. Examples of such early childrens' art nearly always bear telltale faded ink writing on one or both sides. Gradually, even simple antique paper cuttings were recognized as valuable folk art objects, too intriguing to be thrown away. Today the oldest examples may be found in exhibitions and private collections.

Scherenschnitte animal designs can provide quilters with a helpful source of flat, one color motifs. You might want to try cutting some designs of your own just for practice. (A sharp, pointed surgical scissors works best.) Cutting out your animal subjects in paper first can also be a helpful pre-design activity when planning a new quilt or wall hanging.

Stencils

Eighteenth- and nineteenth-century homes were adorned with a multitude of personal folk art touches which we seldom see today outside museums. Faced with the social limitations of the age, women with artistic yearnings usually settled for a domestic life and turned to decorative arts as a means of brightening their homes and their lives. One such method of decoration closely related to the paper-cutting arts was that of stencilling or theorem painting.

Stencils or theorems were cut paper patterns that could be painted over with a blunt brush, producing the cut-out image on paper, fabric or wood. Some theorem paintings consisted of solid color shapes stencilled in, with shading added later. Despite the shading, these basic shapes, with their crisp outlines, suggest many uses as individual quilt motifs.

Following the Revolution, patterned wallpapers imported from Europe became the rage among well-to-do Americans. The fancy wallpapers were prohibitively expensive, however, for most rural families. Yankee ingenuity responded with a more economical procedure—that of stencilling bright, colorful patterns directly on plaster or wood walls. Although fruits, flowers and geometric shapes predominated, animal stencils were also used. A number of them have survived in historic homes and museums, occasionally revealed under successive layers of wallpaper. These include songbirds, ducks and geese, butterflies, and the distinctive horse and rider.

Stencils, like country fashions in general, are currently enjoying a strong revival. Country style stencils of animals, birds, and insects can provide a resource of bold, stylized design for imaginative quilters. Often the stencils themselves may be purchased at quilt and craft stores. Plastic Mylar® cutouts are useful for both stencilling and pattern purposes. Books of traditional stencils and antique theorems are also helpful idea-makers.

Weather Vanes

Many antique picture quilts include animal motifs that suggest the same designs the village blacksmith once used in making weather vanes. For modern quilters, the old-time vanes can supply a host of expressive ideas.

The early American weather vane did more than announce the direction of the wind. Whether it was a cow vane atop a farmer's barn, a fish vane on a whaling village roof, or a fanciful winged Pegasus perched on a colonial mansion, the weather vane told a story of its owner and its maker. Many vanes were created by professional blacksmiths. Others were made by self-sufficient farmers who cut or carved their vanes from left-over scraps of sheet iron or wood—occasionally resulting in some unorthodox-looking animal shapes.

Weather vanes have been used in many countries down through the ages from their first recorded use in ancient Greece. In colonial America, however, they took on new and exciting design characteristics. The sharp outlines of a rooster weather vane against a bright sky must have prompted Pablo Picasso to observe: "Cocks have always been seen, but never as well as in American weather vanes."[5]

The early American weather vane was more than decorative. It was an important tool with respect to the agricultural and sea-faring lifestyles of the colonies. In addition, national pride in our new country fostered some unusual animal symbols of patriotism—all of which eventually appeared in weather vane form. The eagle, a symbol of ancient Rome, was in keeping with the classical fervor of colonial America. As the new nation looked to the Roman republic, rather than to traditional monarchy as its mentor, the eagle quickly found itself the emblem of democracy. The choice of a national bird rested with the bald eagle, believed then to be indigenous only to America. In no time at all, this magnificent raptor developed into a well-loved subject for weather vane crafters, as well as other folk artists and needleworkers.

In addition, the unlikely rattlesnake, a patriotic motif in the New World, inspired numerous graceful, coiling snake vanes. A horse with rider was also popular and patriotic—particularly when the rider was intended to represent General George Washington.

By 1800, life in America was largely centered around agriculture. Farmers chose farm-related animal subjects for their barn and homestead roofs—among them, cocks, horses, pigs, cows, oxen, goats and sheep.

Weather vanes found in New England whaling and fishing villages often suggested the sea-faring life. Animal vanes from these towns included codfish, swordfish, dolphins, whales and seahorses. In some areas, vanes representing wild and exotic animals were also displayed. Some of the more popular examples included deer, elephants, butterflies, squirrels and marsh birds.

Even the simplest weather vane displays a purity of line which modern artists might envy. Folk art weather vane crafters did not consciously work with well-defined aesthetic principles in mind. Yet the vanes they produced reveal a sensitivity to design that makes them appealing to a modern audience. The satisfying contours of a silhouetted whale, a galloping horse, or an eagle in flight readily lend themselves to successful quilt images.

Cookie Cutters and Kitchen Tools

Around the turn of the 19th century in America, sheet tin was cheap and plentiful. Itinerant tinsmiths traveled from town to town seeking work. Like other craftspeople, the tinsmith would visit a household and remain for a few days to make whatever implements and utensils the family required—lanterns, candle molds, funnels and more.

Early Americans wasted nothing. The scraps which resulted from the tinsmith's labors were worked into pleasing shapes and soldered to tin backs to make cookie cutters. A few holes in the back allowed the dough to be released easily. With a handle attached, the cookie cutter was complete.

Many families boasted from one to four dozen cutters accumulated over the years. From one holiday to the next these were strung together on a length of twine and hung in the attic. Animal

shapes, more than any others, were always popular.

Antique cookie cutters depict elephants, birds, dogs, deer, horses, fish and rabbits. Less easy to find are cats, pigs, bears, turtles and squirrels. Sometimes a tinsmith was called upon to design a cutter in the shape of an animal he had never even seen— a tiger, or a camel perhaps.

With nearly all food prepared at home by the women of the house, countless implements were devised to ease the drudgery of kitchen chores. Fanciful animal shapes were incorporated into cookie cutters as well as other utensils to add a decorative touch. If early American housewives spent more time in the kitchen than their modern counterparts, at least they were surrounded by cheerful, attractive tools with which to accomplish their tasks.

The images of everyday life were celebrated in uniquely shaped handles for spoons, spatulas and knives. Pot lids were adorned with easily-gripped stylized birds. Intricately carved wooden pastry prints were devised to leave their raised impressions of animal shapes on cookies, candies and cakes.

Traditional and modern cookie cutters are a good source for animal cutouts. Browse at your local kitchen store for unusual animal cutters. In addition, quilters will find two-dimensional animal motifs in books featuring examples of antique utensils of all kinds.

Children's Toys

The folk art revival is by no means limited to adults and the things that appeal primarily to them. Many animal toys continue today to be designed in primitive two-dimensional format as they were in years past. The simplicity of a wooden Noah's Ark set, an animal pull-toy, or a primitive antique rocking horse may provide you with any number of successful country-style quilting motifs. Children's plastic template farm animals, developed to stimulate creative play on the part of primary students, can play a dual role by offering design ideas for quilt-making adults as well.

Keep on the lookout for other animal motif idea-makers like calico cats (overstuffed with fragrant leaves and spices), whirligigs (old-fashioned wind toys, often based on simple, flat animal shapes) and wooden animals that come as part of village, farm or zoo toy collections. All of these items hold hidden design possibilities for ambitious makers of animal quilts.

Graphic Symbols

The letters of our alphabet are so much a part of our twentieth-century lifestyle that we take them for granted. But they are really a form of graphic symbol.

There are several kinds of graphic symbols. Some are abstract like the letters of the alphabet and have no visual connection with the idea they represent. Some are image related and share a limited relationship with the concept they convey—like double, wavy lines used to indicate water. Still other symbols are pictorial or "iconic," providing a simple, yet complete visual form of an object or thought. All of these are being used more and more by quilters, as needleworkers explore new levels of expression through their artistic medium.

Centuries ago, pictorial symbols enabled a largely illiterate populace to locate different establishments. A stranger might have relied on an animal symbol like a red lion to locate an inn of that name.

Today, pictorial animal symbols are used in graphic art and advertising to symbolize many ideas. Reduced to their most informative elements, they are appealing and successful attention-getters. Pets are used to suggest hominess. Farm animals might announce healthful products. Exotic animals often advertise travel to foreign lands. Modern animal symbols are rapidly forming a kind of universal language.

You might want to start an animal graphics collection as a resource for quilting designs. Try looking for animal silhouettes in newspapers and magazine ads, on notecards, fabric, and packaging materials. You'll be surprised at the many different animals that are turned up by even a casual search. One of them may be just the animal motif you are looking for.

Matisse Cutouts

Much of artist Henri Matisse's work reveals a concern with two-dimensional representation. In his later years, too ill to stand at his easel and paint, he turned to the medium of paper cutouts. He did so partly out of physical necessity, partly to satisfy a need to achieve a new simplicity in his work. His cutouts included birds, snails, fish, monkeys and other natural forms, many of which can provide quilters with ideas for imaginative animal patterns.

Earlier in his career, Matisse had used the paper cutout as a humble tool to aid him in designing paintings and large frescoes. The sophisticated cutouts of his final years were characterized by exuberance, simplicity and brilliant color. They reflect a celebration of life, energy and love of nature. It is appropriate that quilters find inspiration in the work of this French artist, since he was himself influenced greatly by decorative textile arts. Egyptian and African appliques decorated the walls of his studios and left their mark upon his designs. Many of his larger cut paper works are actually suggestive of symmetrical, applique block quilts.

Matisse's cutouts are a testament to the combined use of expressive color and simple, dynamic design. They allowed him to perfect the exciting, flowing movement of natural forms in action. They also serve as a personal tribute to the artist who, though bed-ridden, refused to succumb to self-pity. Matisse was active in his art to the last day of his life and managed, because of his physical handicap, to find a medium that has since become popular with artists around the world. Examples of his cutouts can be found in many museums. They are also reproduced in books on works of his art—particularly those that feature the works of his later years.

Like so many quilts created by generations of women, the Matisse cutout compositions are meaningful for the warm, peaceful, human values which they convey. At the age of 39, Matisse explained what he was trying to capture in his art:

> *What I dream of is an art of balance, of purity and serenity, devoid of troubling or depressing subject matter, an art which could be for every mental worker, for the business man as well as for the man of letters, for example, a soothing, calming influence on the mind. . . .*[6]

Forty-three years later, his ideal remained virtually unchanged: "I believe my role is to provide calm. Because I myself have need of peace."[7] His observations speak eloquently to those of us who strive to create a "peaceable kingdom" of our own through our quilt art and our lives.

Creating Your Own Designs

Your animal motifs can be combined in many different ways. You'll find that often it is the way in which motifs are arranged, and not the motifs themselves, that provides for a satisfying design.

Block quilts provide the quilter with several options. A single motif can be repeated block by block. Or a number of motifs can be repeated in different groupings. Blocks connected by strips of solid cotton or calico can help to unify many separate animal motifs into one complete design. Motifs with a similar theme can be grouped into a creative block pattern: farm animals, animals from the Bible or songbirds from your own garden, for instance.

Another alternative is to place motifs randomly on a single background fabric. If you opt for this plan, you might want to break the background into separate blocks to be quilted and eventually sewn together. The end result is still an unbroken color field, yet is much easier to manipulate than a single, large piece of fabric.

You might want to combine your appliqued ani-

mal motifs with patchwork. Individual motifs can alternate with patchwork blocks to make a striking sampler quilt. Appliqued designs can be used to enhance a large patchwork centerpiece. Or just the reverse. A patchwork border may be just the thing to set off an uncomplicated appliqued center. Small silhouetted animals can function nicely as corner designs to break up the routine of a patchwork border. You may also decide to adapt your animal motifs into a unique border pattern, complimenting a traditional central design.

Fabric Pictures

Animal motifs can be used to create simple, yet striking fabric "paintings." Placing motifs in a specific context is the key. Rolling green fabric "hills" can work as the backdrop for animal or nature motifs.

In planning a fabric picture, you may want to concentrate on an animal theme that holds special meaning for you, like endangered species, the wildlife in your backyard or animals encountered in a favorite vacation spot, for example.

Try juxtaposing different widths of blues and greens to create the effect of waves on the sea. Add animal motifs with an ocean theme: porpoises, whales, fish, shells. Varying widths of brown and

orange fabric, on the other hand, can give the sense of autumn fields. House and farm motifs can be added to farm animal or wild animal motifs to create an original fabric picture. Such abstract backgrounds can provide a successful, recognizable context for animal patterns. But be sure that color contrast is maintained to allow the animals to stand out.

Original Designs

In experimenting with your own designs and motifs, concentrate on simplicity. Simple forms and combinations make the most successful quilts. Look through a magazine and think about how various photographed objects would appear in silhouetted form. Cut out animal shapes from magazines or from colored paper and combine them in ways that seem interesting to you. Experiment with combining shapes in lines, in groups, or randomly. Lights and darks create contrast and add interest. Remember, discovering a favorite animal motif or theme is not enough. Individual motifs have to be combined creatively in order to establish a satisfying quilt design.

Contrast

There are many facets of successful quilt-making.

Choosing or creating an imaginative pattern, using a pleasing color combination and carefully crafting the stitches that go into a quilt are all part of the process. One key to making a successful quilt, however, is frequently overlooked. That feature is contrast. Maintaining a high contrast between background and motif fabric is one of the unspoken rules of good quilt design.

Some of the simplest traditional patterns demonstrate what careful attention to contrast values can do. It is no accident that so many traditional appliqued designs are always executed in color on a white background. However uninspired this may sound in the telling, the actual result is always bold and striking—and the reason is contrast.

Contrast literally means "to stand against." When two elements of a design contrast, each points to the difference in the other. Often, it is the difference between two facets of a design (such as colored motif and muslin background) and not the design elements themselves, that grabs the eye and holds attention.

Heightened color contrast is the principle ingredient in making a successful silhouetted motif. Combining light and dark colors within a single hue yields successful results. A dark blue motif on a light blue background, a cranberry motif on pink are examples. Warm colors and cool colors make each other stand out well. Contrasting colors of the same intensity can also give good results. A deep red animal motif on royal blue or a dark green motif on

gold make for eye-catching color combinations.

Contrast is an important tool in good over-all design as well. When you combine elements of pieced work with appliqued animal motifs, that is a kind of contrast. Some of the most prized heirloom patchwork quilts used small applique elements to enhance large-scale pieced work. Sometimes, skillful quilters used small animal appliques to soften the boldness of pieced geometric designs.

Juxtaposing prints and solids can offer another kind of contrast. Solid color animal appliques work well on calico backgrounds. The tiny print calicos have a tendency to merge into one another, to create an "impressionistic" background landscape effect.

In fabric pictures, contrast of perspective allows for some outstanding design possibilities. Up to now, our emphasis has been on two-dimensional animal motifs. These can be combined with printed three-dimensional fabric images to create interesting and offbeat designs. Fabrics displaying printed three-dimensional designs are easy to find. The print might portray a person, animal, place or object. This motif can be carefully cut out and appliqued. Combined with flat, animal cutouts, the three-dimensional elements confuse the eye and are good attention-getters. Mixing two perspectives in a single work lends a dreamy, fanciful quality to the finished piece. One perspective can even be used to symbolize a real world object, while the other suggests an imagined realm of dreams or memories.

Getting Started

Styles of Working

There are many different ways to construct a quilt. The important thing is to find the method that works for you. You can work spontaneously, or you can work from a carefully organized plan.

Many people prefer to plan their designs on a small scale, trying out many different possibilities and discarding those that are less successful. The final choice can then be worked out by a transfer-grid process. To do this, you must work out your design in grid square form (whether the final piece will be completed in actual blocks or not). Work in a comparable scale—one inch to one foot, for instance. Then, square by square, recreate your design. Make paper templates based on your hand-drawn grid plan. The grid outlines will guide you in recreating your shapes accurately.

If you find yourself with a free wall and the means to tack up your background fabric so that it is flat, secure, and free from wrinkles, you can work in a design-as-you-go method. You might plan your design in a cursory way or work straight from your mind's eye. Cut and pin your animal cut-outs as you go, changing their positions in the overall picture as you find it necessary.

While mapping out your design, look ahead to the final stages of its completion. If you are making a large quilt, you may want to take advantage of the option of quilting it by sections. However, some designs are not easily handled by this method. If you like to take your sewing wherever you go, you will

want to plan a design that can be quilted separately and all units sewn together at the very end. If you choose to do that, plan your quilt so that the seams between the separate sections form part of the overall design.

Estimating Size

There is no set rule for sizing a wall hanging or a quilt. The best rule for wall hangings is to have a planned wall space in mind when mapping out your design.

Beds come in all different sizes and new sizes become fashionable every decade or so. The best gauge is to measure for the bed for which the quilt is to be made. To do this, drape a sheet over the bed and take your measurements from it. This allows you to estimate the length of quilt needed to cover the pillows and the foot end, and the width needed for overhang. Some people like a quilt to hang a few inches over the edge of the bed and others let it drape nearly to floor level. Decide what length best suits you.

Choosing Fabric

Tightly woven cottons and cotton blends are the easiest fabrics to work with and create pleasing results. Heavier fabrics like velvet and corduroy are good for larger projects. Be careful in mixing heavy and light fabrics, as heavier ones tend to pull lighter weaves out of shape. Synthetics and loosely woven materials are particularly difficult to handle.

Test all fabrics for color fastness by washing before sewing them into your quilt.

Templates

Make templates by tracing individual patterns onto tracing paper first and from there, onto cardboard, oaktag or sandpaper. Sandpaper works especially well since its gritty side clings gently to fabric without slipping as you use the template.

When making templates from the patterns offered here, trace the lighter outer line of each animal. This will give you a thin edge for turning under your applique as you attach it to the background fabric. If you're an experienced pro, of course, you can instead trace from the thick inner line and choose for yourself, as you cut, how much or how little fabric you want to later turn under.

Sprightly animal motifs can also be created by cutting freehand. (Take a look at some of the paper cutouts of Henri Matisse, as discussed earlier, to get a feel for the exceptional quality of freehand cuttings.)

Bright origami or construction paper cutouts can be useful planning tools. In planning for color, re-member to distribute light and dark colors so that they appear evenly over the entire project area.

Estimating Fabric

Unless your quilt will be made entirely from fabric scraps, you will want to estimate how much yardage is required. First cut out all templates for your project and be sure you know how many of each motif you will need. Then determine how many times each template (with its seam allowances) can be laid across the width of the cloth. Fabric is usually 36″ or 45″ in width.

For instance, if your fabric is 36″ wide and your template roughly 3″ × 4″, divide 36 by 4 (the larger of the two motif dimensions) to get 9. Your template will fit across the width of the fabric 9 times.

To get the total length of fabric required, divide the number of motifs you will need by the number of times the template will fit across the width of the fabric and multiply the result by the largest width of the template. For example, if you know you need 36 motifs and that your template is 3″ × 4″, it will fit across the width of the fabric 9 times (as above). You will need 4 such widths to yield 36 motifs. Four 4″ widths comes to 16 inches. So you would need a 16″ length of fabric 36″ wide for this particular motif. Since it is best to allow a little extra, you should plan for 18″ or one-half yard of fabric. You can also estimate borders and connecting strips in a similar manner.

Basic Sewing Techniques

To begin sewing your animal quilt, you will use basic applique techniques. After drafting your design and making templates, you will have to cut out your animal patterns and other motifs. Iron all your material, including scraps, before you begin transferring designs onto fabric. Draw your designs on the wrong side of the fabric. Use a pencil to draw around designs on light-colored fabric; use white dressmaker's chalk or white colored pencil on dark fabrics. Be sure to allow ¼ inch on all sides of your design (indicated by the lighter outer lines on the templates in this book) so that you can turn the raw edges under (or use as a seam allowance on patterns to be pieced).

Cut out your animals and other motifs carefully to ensure correct size and shape. As each motif is cut, be sure to clip all in-turning angles and concave curves to keep the outline of the applique from stretching as its edge is turned under. Follow the clip lines as indicated on the patterns in the book and be sure to clip accordingly when devising your own patterns.

Now you are ready to position your appliques

on the background fabric. When you pin the motifs in place, be sure not to pin them too close to the edge of the background fabric. Note the finished size of your project and make sure all motifs lie well within edges that will be trimmed. You are now ready to applique.

The applique stitch is done by hand-sewing short tight stitches. The stitches are hidden underneath the appliqued pieces with only a tiny section of each stitch showing on top where the stitches hold the applied piece of fabric to the background. The thread used should always match the color of the piece being appliqued. As you stitch, turn under with your thumb and forefinger the ¼″ raw outer edge of each appliqued piece.

When appliqueing by hand, turn under the raw edge of the appliqued patch while sewing it with short, tight, partially hidden stitches onto the background fabric.

Beginners may want to baste under the ¼″ raw outer edge before appliqueing the patch to the background fabric. If you plan to remove the basting stitches later, use thread of a contrasting color and be sure the knot of the thread is on top so the thread can be easily removed. If you use blind basting stitches, be sure the thread matches the appliqued patch fabric color.

When sewing together decorative areas of pieced work, be sure to measure and trace the patterns accurately. A little carelessness can be disastrous to the crisp, geometric look of finished pieced work. Match the seams carefully as you sew. Take time to check the right side of your work often, as you sew along the pencil lines marked on the wrong side of your fabric shapes.

Machine Applique

Most modern sewing machines can produce var-ious decorative embroidery stitches. Machine applique has the advantage of being quick and particularly sturdy. It can also provide many creative possibilities. Machine-sewing is generally faster than hand-sewing but not always easier.

First, baste under the ¼ inch outer edge of each piece to be appliqued. You can choose to baste patches loosely in a contrasting color from your fabric for easy removal later. Again, be sure the knot of your thread is on the outside so you can pull it out when you want to. You may decide to use blind basting stitches and leave them in. Use tiny stitches on the top side and longer ones on the reverse side of the patches. If you do not plan to sew removable stitches, use thread that matches your patches exactly.

When your edges are turned under, tack the pieces into place on the background fabric. Then use a straight stitch or decorative zigzag stitch to attach them securely. You might also opt for a satin stitch, in which case you need not turn under the raw edges of the motif. Take the threads to the back when beginning and ending a line of stitching, rather than using a back stitch.

Borders

Many traditional appliqued quilts were based on a central motif design with a wide, fairly elaborate border. Today's modern fabric pictures break all rules and you may want to dispense with a border altogether. A thin binding of wide, cotton hem facing will finish off your quilt easily and attractively. If, however, you decide to include a border, you have a number of options.

A simple pieced border can be made to contrast successfully with your animal appliques. Pieced triangles, squares or diamonds create a pleasing complement to a central design. A complicated center, however, is too busy to sustain the strong bold rhythm created by a geometric border. In this case, a border should probably be eliminated, or a simple, solid color border planned. A good border enhances and reflects the central body of a quilt and never overshadows the rest of the design. In determining size, remember that too narrow a border will make the central part of your design stand out too strongly. A border that is too wide will overpower the rest of the quilt.

Some traditional possibilities for applique borders include curving vines, swags and bows, or an easy, repeated motif like hearts, moons, stars or single leaves. The border may also echo an animal motif that already appears in the central design.

If you decide on a patchwork border, cut and

piece the patches together. Sew them in long rows to the length that you want the border to be. For an appliqued border, cut, pin in place, turn under, and applique your border motifs just as you did the animal cutouts earlier. Remember to leave at least ½ inch extra on all sides to make binding your quilt easier.

Depending on your design, border corners may have to be completed after all blocks and strips have been attached to the quilt top. To create a continuous border design, you may have to adapt your pattern at the corners. You might want to miter the edges of the border, joining them at an angle like on a picture frame (see "Binding" section, page 25). A corner motif can be sewn over the mitered seam after all pieces have been joined. Or you can join the borders at the sides.

Setting

If you are working in blocks, lay the finished pieces on the bed to get an idea of how they look together. If you have sewn your blocks randomly, according to color and shape, this is the time to decide in what order you want them to fall. Alternate your blocks so that lights and darks are balanced throughout.

Whether you are working in blocks, in larger units, or on a single over-all pattern, take the time to determine how close your design comes to the original plan. You may find that your pieces do not cover the entire area of the bed. This can be overcome by adding strips of colored or patterned fabric between the blocks or by using a wider border. If, on the other hand, the design is larger than you had intended, you may want to use a wider seam in sewing the blocks together. Just watch that your seams do not intersect the appliques.

You can join your quilt blocks by hand or on a machine. Allow a ¼ inch seam between all blocks and strips. You may want to join the pieces into four, five, or six large, workable units rather than one finished quilt top to enable you to quilt each unit separately and more conveniently.

Quilting

When your quilt top is fully sewn with borders added, you are ready to do the actual quilting. Quilting is simply the process of joining together all three layers of your quilt—top, lining and backing. Light-colored thread is frequently used on light fabrics and dark thread on darker toned fabrics.

You can use contrasting quilting thread, such as dark thread on light fabric, or you can match quilt-ing thread to applique patches to create "invisible" quilt stitches. Invisible quilting is useful in some designs where the stitches would steal attention away from the central motif.

Arrange the backing of the quilt on the floor or some other spacious work area. Place the backing right side down. Next, arrange the lining on top of the wrong side of the backing. Traditionally, many different materials have been used as quilt fillers or linings, among them, cotton, wool, flannel, down, kapok, felt and rags.

Polyester batting is lightweight and warm. It does not mat together (like cotton) or shift (like loose fillers). It is also easy to wash. For a quilt that is to undergo relatively hard, everyday use this is an important consideration. Quilts with wool fillers should not be washed and those with cotton batting cleaned only with great care. Both laundry machines and dry cleaning equipment can wear on quilt stitches. Quilts should be subjected to washing and/or dry cleaning infrequently.

Polyester batting comes in wide lengths in high and low loft varieties. If you want a thin, low-relief coverlet, you may want to use low loft or "traditional" batting. High loft batting will give your quilt a puffy, airy look. Lay the batting evenly over the backing fabric. Do not overlap lengths of batting or leave any gaps. Let batting extend beyond the edge of the backing at least two inches.

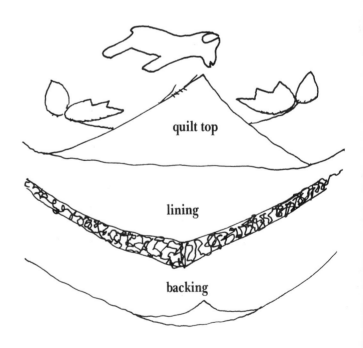

Quilting is the joining together of all three layers of a quilt—its top, lining (or batting), and backing.

Next, lay the finished quilt top on the batting/ backing. Be sure the edges are even all around and carefully match corner to corner. Baste all three layers together to keep them in place as you quilt. Use quilt basting or soft sculpture needles. These are long needles, like the kind used in tapestry making, but with a sharp point, and are available at most quilt shops. Baste in diagonal lines from the center to each corner, and to the middle of each of the four side edges. Use thread that contrasts as sharply as possible with your over-all design to allow for easy removal later.

The above directions hold true for those who are quilting wall hangings or who choose to quilt in large units and sew the units together at the very end. Treat each unit separately, laying out backing, batting and top, and pinning or basting to hold the three layers in place.

Quilting Hoops and Frames

When all three layers of your full-size or wall quilt have been basted, you are ready to begin quilting. If you are quilting the entire design at once, you can use either a large quilting hoop or a frame. If you are quilting separate units to be joined together later, a smaller hoop may be the answer. Quilting hoops come in various sizes, from 24 to 14 inches in diameter. Frames can be large or small, depending on how much space is available. They are usually free-standing.

If you are using a frame, attach the sides of the quilt to the side bars of the frame. The frame should hold the layers taut but not pull or stretch them. Some needle-craftswomen roll both ends of the material and begin quilting in the center. Depending on the size of the frame and how many people are working on it at once, you may also choose to begin quilting on one end.

If you are quilting with a hoop, lay the fixed circle of the hoop on the floor, place the quilt layers over it, and fit the adjustable circle over the fixed one, pulling one section of the material taut. Begin quilting in the center and work outward when using a hoop. A hoop tends to pull the fabric more tightly than a frame, so allow for this when adjusting the tautness of your quilt layers.

Beginning to Quilt

To quilt, you will need "betweens," quilting needles that are shorter than conventional sharps, thread, scissors and a thimble or thumb guard. Adhesive tape provides satisfactory protection. A commercial finger guard allows you to feel the presence of the needle without being pricked by it. Coating the thread with beeswax keeps it from becoming tangled as you sew.

You can do your hand quilting by one of two methods. A very fine running stitch is accomplished by first holding the needle at an acute angle and then bringing it up near the point of entry. Before long, you will have learned to take several stitches before drawing the needle away from the material.

Another method of quilting is done by taking two separate stitches, one down and the other up, with one hand kept beneath the quilt to receive the needle. This approach is more time-consuming, but unfailingly accurate and especially useful when quilting on heavy materials.

Your quilting stitches should be as tiny as possible. An inch of quilting should ideally contain between five and nine stitches. No more than four to six square inches of quilt should be left unquilted.

Ideally, the knot of your quilting thread should pass through the bottom layer of fabric and become lost in the batting. If you have trouble with this, you can make an invisible knot by passing your thread through the bottom layer, and leaving up to an inch of thread beneath the fabric. Make a loop and knot it. Make a second loop, knot it and you are ready to begin your quilting stitches. To finish a line of thread, make one or two back stitches, run the thread through the batting and cut.

Some quilters use templates for their quilting patterns. Fine sandpaper, like that suggested for the animal cutouts, makes a good quilting template because it is sturdy, easy to cut and clings to the fabric when pinned sand side down. Quilting lines can be drawn on the fabric, using pencil, tailor's chalk, or an invisible ink quilter's pen. Another method for quilting straight lines is to put a piece of masking tape directly on the quilt and use the edge as a guide.

Most quiltmakers use quilting stitches about ⅛″ from the outside edge of their applique and quilt all around the design, then add filling stitches in unpatterned areas. If unpatterned sections of your quilt are not too large, they can be left unquilted to form a relief pattern of their own.

Contour Quilting

Contour quilting is particularly successful in creating landscape fabric pictures. In contour quilting, a line of stitches outlines the edge of the design. Successive lines of stitching repeat the pattern of the first at intervals of one to three inches apart, depending on the size of your image. Contour quilting gives the impression of raised levels, lending a hint of perspective to a design.

Use contour quilting to create designs beyond the appliqued ones and to fill large open areas of space.

Outline Quilting

Outline quilting may be done around pre-painted or printed fabric pictures. The picture may represent a three-dimensional landscape, human figures, animals or any subject at all. When it is carefully cut out, turned under, and appliqued to a background fabric, it can then be quilted in such a way as to bring out the pictorial characteristics.

In such a picture, the quilting follows the edge of the design and may be used to enhance details in the design itself. The three-dimensional quality of painted or printed fabric pictures allows the quilter some interesting effects when combined with flat, two-dimensional animal motifs.

Quilting by Section

This process is often referred to as the "quilt-as-you-go" method. It can be done with individual blocks or with larger sections of a quilt. The only difference in appearance between a quilt done by this method and one using the all-over style of quilting is the seams. A quilt that has been quilted in sections will show seams around each separate block or section.

If you decide on this method, be sure you do not quilt right to the edge of your project. Leave at least a 2″ margin unquilted all the way around the outside of the project. If, when you are done, you find the quilting stops short of your binding, you can add a few quilting stitches after binding the project to complete the unfinished lines of quilting.

As with the all-over design method described above, for a single section of your quilt, lay the fabric backing flat (wrong side up) followed by batting and top layer (right side up). Baste along the diagonals and repeat for each section, quilting the sections separately.

To join the sections, trim excess fabric around the edges. Fold the fabric edges on one side inward ½ inch. Trim batting so that it is level with the fold. Trim *the same amount* of batting from the adjacent section to be joined to this one but do not fold the fabric edges. Instead, place them between the folded edges of the first section, running the edges of the batting together but without overlapping them. Pin, baste and then sew, using a blind hem stitch. Repeat this procedure until all sections are joined into long strips and then join the strips in the same manner.

Binding

When you have completed your quilting, release the quilt or quilted hanging from the frame or hoop. If several "quilt-as-you-go" units are to be

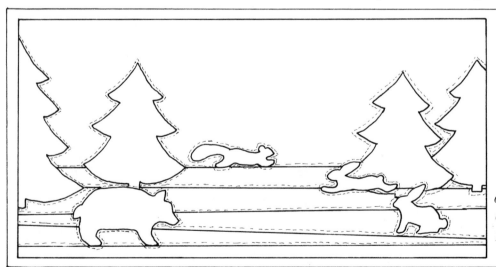

Outline quilting simply follows the outer edge of appliqued patches and adds dimension and texture to the finished piece.

joined, they should be sewn together at this point as described above. If you are quilting the entire piece at once, trim the edges, evening out all four sides. You can turn the two raw edges in and blind stitch all around the outside, or, finish it off with a colored binding. Wide hem facing comes in two-inch widths with raw edges already turned under and pressed. You can also use pre-cut and ironed quilt binding or you can make your own binding, using a fabric echoed in your design. Be sure to choose a binding that complements your over-all pattern. Having chosen the fabric for your binding, take a moment before you begin to measure your quilt. You will need to be sure that each of the four corners forms a 90 degree angle. If they do not, you may have to re-do any blocks or sections that make the corners crooked.

You will be mitering the corner edges of the binding on the back of the quilt. The end result will be a little like a picture frame. Measure so you have the correct amount of binding to go all the way around the quilt. Add an additional 6" for each side for mitering. Then cut each strip to the proper length.

With right sides together, lay one binding strip on top of the quilt, matching its one outer edge to the outer edge of the quilt and centering it lengthwise so that it extends 3" beyond the quilt at each corner. Then, starting in the middle and working toward

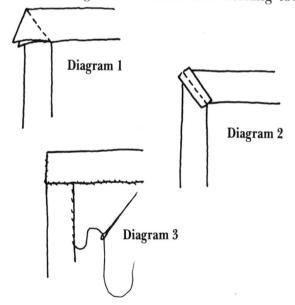

Diagram 1

Diagram 2

Diagram 3

the corners, pin the binding to the front of the quilt. You are now ready to sew it down, stitching ¼ to ½ inch from the edge, but stopping ¼" from each corner to create the seam allowance needed to form the diagonal seam at each corner. You can use a sewing machine to stitch the binding in place, or sew by hand using a running stitch.

When you have sewn each binding strip in place, fold a triangular pleat in one corner (Diagram 1). Pin the pleat and stitch with a running stitch. Trim the seam (Diagram 2). Do this for each corner. Then turn under the binding to the back of the quilt. Pin carefully, being sure the binding does not pucker. Then turn under the raw edge and sew down the binding edge to the back of the quilt by hand, using an applique stitch (Diagram 3).

Animal Patterns

Use the animal patterns in the back section of the book to create your own unique designs. You will find that, while most of the patterns represent animals, a few non-animal patterns (trees, plants and buildings, for instance) are included to help you design your own quilted fabric scenes.

The animal patterns have not been drawn in direct proportion to each other. The animals in most quilts seldom appear that way. It is quite normal to find a quilt that features doves as large as the horses or other large mammals portrayed in the design. If you find, however, that you would like to make one of the patterns larger or smaller before tracing it, your local copy center or library will probably have a photocopy machine with enlargement and reduction features. Have the patterns enlarged or reduced to a percentage of the size they appear in the book.

When tracing the patterns offered here, remember to trace both the outside and inside pattern lines first onto tracing paper, and then onto your fabric. When cutting the fabric, cut the outside line and use the inside line to help guide you in how much fabric to turn under to create each animal applique. Be sure to clip all concave curves, as indicated on the patterns themselves, in order to make the fabric turn under smoothly.

Good luck with your animal designs, and ENJOY!

Notes

1. Michael Godfrey, **A Closer Look** (San Francisco: Sierra Club Books, 1975).

2. Patsy and Myron Orlovsky, **Quilts in America** (New York: McGraw-Hill Book Company, 1974), p. 31.

3. Alice Morse Earl, **Customs and Fashions in Old New England** (Rutland, Vermont: Charles E. Tuttle, 1973), p. 128.

4. Johanna Stratton, **Pioneer Women** (New York: Simon and Schuster, 1981), p. 150.

Schuster, 1981), p. 150.

5. Robert Bishop and Patricia Coblentz, **A Gallery of American Weathervanes and Whirligigs** (New York: E. P. Dutton, 1981), p. 7.

6. John Hallmark Neff, et al., **Henri Matisse Paper Cut-Outs** (St. Louis, Missouri: St. Louis Art Museum and Detroit Institute for the Arts, 1977), p. 22.

7. Ibid.

Project 1
The Animal Tree

Project Diagram

Finished size: 34" × 38"

About the Project

This wall hanging project is featured on the cover of the book. You may want to use the animal patterns suggested in the directions, or substitute other animals appearing in the book. Remember, if you want to use an animal pattern that is too large or too small for this project, you can change the pattern you need on a photocopy machine that reduces and enlarges. Most printers and copy centers have one. If you reduce a pattern on a copier, you will have to add a little more seam allowance to the reduced pattern—but you can do this by eye when tracing your pattern on the fabric.

Take a look at the variations for this project before you begin. You may get some additional ideas on how to make the project uniquely your own. Note: all measurements in this and the following projects are given with the width first and the height second (w × h).

Materials

Background fabric rectangle (tan)—38″×42″
Batting rectangle—38″×42″
Backing fabric rectangle—38″×42″
¾ yard calico for tree trunk (brown)
½ yard fabric for leaves (green)
Assorted solid color fabrics for different animals

(Note color suggestions for this project.)
Thread to match applique fabrics
Quilting thread
Quilt binding to match applique fabrics (approximately 5 yards)

Color Suggestions for Project 1

Background—tan
Leaves—teal blue
Tree trunk—brown (calico)
Rabbit with back turned—rust brown
Tail of rabbit with back turned—white
Snake—blue (flowered)
Snake's tongue—red
Butterfly—pink

Lefthand bird—orange
Cardinal (righthand bird)—red
Dragonfly—blue (calico)
Squirrel—russet brown
Opossum—gray
Opossum's face—white
Side-turned rabbit—brown

Directions

1. Photocopy or trace the pattern pieces for the tree trunk and branches (Figures 01–09) onto heavy paper or sandpaper and cut out. Tape the paper pieces together to make a template as indicated in the Tree Trunk Diagram. Use the full-size tree template you have made to trace and cut the tree trunk from a single piece of fabric.

2. Photocopy or trace the remaining pattern pieces (Figures 10–25 and Figure 28) and cut out. Use these templates to mark and cut out the fabric pieces.

3. Pin and applique in place on the background fabric.

4. Use embroidery or small bits of felt to add details like eyes, whiskers, the snake's tongue and the nut in the squirrel's paws.

5. Quilt the project, doing outline quilting around the appliqued pieces.

6. Trim to the finished size and bind the quilted project. Add loops at the top of the project for hanging if desired.

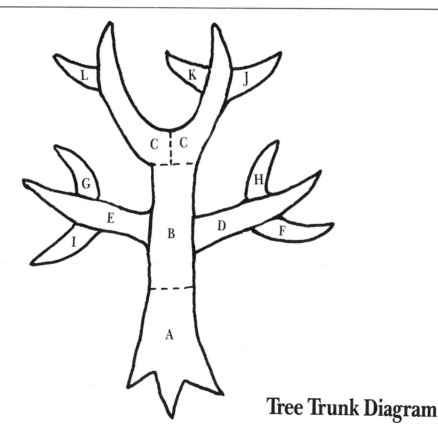

Tree Trunk Diagram

Variation 1

Album Tree

Follow the directions for the basic project to make the tree trunk and any animals you would like to include. Cut out and turn under the leaves and pass them out to your friends, to members of a club, or to any special group of people that you would like to recognize in your wall hanging. Ask them to sign the leaves, using a laundry marker or other permanent ink pen. When the leaves have all been signed, position and sew them in place and complete your project. If you like, you may finish by going over the ink names with embroidery.

Variation 2

Tree Full of Birds

Looking for a gift for the bird lover in your life? Follow the directions for making the tree trunk and leaves. Then look through the patterns for the different projects in this book to find the bird patterns you want to include. Use the crested bird pattern from **Project 1** (Figure 14) to make a cardinal (red fabric) and a blue jay (slate blue fabric).

Try adding different birds from your area. A small bird might become a sparrow when done in brown fabric or a goldfinch when done in yellow with black wings. Use a larger bird pattern for a bluebird (light blue with orange chest) or mockingbird (gray). You might also want to include a flying bird at one upper corner. All of the patterns you need for this variation are included among the patterns for the different projects in the Pattern Section. If you like, try designing a couple of your own patterns.

Variation 3

Crib Quilt

Add a border to turn your wall hanging into a crib or single bed quilt. Measure the crib or bed mattress you want to cover and add extra fabric for the overhang. Use the vine pattern included with the patterns for Project 1 (Figure 27). Photocopy or trace the vine and cut out as many as you need from heavy paper or sandpaper, taping them together at the ends to make a template of the desired length. Use the vine template to cut the fabric. Use the large leaf included for Project 1 (Figure 10) for the vine border leaves. Pin and applique the border, and finish as in Project 1.

Variation 4

Partridge in a Pear Tree

Celebrate the holidays with this variation in which you follow the basic project directions, but leave out the animals. Do not quilt the project. Add the partridge (Figure 26) and nine or ten pears (Figure 29) and finish the wall hanging as directed.

Project 2
The Folk Tree

Project Diagram
Finished size: 30" × 35"

About the Project

The folk tree on which this wall hanging project is based is much more stylized than the tree design in **Project 1.** This folk design, inspired by a Swedish embroidery pattern, would work well in a primitive or American country-style setting. The Fruit Tree variation for this project is reminiscent of the "spirit tree" of Shaker artist Hannah Cohoon.

Materials

Background fabric rectangle (unbleached muslin)—34″ × 39″
Batting rectangle—34″ × 39″
Backing fabric rectangle—34″ × 39″
¾ yard solid fabric for tree trunk (brown)
½ yard calico for leaves (dark green)

Assorted color fabrics for different animals
Thread to match applique fabrics
Quilting thread
Quilt binding to match applique fabrics (approximately 5 yards)

Color Suggestions for Project 2

Background—white (muslin)
Tree trunk—brown
Leaves—dark green (calico)

Bird on ground—red
Bird in tree—light blue
Sun, moon—yellow (calico)

Directions

1. Photocopy or trace the pattern pieces for the tree trunk and branches (Figures 30–35) and cut out. Tape the pieces together as indicated in the Folk Tree Diagram. Use the full-size tree template you have made to cut the tree from a single piece of fabric.

2. Photocopy or trace the remaining pattern pieces (Figures 36–39 and Figure 44) and cut out. Use these templates to mark and cut out the fabric pieces.

3. Pin and applique in place on the background fabric.

4. Quilt the project, doing outline quilting around the appliqued pieces.

5. Trim to the finished size. Bind the quilted project. Add loops at the top of the project for hanging if desired.

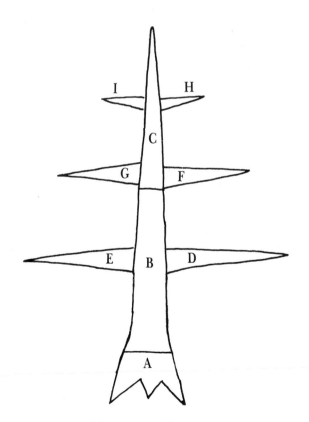

Folk Tree Diagram

Variation 1

Fruit Tree

Follow the directions for the basic project to make the tree and dark calico leaves. Add red calico apples (Figure 41) in place of some of the leaves and add animals of your choice.

Variation 2

Flower Tree

Follow the directions for the basic project to make the tree and leaves. In place of some of the leaves, try adding flowers (Figure 42).

Variation 3

Crib Block Quilt

Use the tree design as a centerpiece for a block-style crib quilt. Otherwise, follow the directions for the basic project, or one of its variations. However, before quilting the project, surround the appliqued tree rectangle with small muslin blocks to which fabric hearts (Figure 45) have been appliqued. Then, complete as directed.

Since cribs come in different sizes, it is impossible to provide fabric measurements here. You will need to measure the crib for which the quilt is intended. Then, add one or more rows of 5″ square blocks as are needed to arrive approximately at the desired measurements.

Variation 4

Strip-Pieced Tree

Follow the basic project directions for making the tree and leaves and any animals you want to include. Using a sewing machine (if possible) make a strip-pieced background for your wall hanging. The strips should be 34″ long and 3″–5″ wide and in solid colors. You might want to try the following color suggestion from top to bottom: pale blue to light blue-green to pale green to medium green. When you begin doing the green strips, vary the widths of the strips at either end to create a slanted "hill" effect in contrast to the straight blue "sky" strips. Complete the project as directed.

Variation 5

Animals' Christmas Tree

Follow the basic project directions. Use the animal patterns from **Project 1** (Figures 12, 13, 15, 16 and 28). You may want to trace the squirrel from the "wrong" side of the template to position it facing left as indicated in the diagram. Cut out the round tree ornaments (Figure 40) from different solid colors of fabric. Complete the project as directed.

Project 3
Animal Town

Project Diagram
Finished size: 36" x 18"

About the Project

Reminiscent of a wooden toy village and the primitive animals that accompany it, this wall hanging would be a delightful addition to a child's room or playroom. The large strips and shapes make up quickly. The basic project directions call for cutting out the windows and doors on the buildings and placing a different color of fabric behind the open areas. You may choose to simplify this by doing the windows in embroidery or by painting them on the fabric instead of cutting them out.

Whatever method you use, you might also want to try adding embroidery details like window panes, features on the animals, and stars, half-moons or clouds in the sky.

Materials

Background fabric rectangle (light blue)—40" × 22"
Batting rectangle—40" × 22"
Backing fabric rectangle—40" × 22"
Large fabric strip for foreground (green)—7" × 40"
¼ yard fabric for Buildings A and D (brick red)
¼ yard fabric for Building C (brown)
¼ yard fabric for Buildings B and E (yellow)
¼ yard fabric to place behind cutout windows (black)

Assorted large fabric scraps for remaining appliques including doors and animals
Thread to match applique fabrics
Quilting thread
Quilt binding to match applique fabrics (approximately 3½ yards)

Color Suggestions for Project 3

Sky—light blue
Ground—green
All windows—black
Duck—white
Cat—tan
Dog—brown
Dog's ear—black
Beginning with lefthand house: doorway #1, #3—
          yellow

doorway #2—
black
doorway #4—tan
doorway #5—
light blue
Beginning with lefthand house: house #1, #4—
brick red
house #2, #5—
yellow
house #3—brown

Directions

1. Photocopy or trace the patterns for the buildings (Figures 47–49). Mark fabric and cut out. Note that you will be cutting three buildings from one pattern. One of these three buildings (Building C) is merely one inch shorter than the other two (Buildings A and E).

2. Photocopy or trace the patterns for the animals (Figures 50–52). Mark and cut out fabric.

3. Lay out the background fabric. Position the foreground fabric over it at the bottom of the design. Position the buildings, using the Building Placement Diagram as a guide, but do not pin yet. Be sure the bottom edge of each building covers the ragged upper edge of the foreground fabric strip.

4. You will use a cut-away applique technique to fill in the area behind the cutout windows and doors. Cut "filler" fabric scraps to go behind each door and window. Each window "filler" should be 2″ × 2″ square. Each door "filler" should be 4″ × 4″ square. This will leave plenty of overlap when you fit the "filler" behind the opening.

5. Turn under one edge of each door filler, then position and pin each window and door filler in place. Applique the buildings, including the windows and doors.

6. Position the animals on the foreground fabric strip. Pin, then applique in place.

7. Quilt the project, doing outline quilting around each appliqued piece.

8. Trim to the finished size and bind the quilted project. Add loops for hanging if desired.

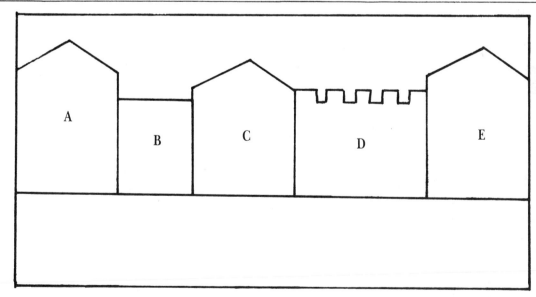

Building Placement Diagram

Variation 1

Wild Animals in Town

Follow the directions for the basic project, but substitute different animals. You might want to include such urban wildlife as a squirrel, bird and butterfly, for instance. See the patterns for **Project 1: The Animal Tree** (Figures 15–17.)

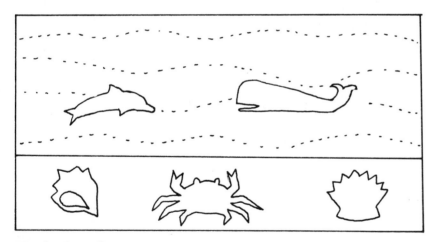

Variation 2

At the Seashore

Follow the directions for the basic project, but substitute a solid color ocean with quilted waves for the buildings. Use a foreground fabric that suggests sand—such as tan calico. Add seashells and a crab (Figures 53–55) along the foreground fabric strip instead of the domestic animals from the basic project. Add a porpoise (Figure 56) and whale (Figure 57) on the ocean strip. Complete the project as directed.

Project 4
Seal Mother and Baby

Project Diagram
Finished size: 30" × 35"

About the Project

This project is similar in construction to **Project 6: Gulls in the Water.** Cool background colors are used to give a feeling of an arctic setting. Also, notice how the grouped animals in this project and **Project 6** act as symbols for different feelings: two full-size animals for love or companionship, one single animal for solitariness, a large animal paired with a smaller one for caring and motherhood. Choose the feeling you want your wall hanging to impart and group your animal designs accordingly.

You may want to use colored quilting thread to bring out a design of waves in the water.

Materials

Background fabric rectangle (cream)—34″×39″
Batting rectangle—34″×39″
Backing fabric rectangle—34″×39″
½ yard solid fabric for mother seal (light brown)
Large scrap or quilter's quarter of fabric for baby seal (cream)
Large scrap of solid fabric for sun (red)
One 34″ long, 3″ wide strip of fabric for the land (tan)

Three or four 34″ long, 6″–8″ wide strips of fabric for ocean (shades of light to medium green—from pale green just underneath the land strip to medium green at the bottom of the wall hanging)
Thread to match applique fabrics
Quilting thread
Quilt binding to match applique fabrics (approximately 5 yards)

Color Suggestions for Project 4

Sky—cream
Top layer of water—pale green (calico)
Middle layer of water—light green (calico)
Bottom layer of water—medium green (calico)

Sun—red
Land—tan
Larger seal—light brown
Smaller seal—cream

Directions

1. Photocopy or trace the pattern pieces for the large seal (Figures 58–59). Tape them together to make a template for marking and cutting the seal out of a single piece of fabric. Photocopy or trace the pattern for the baby seal (Figure 60).

2. Photocopy or trace the pattern for the sun from **Project 6: Gulls on the Water** (Figure 79).

3. Using the Cutting Diagram as a guide, cut out the fabric strips for the land and the ocean. Cut only the top edge of each strip with curves. The bottom edge of each strip should be left straight since it will not show. (If you have trouble, please see the directions and diagrams for **Project 6**.) Be sure to clip all inward-turning curves for ease in turning under.

4. When the land and ocean strips are cut out, lay them in position on the background fabric. One at a time, turn under the top edge of each strip and secure it with pins, then lay it back down in place so that the sewn top edge covers the ragged unsewn edge of the strip before it. (Again, if you have trouble, please see the directions and diagram for **Project 6.**)

5. Pin and applique the remaining pieces in place.

6. Quilt the project, doing outline quilting around each appliqued piece.

7. Trim to the finished size and bind the quilted project. Add loops at the top of the project for hanging if desired.

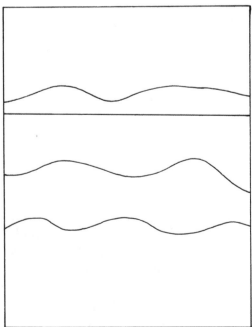

Cutting Diagram

Variation 1

Porpoise Mother and Baby

Follow the directions for the basic project, but substitute the porpoise patterns (Figures 61–62, 56) for the seals. You will have to tape together the pieces of the porpoise pattern to make the large porpoise template. Complete the project as directed.

Variation 2

Penguin Mother and Babies

Follow the directions for the basic project, but substitute the penguin patterns (Figures 63–64) for the seals. After the ocean strips have been appliqued in place, applique the extra land shape on top of them for the penguins to stand on. The extra land shape will partially cover the sewn ocean strips. Position the penguins on the extra land shape (Figure 65) and complete the project as directed.

Project 5
Hummingbird and Flowers

Project Diagram
Finished Size: 25" × 20"

About the Project

The smallest of all birds, the hummingbird, is the subject of this project with its "hummingbird's eye view" of large, exotic flowers. Try using a patterned fabric or embroidery to simulate the hummingbird's colorful, iridescent plumage. Lines of colored quilting thread will bring out the soft curves of the flower petals.

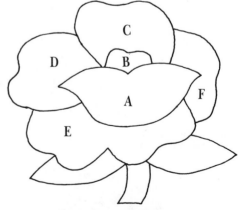

Flower Diagram

Materials

Background fabric rectangle (pale green)—29″ × 24″
Batting rectangle—29″ × 24″
Backing fabric rectangle—29″ × 24″
¼ yard light fabric for left flower (light pink)
¼ yard dark fabric in same color tone for left flower (dark pink)
¼ yard light fabric for right flower (light yellow)
¼ yard dark fabric in same color tone for right flower (dark yellow)
¼ yard for leaves and stems (medium green)
Assorted large scraps for hummingbird, butterfly, and flower centers
Thread to match applique fabrics
Quilting thread
Quilt binding to match applique fabrics (approximately 3 yards)

Color Suggestions for Project 5

Background—pale green
Butterfly—purple
Hummingbird—crimson
Stems and leaves on both flowers—medium green
Centers on both flowers—peach

Lefthand flower: petal next to leaves, petal next to hummingbird—light pink
    remaining petals—dark pink
Righthand flower: petal next to leaves, petal next to hummingbird—light yellow
    remaining petals—dark yellow

Directions

1. Photocopy or trace the pattern for the butterfly from **Project 1: The Animal Tree** (Figure 17). Use the template to mark and cut out the fabric.

2. Photocopy or trace the patterns for the hummingbird (Figure 74) and the flower leaves and stems (Figures 66 and 71). Mark and cut out the fabric.

3. Photocopy or trace the patterns for the flower petals (Figures 67–70 and 72–73). Mark and cut the two sets of light and dark colors for the flowers. In cutting, follow the broken lines indicated on the patterns. The sides of the flower petals with the broken lines, however, will not need to be turned under when it comes time for appliqueing. They can be left ragged, since they will be covered by other appliqued pieces of fabric.

4. Assemble and pin the two flowers on the background fabric. Use the Flower Diagram as a guide in positioning the petals. When the flowers are pinned in place, pin the hummingbird and butterfly, and applique all pieces.

5. Quilt the project, doing outline quilting around each appliqued piece.

6. Trim to the finished size and bind the quilted project. Add loops at the top of the project for hanging if desired.

Variation 1

Hummingbird and Butterflies

You might want to try this variation if you are looking for a square hanging to fill a particular wall area. Or you may like a design with a more traditional feel to it. For this variation, follow the directions for the basic project, but use batting and backing, each measuring 29″ × 29″. Finished size of the large center square will be 20″ × 20″. Add a row of 5″ × 5″ butterfly blocks around the outside. Use the 5″ × 5″ block from the pattern variations for **Project 2: The Folk Tree** (Figure 43). Use the butterfly applique from **Project 1: The Animal Tree** (Figure 17). Complete the project as directed, but plan for approximately 4 yards of binding.

Project 6
Gulls on the Water

Project Diagram
Finished size: 30" × 35"

About the Project

Use calico and solid color fabrics to create a striking waterscape effect in this project and its variations. Solid pastel fabrics for the sky give a feeling of calm, while tiny print calicos for the water strips fool the eye and provide an impressionistic-style image.

Remember contrast! Be sure to use colors for the background that will make your silhouette animals stand out well. In using light-colored animals on dark backgrounds, however, you may need to choose slightly heavier fabrics for the silhouettes, or use an extra layer of fabric underneath your animal design to avoid show-through.

Try using colored quilting thread to bring out the designs of the waves on the water.

Materials

Background fabric rectangle (medium light blue)—34″ × 39″

Batting rectangle—34″ × 39″

Backing fabric rectangle—34″ × 39″

½ yard solid fabric for gulls (white)

Large scrap or quilter's quarter of fabric for sun (gold calico)

Three or four 34″ long, 4″–7″ wide strips of calico for ocean (several shades of aqua—from pale blue-green at the top of the water to dark turquoise at the bottom of the wall hanging)

Thread to match applique fabrics

Quilting thread

Quilt binding to match applique fabrics (approximately 5 yards)

Color Suggestions for Project 6

Sky/background—light blue

Top layer of sea—light blue-green

Middle layer of sea—medium blue-green

Bottom layer of sea—dark blue-green

Sun—gold (calico)

Birds—white

Directions

1. Photocopy or trace the pattern pieces for the gull (Figures 76–78) onto cardboard or sandpaper and cut them out. Tape the body and the two wing pieces together. Use the full-size gull template you have made to mark and cut out two gulls from a single piece of fabric.

2. Photocopy or trace the pattern piece for the sun (Figure 79). Use this template to mark and cut out your fabric.

3. Using the Cutting Diagram as a guide, cut out your three or four strips of fabric for the water. Cut only the top edge of each strip with curves. Leave the bottom edge straight since it will not show—as you will see. (Remember, each strip should be 34″ long, the same as the *width* of your background fabric.)

Each strip should be from 4″–7″ in width, with the thinnest and lightest color strip near the middle of the wall hanging. The widest and darkest "ocean" strip should appear at the bottom. You can cut your strips with more curves for large waves or cut as in the diagram for calmer waters. Be sure to clip all inward-turning curves for ease in turning under the fabric edge.

4. When the ocean strips are cut out, lay them in position on the background fabric. One at a time, turn under the top long edge of each strip, secure it with pins, and lay it back in place. As you lay down the second strip, be sure the turned-under edge covers the ragged, straight bottom edge of the strip above it. See the Strip Placement Diagram. Do the same for any succeeding strips, making sure that a turned-under top edge covers each ragged bottom edge. (Leave the ragged left and right edges unsewn.)

5. Pin the sun and gull in place and applique.

6. Quilt the project, doing quilting around each appliqued piece.

7. Trim to the finished size and bind the quilted project. Add loops at the top of the project for hanging if desired.

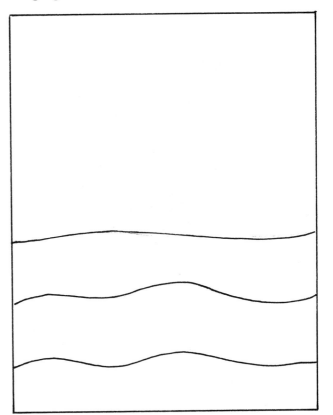

Cutting Diagram

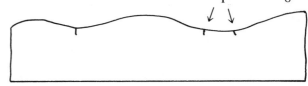

clips for turning under curves

Sample strip with curves cut in top edge only

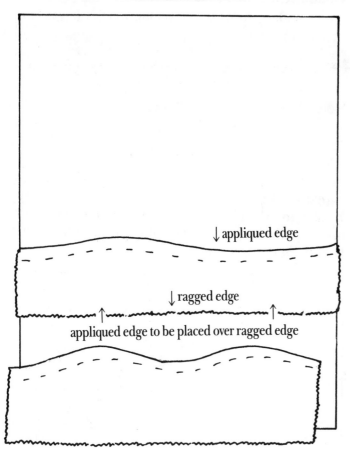

Strip Placement Diagram

↓ appliqued edge

↓ ragged edge

↑   ↑

appliqued edge to be placed over ragged edge

Variation 1

Pelican on the Ocean

Follow the directions for the basic project, but instead of making a gull template, trace and cut out the pattern pieces for the pelican (Figures 80–82). Use them to make a template, then use this template to mark and cut the pelican from a single piece of fabric. (Don't forget the pelican's wing, to be appliqued onto the body.) Trace and cut the wooden piling (Figure 83). Complete the project as directed.

Variation 2

Ducks in the Marsh

Change the setting of your project from a seascape to a marsh scene. Follow the basic project directions, but use the flying duck patterns (Figure 75) cut out of brown fabric in place of the gulls, and add brown calico reeds and green grasses (Figures 84–85) to the bottom of the design. Complete the project as directed.

Variation 3

Night Scene

Change any of the variations for this project into a night scene by using dark, rich colors for the background, and slightly lighter colors for the animal silhouettes (Figure 75). Try a red setting sun (Figure 79) in a pink sky, or a pale white moon (Figure 79) in a dark blue sky. For a nighttime marsh scene, use solid black for the reeds and grasses (Figures 84–85) in the foreground, instead of brown and green calico.

Project 7
Wolves and the Rising Moon

Project Diagram
Finished size: 20" × 25"

About the Project

When you make this wall hanging, you will be drawing attention to one of our most endangered animals—the wolf. Be sure to use fabrics for the landscape that make the wolf silhouettes stand out clearly. If you would like to enlarge the rising moon, try adding additional outer rings to the moon applique.

Materials

Background fabric rectangle (dark blue)—24″ × 29″
Batting rectangle—24″ × 29″
Backing fabric rectangle—24″ × 29″
¼ yard fabric for stars (gold)
¼ yard fabric for outer moon ring (yellow)
Four 24″ long strips of calico, each 3″–7″ wide for landscape (several shades of green ranging from medium at the middle of the wall hanging to dark at the bottom)

Large assorted fabric scraps for remaining moon rings and wolf silhouettes
Thread to match applique fabrics
Quilting thread
Quilt binding to match applique fabrics (approximately 4 yards)

Color Suggestions for Project 7

Sky/background—dark blue
Top layer of ground—gray-green (calico)
Second layer of ground—medium dark green (calico)
Third layer of ground—dark green (calico)
Bottom layer of ground—darkest green (calico)
Front wolf—black

Back wolf—gray
Stars—gold
Top arch of moon—gold
Second arch of moon—red
Third arch of moon—orange
Bottom arch of moon—red

Directions

1. Photocopy or trace the patterns for the two wolves (Figure 86) and the eight stars (Figure 46).

2. Using the Cutting and Placement Diagram as a guide, cut out the four landscape fabric strips. (If you have difficulty, please see the more detailed instructions for treating the fabric strips in **Project 6: Gulls on the Water.**)

3. When the landscape strips are cut out, lay them in position on the background fabric, using the Cutting and Placement Diagram as a guide. Remember, the widest, darkest strip goes at the bottom. The narrowest, lightest strip goes at the top of the strips. One at a time, turn under the long top edge of each strip, secure it with pins, and lay it back in place. Be sure the ragged bottom edge of each strip is covered by the sewn edge of the next strip that goes on top of it. (Again, if you have difficulty, please see **Project 6.**)

4. Pin the strips and the wolf appliques in place on the background fabric.

5. Use a similar method for the moon rings (Figures 89–92). Photocopy or trace the patterns, then mark and cut out the fabric. When cutting, be sure to place your moon ring template on the *fold* of a folded piece of fabric to get both halves of each ring. Seam allowance is provided in the patterns for all edges of the moon rings. However, you should turn under the outer edge *only* of each ring.

6. Position the rings, using the Cutting and Placement Diagram as a guide. Begin with the center half circle in about the middle of the wall hanging. Be sure the ragged inner edge of each ring is cov-

ered by the turned down outer edge in front of it. Pin all rings in place and applique.

7. Pin and applique the stars in place.

8. Quilt the project, doing outline quilting around each appliqued piece.

9. Trim to the finished size and bind the quilted project. Add loops for hanging if desired.

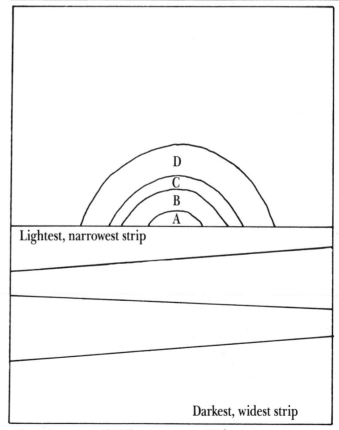

Cutting and Placement Diagram

 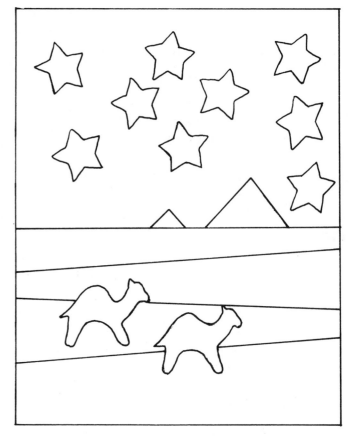

Variation 1

Wolves and Crescent Moon

You might like to substitute a crescent moon for the rings of the rising moon. If so, follow the directions for the basic project, but substitute the crescent moon from **Project 2: The Folk Tree** (Figure 44). This makes for a quicker project that is still very attractive.

Variation 2

Under Sahara Stars

Camels are unique animals, able to go without eating or drinking quite comfortably for days. Use them in this variation to create a wall hanging with a unique, mystical quality. Follow the directions for the basic project, using 9 stars instead of 8 (Figure 46), and black pyramid silhouettes (Figures 87–88) to replace the rings of the rising moon. Use tan calicos for the land strips, instead of greens. Use brown for the camels (Figure 93). Try making one of your stars an unusual color—red, for instance, just for fun.

Project 8

Down on the Farm

Project Diagram
Finished size: 25" × 20"

About the Project

Although most farm animals today are raised in confinement, the old-time family farm has plenty of visual appeal for quilters. Make paper templates and try out the different animals offered here in various combinations to create your own individual landscape design. Contour quilting in the green calico land areas is sure to enhance your fabric picture.

Materials

Background fabric (light blue)—29″ × 24″
Batting—29″ × 24″
Backing fabric—29″ × 24″
Four quarter-yard strips green calico in shades from light to dark. These strips should be between 4″ and 6″ wide and 29″ long.

Assorted large fabric scraps for sheep, pig, farmhouse, clouds, and sun
Thread to match applique fabrics
Quilting thread
Quilt binding to match applique fabrics (approximately 4 yards)

Color Suggestions for Project 8

Sky/background—light blue
Top layer of ground—light green (calico)
Second layer of ground—medium green (calico)
Third layer of ground—medium dark green (calico)
Bottom layer of ground—dark green (calico)
Sun—yellow

Clouds—white
House, roof—red
Window of house—black
Lefthand sheep—white
Righthand sheep—black
Pig—pink

Directions

1. Photocopy or trace the patterns for the sheep, pig, farmhouse, clouds, and sun (Figures 94–98). Mark and cut your fabric.

2. Using the Cutting Diagram as a guide, cut curves in the long top edge of each green calico strip. Clip inward-turning curves for ease in turning under. You will need to turn under only the top edge of each calico strip. The ragged bottom edge will be covered by the strip in front of it. (If you need help with this, see the directions for **Project 6: Gulls on the Water.**)

3. Arrange and pin the calico strips and cutouts in place and applique. Leave a 2″ margin around your design area. Remember, you will be trimming to a finished size of 25″ × 20″.

4. Quilt the project, doing outline quilting around each appliqued piece.

5. Trim your project to the finished size and bind the project. Add loops for hanging if desired.

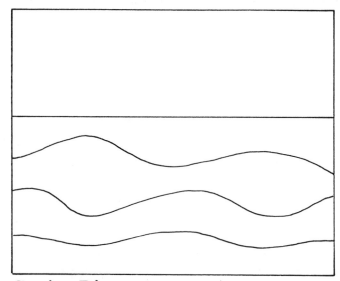

Cutting Diagram

Variation 1

Cider Time

Follow the project directions, but use red, gold, orange and brown in the landscape to create an effect hinting of late autumn. Take out the clouds and add a leafless tree (Figure 100) for a touch of autumn melancholy.

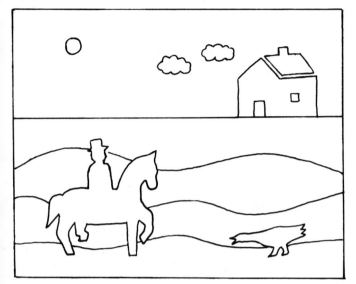

Variation 2

Riding Scene

The horse and rider is a traditional colonial silhouette used to decorate walls and furniture in stencil form. Substitute the horse and rider (Figure 101) and the angry goose (Figure 99) for the sheep and pig.

Variation 3

Mothers and Babies

Follow the basic project directions, substituting large and small animals (Figures 101 without rider, 102–104) in your landscape. You might want to make your landscape of lighter greens to suggest the early months of spring when animal babies generally appear on the farm.

Variation 4

Teasing the Cows

Substitute the bull, cow and dog (Figures 105–106, 108) for the animals in the basic project and complete as directed.

Variation 5

Hen, Rooster and Chicks

Follow the basic project directions, but substitute a hen, rooster and chicks (Figures 107, 109–110) for the animals. Complete as directed.

Project 9
Night in the Forest

Project Diagram
Finished size: 30″ × 15″

About the Project

Who has not experienced a night of camping in the woods and heard the rustlings of the animals that live there? Use thin brown calico strips for the forest floor in this project, with a light green background to suggest trees farther in the distance. As in the preceding wall hanging, try using paper patterns to plan a landscape with your own combination of animals. Look through the animal patterns from other projects for the possibilities they offer as well.

Materials

Background fabric—34″ × 19″
Batting—34″ × 19″
Backing fabric—34″ × 19″
Five strips of brown calico ranging in shades from light to dark. Each strip should be from 1½″ to 3″ wide and 34″ long.
¼ yard calico for pine trees (dark green)
¼ yard calico for pine tree (medium-dark green)
¼ yard calico for pine tree (medium green)
Assorted large scraps for remaining appliques
Thread to match applique fabrics
Quilting thread
Quilt binding to match appliques (approximately 3½ yards)

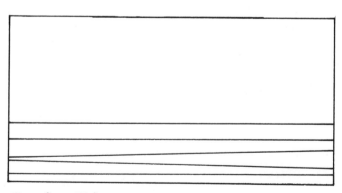

Cutting Diagram

Color Suggestions for Project 9

Background/sky—gray-green
Lefthand half-tree—dark calico
Righthand half-tree—medium-dark calico
Lefthand full tree—medium calico
Righthand full tree—dark calico
Top layer of ground—light calico
Second layer of ground—light-medium calico
Third layer of ground—medium calico

Fourth layer of ground—medium-dark calico
Bottom layer of ground—dark calico
Moon, star—yellow
Bat—brown
Fox—orange
Deer—rust
Skunk—black

Directions

1. Photocopy or trace the patterns for the fox, deer, skunk, and bat (Figures 111–114). Mark and cut the fabric.

2. Trace the patterns for the star and the moon from **Project 2: The Folk Tree** (Figures 44 and 46). Mark and cut the fabric.

3. Trace the pattern for the pine trees (Figure 115). Note that both trees are traced from the same pattern. Use the short version of the pattern for two trees and the long version for two other trees. Mark the fabric, cut out, and set aside.

4. Organize your thin strips of brown calico. Use the Cutting Diagram to aid you in making some strips narrower at one end than at the other for interest value. Turn under the top edge only of each strip since the ragged bottom edge of each will be covered by the strip placed in front of it. (See the directions for **Project 6: Gulls on the Water** if you need help.)

5. Lay out and pin the strips and the appliques in place. Remember to leave a 2″ margin around the design area since you will be cutting to a finished size of 30″ × 15″. Then applique the design.

6. Quilt the project, doing outline quilting around each appliqued piece.

7. Trim to the finished size and bind the project. Add loops for hanging if desired.

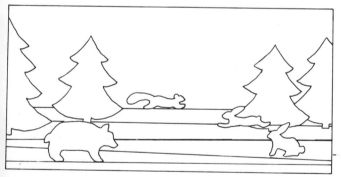

Variation 1

Bear in the Woods

Follow the basic project directions, substituting different animals like the bear, running rabbit and running squirrel (Figures 116–118). The sitting rabbit is from **Project 1: The Animal Tree** (Figure 28). The pictured variation uses three small trees and one large one.

Variation 2

Fairy Tale Castle

Follow the basic project directions, but add a castle (Figure 119) and a frog waiting to be kissed into a prince (Figure 120). Substitute a deer (Figure 113) for some of the other forest animals if you like.

Project 10
Noah's Ark

Project Diagram
Finished size: 30" × 20"

About the Project

The Bible story of Noah's ark provides a wonderful theme for an animal quilt. You can make a simple wall hanging, a crib quilt or a three-dimensional fabric picture that combines traditional applique with pull-out animal toys. Choose the variation you like best and experiment with colored quilting thread and different animal shapes.

Materials

Background fabric—34" × 24"
Batting—34" × 24"
Backing fabric—34" × 24"
One 9" wide × 34" long strip of fabric for water (green)
¼ yard fabric for ark (light brown)
One small 3" wide × 10" long fabric strip for cabin of the ark (red)
Assorted large fabric scraps for remaining appliques
Thread to match applique fabrics
Quilting thread
Quilt binding to match applique fabrics (approximately 4 yards)

Color Suggestions for Project 10

Background/sky—gray-blue
Sea—green
Dove, cloud—white
Sun (behind cloud)—yellow
Ark bottom—light brown
Ark top—red

Octopus—pink (calico)
Dolphin—light blue
Cat—orange (calico)
Camel—tan
Elephant—gray (calico)
Giraffe—yellow (calico)

Directions

1. Photocopy or trace the pattern pieces for the ark (Figure 121). Mark and cut the fabric. When cutting, place the template edge of the ark on the fold of your fabric as indicated in the pattern and cut the main part of the ark from a single piece of fabric.

2. Trace the pattern for the rectangular cabin of the ark, the dove, and the octopus (Figures 123–125). Mark fabric and set aside.

3. Trace, mark and cut out the following patterns: the baby porpoise (Figure 122), the camel from the variations for **Project 7: Wolves and the Rising Moon** (Figure 93), the cloud and small sun from **Project 8: Down on the Farm** (Figures 94–95), the giraffe and elephant from **Project 11: Out of Africa** (Figures 140 and 131) and the sitting cat from **Project 12: Animals at Our House**

(Figure 150).

Note: Some of the animals in this project are only partly visible, so you may not need to cut out the entire animal pattern.

4. Assemble all of the pieces for the wall hanging. Pin the water strip to the background fabric, then pin the ark and the animals in place. When appliqueing, turn under the main part of the ark all the way around. Turn under the ark cabin strip along the two short sides and one long side. Be sure the sewn edge of the main part of the ark covers the one ragged edge of the ark cabin strip.

5. Quilt the project, doing outline quilting around the appliqued pieces.

6. Trim to the finished size and bind the project, adding loops for hanging if desired.

Variation 1

Noah's Ark Border Quilt

Use the basic project as a centerpiece for a crib quilt or larger quilt. Measure the crib or bed for which the quilt is intended. Plan for wide borders to be covered with the animals of your choice. You might want to portray the animals singly or in pairs like in the Old Testament tale. Remember, if an animal silhouette is facing the wrong way, simply turn the template over and draw from the other side. Also, if a pattern you want to use is too large or too small, change the size of the pattern on a photocopying machine that reduces and enlarges.

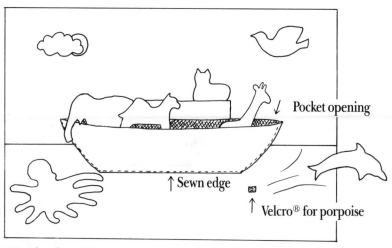

Pocket opening

↑ Sewn edge

↑ Velcro® for porpoise

Variation 2

Noah's Ark with Removable Toy Animals

Children love this fabric picture with animal toys that come out of their Noah's ark pocket. Trace, mark, and cut out the pieces as directed for all of the flat motifs to be appliqued—the sun and cloud, the ark cabin strip (Figures 94, 95 and 123) and the water strip.

Do the same for each animal; however, cut not one, but two of each. You may want to simplify these for ease in sewing. Please see the **Simplified Animals Diagram** for examples.

Cut the water strip and pin on the background fabric.

For the ark, cut three arks—one for the sewn down ark backing and two for a quilted pocket top. Turn under the edges of each ark cutout. Applique

one ark in place on the background. Position and applique the ark cabin strip in place as well. This forms the back of the ark. Cut a piece of batting slightly smaller than the remaining ark cutouts, sandwich it between the two cutouts, and quilt the three layers together. Finally, join the quilted ark top to the ark backing along three sides, leaving the top of the ark open like a pocket. See the **Ark Assembly Diagram**.

Sew and stuff the two-sided animal toys. Put some animals inside the ark pocket. Use Velcro™ to attach the bird and the water animals outside the ark. Quilt the background, trim and bind your wall hanging.

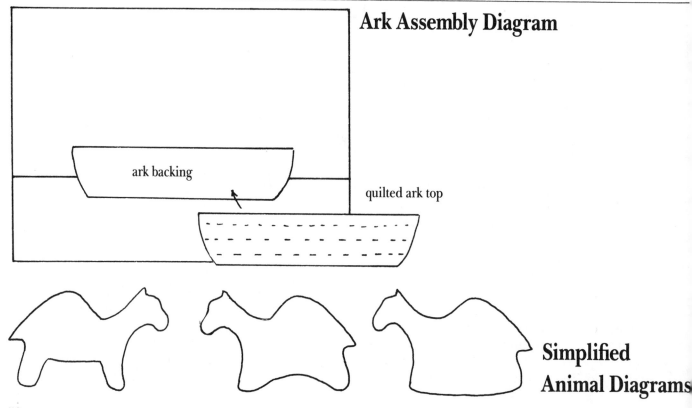

Ark Assembly Diagram

ark backing

quilted ark top

Simplified Animal Diagrams

Project 11
Out of Africa

Project Diagram
Finished size: 30" × 30"

About the Project

One of the most beautiful animal quilts ever made is in the Museum of American Folk Art in New York City. It is also reproduced in Jean Lipman and Alice Winchester's classic work, *The Flowering of American Folk Art* (New York: Viking Press, 1974). The central figure in this well-known antique "Bird of Paradise" coverlet was the inspiration for the bird in this project. If possible, take a look at a reproduction of the original antique coverlet to spark ideas about combining solids and calicos to create a colorful and striking bird of paradise of your own.

Materials

Background fabric (light green)—34" × 34"
Batting—34" × 34"
Backing fabric—34" × 34"
½ yard for tree (brown)
¼ yard for large leaves (green)
¼ yard fabric for elephant mother and baby (gray)

Assorted large scraps for remaining appliques
Thread to match applique fabrics
Quilting thread
Quilt binding to match applique fabrics (approximately 4 yards)

Color Suggestions for Project 11

Background/sky—light green
Tree trunk—brown
Large leaves—medium green
Monkey—rust
Elephants—gray
Flower leaves—dark green

Bird—yellow
Bird's wings—orange
Bird's Tail Feathers—see Bird Diagram below
Flower Petals—see Flower Diagram below

Directions

1. Photocopy or trace the pattern pieces for the elephants (Figures 126 and 131), the monkey (Figure 135), the bird (Figures 132–134) and the flower petals (Figures 127–130). Use your templates to mark and cut out fabric. When cutting out the tail feathers for the bird (Figure 134) be sure to cut three feathers from one color and two feathers from a contrasting color.

2. When turning under the raw edges it is not necessary to turn under the edges marked in the pattern with a dotted line since they will be covered by other fabric pieces.

3. Trace the pattern piece for the large flower leaf from **Project 5: The Hummingbird and Flowers** (Figure 66). Mark and cut 6 leaves and set aside.

4. Trace the pattern piece for the small leaf from **Project 1: The Animal Tree** (Figure 11). Mark and cut 16 leaves and set aside.

5. To make a template for the tree, cut a strip of heavy paper 4″ × 20″. Trace the tree trunk pattern for this project (Figure 136) and tape it to your paper strip. Trace the tree branches D and E from **Project 1: The Animal Tree** (Figure 9). (When making your paper pattern, be sure to cut from the thick cutting line of the pattern, not the thin seam allowance line.) Tape the topmost paper branch to the trunk about eight inches from the top. Tape the lower branch about eight inches below this. Use the tree template you have made to cut a tree from a single piece of fabric. When cutting, allow a ¼″ seam allowance all the way around the tree.

6. Cut a short strip of fabric for the flower stem—about 1½″ wide × 4″ long. Cut a slightly larger strip for the front of the mother elephant's leg that shows in the lower right corner of the project (Figure 126a).

7. Assemble and pin the project according to the diagram. See the **Bird Diagram** and the **Flower Diagram** for help in assembling these two motifs. The tail feathers of the bird will overlap slightly. You will need to cut a piece of background fabric for the flower bush. It should not be turned under. Instead, its rough edges should be covered by the turned-under leaves. Only a few small areas of the flower bush background fabric will show between the leaves.

8. Applique the design in place.

9. Do outline quilting around each appliqued piece.

10. Trim to the finished size and bind the quilted project. Add loops for hanging if desired.

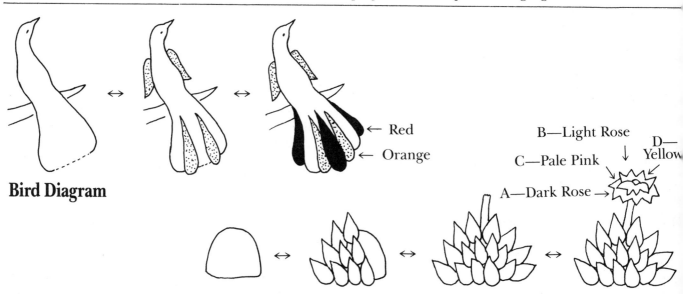

Bird Diagram

← Red
← Orange

B—Light Rose
C—Pale Pink
D—Yellow
A—Dark Rose →

Flower Diagram

Variation 1

Jungle Twin Bed Quilt

To use the **Out of Africa** design as a centerpiece for a larger quilt, complete the project as directed but do not quilt. Cut 16 square blocks, 10½″ × 10½″ each. Mark a ¼″ seam allowance on each side of each block. Mark, cut and applique 12 small elephants to 12 of the blocks. For the corner blocks, mark, cut and applique four flowers (See Steps 3, 4, 6, and 7 above). Join the blocks to the centerpiece. Add a fabric border to enlarge your quilt to the size you would like. Quilt the fabric border with monkeys, exotic flowers and vines or other jungle designs.

Variation 3

Animals Down Under

For a wall hanging that features Australian animals, follow the basic project directions, but leave out the bird, the elephants, the flower and the monkey. Add the Australian animals of your choice. You may want to use a kangaroo (Figure 141), koala bear (Figures 142 and 142a) and the mother and baby emus (Figures 143–144), the Australian relatives of the ostrich.

Variation 2

Elephants on the Move

There are two kinds of elephants in the world and both are endangered. To create a design that celebrates these beautiful, intelligent animals, follow the basic project directions, but leave out the bird, the flower, and the mother elephant. Make five large tree leaves (Figure 66) instead of six. Make two monkeys (Figure 135) instead of only one, but for the second monkey, turn the template over so it will be facing the opposite direction. Use the snake pattern from **Project 1: The Animal Tree** (Figures 22–25). Add a sun, using the pattern from **Project 6: Gulls on the Water** (Figure 79).

Variation 4

African Plains Scene

Some of the animals we often think of as living in the forest jungle, actually live on the African plains. (Elephants, however, may live in both areas.) Follow the basic project directions, but leave out the tree, the bird, the mother elephant, monkey and the flower. Use the lion (Figure 137), hippopotamus (Figure 138), rhinoceros (Figure 139), giraffe (Figure 140), and elephant (Figure 131).

Design a landscape, using a large strip of fabric for the sky—about 34″ wide × 14″ high. Add a piece of fabric for a shallow watering hole by using the "extra land" pattern from the variations for **Project 4: Seal Mother and Baby** (Figure 65). Extend the fabric for the watering hole as far as you like to accommodate the animals you choose to include.

Project 12
Animals at Our House

Project Diagram
Finished size: 25″ × 20″

About the Project

Quilters who especially enjoy the old time School-house pattern will want to complete this project. Try embellishing the large house pattern to look more like your own house, if you like.

The block quilt variations can be used for a large full-size quilt, a wall hanging, or smaller projects like placemats and potholders. Just make as many blocks as you need for the kind of project you want to complete. Join all of the blocks before quilting or set the blocks in groups for the convenient quilt-as-you-go method.

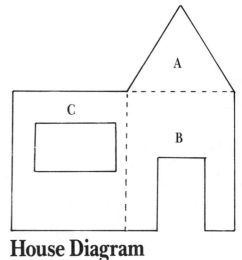

House Diagram

Materials

Background fabric—29″ × 24″ (light blue)
Batting—29″ × 24″
Backing fabric—29″ × 24″
One 5″ wide × 29″ long strip of fabric for grass
½ yard fabric for house (peach)
Large assorted fabric scraps for remaining appliques

Thread to match applique fabrics
Quilting thread
Quilt binding to match applique fabrics (approximately 4 yards)

Color Suggestions for Project 12

Background/sky—light blue
Ground—green
Tree—dark green
House—peach
Window, doorway—white

Cat—black
Dog—brown
Top arch of rainbow—red
Middle arch of rainbow—green
Bottom arch of rainbow—medium blue

Directions

1. Photocopy or trace the pattern pieces for the house (Figures 145–147). Note that one pattern represents two shapes—B and C. For part B, cut out a door. For part C, cut out a window. Follow the **House Diagram** in taping the three pieces of the main part of the house together to make a paper template. Use the template to mark and cut a house applique from a single piece of fabric.

2. Trace the patterns for the small folk tree (Figure 149), the cat (Figure 150), and the dog (Figure 108). Trace the rainbow from the three outer moon ring patterns from **Project 7: Wolves and the Rising Moon** (Figures 90–92). Cut out and set aside.

3. Assemble and pin the project. Lay out the grass strip on the background fabric and follow with rainbow, the house, the animals and the tree. Pin all pieces in place and applique (you need to turn under only the top edge of the grass fabric).

4. Quilt, doing outline quilting around each appliqued piece.

5. Trim to the finished size and bind the project. Add loops for hanging if desired.

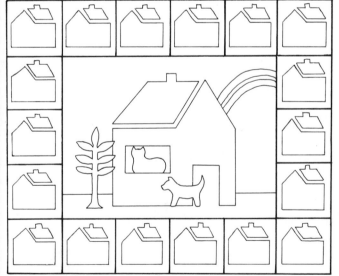

Variation 1

House Block Crib Quilt

To turn the wall hanging into a larger crib quilt, add a single row of 6½″ house blocks all the way around the basic project design. Use the 6½″ square block (Figure 148) provided with this project and the house from **Project 8: Down on the Farm** (Figures 96–96a). Complete as directed.

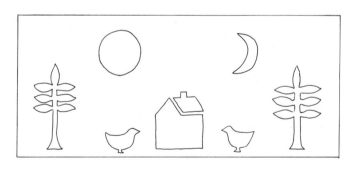

Variation 2

European Style Folk Design

For a wall hanging inspired by European design, follow the basic project, but use a background fabric that measures 30″ × 15″. This means you will need batting and backing fabric that are each 34″ × 19″. Use the house and the chicks from **Project 8: Down on the Farm** and its variations (Figures 96–96a, 107), the round moon from **Project 6: Gulls on the Water** (Figure 79), and the crescent moon from **Project 2: The Folk Tree** (Figure 44). Complete as directed.

Project 13
Animal Alphabet

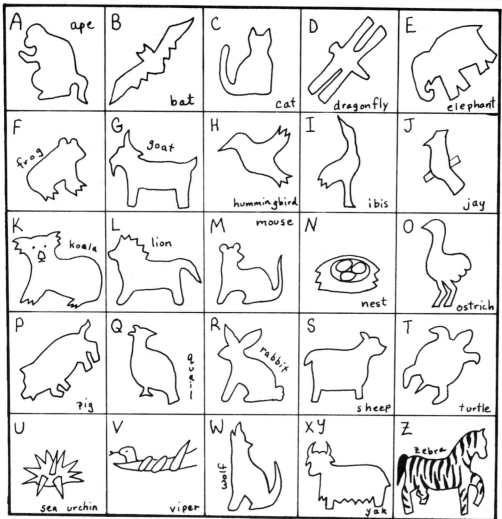

Project Diagram
Finished size: 40" × 40"

About the Project

In pioneer days, young girls often learned their ABCs at the same time they learned to sew—from an alphabet sampler. In some cases, crib quilts were made by adults in imitation of the traditional yarn sampler with its numbers or alphabet.

Today's children will enjoy pointing out the different animal that goes with each letter in the design for this project. No Color Diagram is given, because you will most likely be making this one from fabric scraps. Consequently, a few suggestions are in order. For a traditional look, use unbleached muslin background blocks. Calico or solid animal silhouettes will give a nice folk art feeling to the design.

Try to balance the colors in your alphabet. One trick quilters use to balance color is the Triangle Method. To do this, use the same color fabric in three areas of a quilt—as if each piece of fabric fell at one of the three points of an imaginary triangle.

If you can't find the right color of fabric, don't hesitate to make your own! Experiment with permanent fabric paints available at art and hobby stores. Test them, however, to be sure they will not wash out. Use fabric paints, for instance, to turn a white horse silhouette into a zebra painted with black stripes. Or, paint a cat silhouette to look like a family pet.

Materials

1½ yards fabric for blocks (unbleached muslin)·
Batting square—44″ × 44″
Backing fabric—44″ × 44″
Assorted fabric scraps for animal appliques
Embroidery floss for letters and animal names
(optional)

Thread to match applique fabrics
Quilting thread
Quilt binding to match applique fabrics (approximately 5 yards)

Directions

1. Make a template for the blocks that measures 8½″ × 8½″ square. Mark and cut 25 blocks. Mark a ¼″ seam allowance all the way around each block. Iron the blocks and set aside.

2. Photocopy or trace the animal patterns included for this project: the cat, elephant, ibis, mouse, nest full of eggs, quail, turtle, sea urchin and yak (Figures 151–161a). Mark and cut your fabric. Pin each applique in place on a block. Applique and set aside.

3. Trace the following animal patterns from these projects. Follow the above procedure for each to complete your animal blocks.
Project 1: The Animal Tree—dragonfly (Figure 18), jay (cardinal) (Figure 14), rabbit (Figure 28), viper (snake on a branch) (Figure 22–25); **Project 5: Hummingbird and Flowers**—hummingbird (Figure 74); **Project 7: Wolves and the Rising Moon**—wolf (Figure 86); **Project 8: Down on the Farm**—mother goat (Figure 103), pig (Figure 98), sheep (Figure 97), horse (Figure 104); **Project 9: Night in the Forest**—bat (Figure 112), frog (Figure 120); **Project 11: Out of Africa**—ape (monkey) (Figure 135); koala (Figure 142), lion (Figure 137), small ostrich (Figure 144).

4. Set the blocks together in the correct order, making sure to match the seams between the blocks as you go.

5. Using the embroidery floss, add the letters of the alphabet and the animal names if desired.

6. Quilt the project, doing outline quilting around each appliqued piece.

7. Trim to the finished size and bind the project, adding loops for hanging if desired.

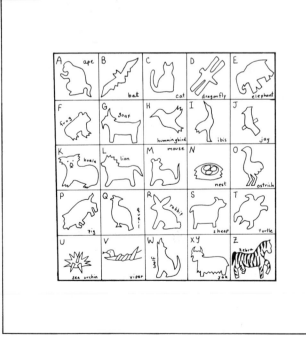

Variation 1

Animal Alphabet Quilt

Follow the directions for the basic project, but do not quilt the design. Instead, add an 8″ or 12″ border around the outside of the joined blocks. For the border use muslin or choose a fabric repeated in the appliques. You will need about 2½ yards of border fabric. For an 8″ border quilt, you will need at least a 60″ square of both batting and backing (includes 2″ extra on each side). For a 12″ border quilt, you will need at least a 68″ square of both batting and backing (includes 2″ extra on each side). You will also need between 7 and 8 yards of binding. When your border is joined to the center block design, bind and quilt your project as directed. Finished size for the 8″ border quilt is 56″ square. Finished size for the 12″ border quilt is 64″ square.

Project 14

Fox and Geese

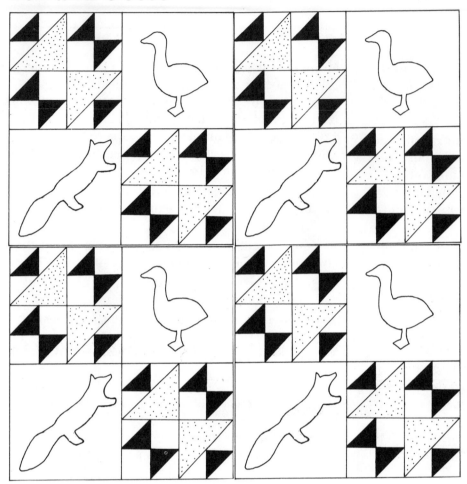

Project Diagram   *Finished size: 40" × 40"*

About the Project

Many traditional pieced-work patterns take their names from animals. You can have some fun combining pieced and applique techniques in this project and the two that follow it. Even if you are a pieced-work or applique devotee and have more experience with one technique than the other, you'll find these projects easy to complete. They may even provide you with a good excuse to sample a quilt-making style with which you are a little less familiar.

Projects 14 and 15 are done in block style, so you can choose whether to make a few blocks to complete a pillow or wall hanging, or many blocks for a full-size quilt. Although the directions call for using the animal patterns to make appliques, you may want to alternate your pieced blocks with plain white ones. If so, try using the patterns to quilt the animals in outline. Use the inner tracing line as your guide when using an animal pattern as a quilting template.

Materials

2 yards background and block fabric (unbleached muslin)

Batting—44" × 44"   Backing fabric—44" × 44"

1 yard fabric for both appliqued and pieced "foxes" (red calico)

½ yard fabric for appliqued geese (yellow calico)

1 yard fabric for pieced "geese" (green calico)

Thread to match applique fabrics

Quilting thread

Quilt binding to match applique fabrics (approximately 5 yards)

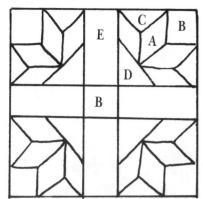

Piecing Diagram, Variation 1

Color Suggestions for Project 14

Background for animals—white (unbleached muslin)
Fox—red (calico)   Duck—yellow (calico)
White squares and triangles in pieced blocks—
white (unbleached muslin)
Black trianges—red (calico)
Dotted triangles—green (calico)

Directions

1. Mark and cut eight background blocks for your appliques. Each block should measure 10½″ × 10½″ square. Mark a ¼″ sewing line on each block. Iron and set aside.

2. Photocopy or trace the patterns for the applique goose from this project (Figure 165) and the applique fox from **Project 9: Night in the Forest** (Figure 114). Mark and cut fabric for four geese and four foxes. Pin and applique each animal in the center of a background block.

3. You will be making eight pieced Fox and Geese blocks to alternate with the fox and goose appliqued blocks you have just completed. For each block you will need ten small white triangles, six small colored triangles, two large colored triangles, and four small white squares (Figures 162–164). Cut out all of the triangles and squares for the eight blocks and iron. Using a running stitch, piece each of the blocks. Think of each one as a group of four small squares and piece each square separately. Then join the four squares into a single block. Be sure to match your seams as you sew the triangles and squares into blocks.

4. Matching seams as you go, join two pieced blocks, one appliqued fox block and one appliqued goose block to make a group of four blocks. Do the same with the remaining blocks until all 16 blocks are joined together.

5. Quilt the project, doing outline quilting around each appliqued piece.

6. Trim to the finished size and bind your wall hanging. Add loops for hanging if desired.

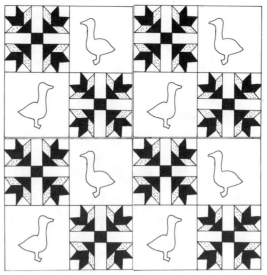

Variation 1

Goose Tracks

Also known as Duck's Foot in the Mud or Bear's Paw, the Goose Tracks pattern is a traditional favorite. Follow the basic project directions, but complete eight goose appliques (Figure 165) and leave out the fox appliques. Piece eight Goose Track blocks. For each block you will need four white rectangles, four white squares, one colored square, eight small white triangles, four large colored triangles, eight diamonds of one color and eight diamonds of another color (Figures 168–172). See the Piecing Diagram for this variation. Alternate appliqued blocks with pieced blocks and complete the project as directed.

Variation 2

Fox and Geese or Goose Tracks Pillow

Make a 20″ square pillow from two appliqued blocks and two pieced blocks of either design. To make a simple pillow backing cut a square 21″ × 21″ (that includes a ½″ seam allowance on all four sides). With right sides together, sew the backing to the quilted pillow front along three sides and along part of the fourth side, leaving a four to five inch opening for stuffing. Then turn right side out and stuff batting well into the corners, distributing it evenly throughout the square until it becomes plump. Finally, close the opening with blind stitches.

Variation 3

Fox and Geese or Goose Tracks Quilt

Follow the directions for either design, but add more blocks to make a twin or full-size quilt. Measure the bed for which your quilt is intended and allow for additional overhang to determine how many blocks you will need.

Project 15

Cats and Mice

Project Diagram
Finished size: 40" × 40"

About the Project

Sometimes the name of a pieced pattern fits its design exactly. Sometimes, a little more imagination is needed to see the connection between pattern name and the arrangement of triangles, diamonds and squares. For instance, it is easy to identify the large triangle "foxes" and the small triangle "geese" in the project that comes before this one. In the Cats and Mice pattern, however, which are the cats and which are the mice? It's hard to say for sure. Yet the ambiguity hasn't seemed to bother quilters.

This pattern is one that has been handed down and used for generations.

Try following the color suggestions offered here. Or use whatever small bits of calico you have left over from other projects to create a unique scrap quilt.

Please read about **Project 14: Fox and Geese** before beginning this project. The two projects are similar and you may find the details included in the preceding directions helpful.

Materials

3 yards background and block fabric (unbleached muslin)

Batting—44″ × 44″

Backing fabric—44″ × 44″

1 yard fabric for appliqued cats and mice (brown calico)

1½ yards fabric for pieced blocks (orange calico)

Thread to match applique fabric

Quilting thread

Quilt binding to match fabric (approximately 5 yards)

Color Suggestions for Project 15

Background to animals—white (unbleached muslin)

Cat, mice—brown (calico)

White areas of pieced blocks—white (unbleached muslin)

Dark areas of pieced blocks—orange (calico)

Directions

1. Mark and cut eight background blocks for your appliques. Each block should measure 10½″ × 10½″ square. Mark a ¼″ sewing line on each side of each block. Iron and set aside.

2. Photocopy or trace the patterns for the appliqued cat and mouse (Figures 166–167). Mark and cut fabric for four cats and eight mice. Pin and applique a cat or two mice in the center of each background block.

3. You will be making eight pieced Cats and Mice blocks to alternate with the appliqued blocks you have just completed. For each block you will need twelve small white triangles, eight small colored triangles, four large white triangles, and five colored squares (Figures 173–175). Cut out all of the triangles and squares for the eight blocks and iron. Using a running stitch, piece each of the

blocks. Begin by joining together the small triangles that make up squares. Next piece the squares into a cross. Finally, add the outer triangles to complete the block. Be sure to match the seams as you go.

4. Again, matching seams as you go, join two pieced blocks, one cat block and one mice block to make a group of four blocks. Do the same with the remaining blocks until all 16 blocks are joined together.

5. Quilt the project, doing outline quilting around each triangle in the pieced blocks and each appliqued piece in the appliqued blocks.

6. Trim to the finished size and bind your wall hanging, adding loops at the top for displaying if desired.

Variation 1

Cats and Mice Pillow

Follow the basic project directions to make a 20″ pillow from two pieced blocks and two appliqued blocks in the Cats and Mice design. See the pillow variation instructions for **Project 14: Fox and Geese** before you begin.

Variation 2

Cats and Mice Quilt

Follow the basic project directions, but add more blocks to make a twin or full-size quilt. Measure the bed for which your quilt is intended and allow for additional overhang to determine how many blocks you will need.

Project 16
Flying Geese

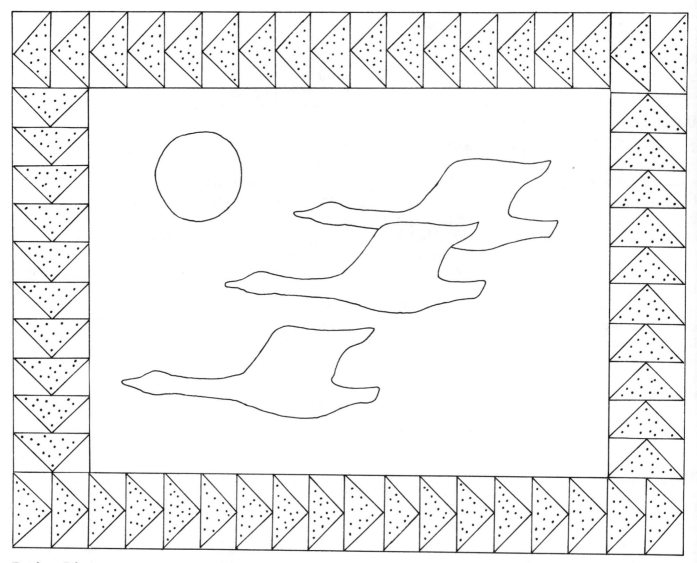

Project Diagram
Finished size: 45" × 35"

About the Project

Geese both wild and tame played an important role in the lives of many of our ancestors. Perhaps that is why geese provide the imagery in so many traditional quilt patterns. The Flying Geese pattern is generally done in long vertical rows that alternate with wide fabric strips up and down the length of a quilt. The pattern, however, lends itself to use as a border design like the one that appears here.

Although this project is similar in visual content to **Project 6: Gulls on the Water,** it has been included here because it combines pieced work and applique techniques like the two projects that come immediately before it.

Materials

Background fabric—33″ × 25″ (medium blue)
Batting—49″ × 39″
Backing fabric—49″ × 39″
1 yard fabric for appliqued geese (black)
1 yard fabric for large border triangles (lavender calico)

1 yard fabric for small border triangles and sun (dusty rose)
Thread to match applique fabrics
Quilting thread
Quilt binding to match (approximately 5 yards)

Color Suggestions for Project 16

Background for geese—medium blue
Sun—dusty rose
Bottom, middle geese—black

Top goose—dark gray
Plain triangles—dusty rose
Dotted triangles—lavender (calico)

Directions

1. Photocopy or trace the pattern pieces for the large flying goose applique (Figures 178–178a). Ignore the dotted lines on the goose pattern unless you are doing Variation 2 for this project. You will need to tape the two pattern pieces together to make a paper template. Then use the template to mark and cut three large geese from your fabric.

2. Trace the pattern for the large sun from **Project 6: Gulls on the Water** (Figure 79). Mark and cut out fabric.

3. Trace, mark and cut 56 large border triangles and 112 small border triangles (Figures 176–177).

4. Using a running stitch, sew a small border triangle on each side of a large border triangle to make a rectangle. See the Border Rectangle Diagram. You will complete 56 rectangles in all.

5. Using a running stitch, piece together the rectangles to form the flying geese borders. To make sure your piecing is accurate, fold each large triangle in half. Put a pin in the middle of the base of the large triangle. Sew the point of the next triangle so that it lines up with the pin in the exact middle of the base of the triangle before it. See the Border Piecing Diagram. Sew two long rows of 18 Flying Geese rectangles each and two short rows of 10 rectangles each.

6. Pin and applique the large geese and the sun to the background fabric.

7. Pin and sew the rows of pieced Flying Geese rectangles to the background fabric. Join the loose border seams at the corners.

8. Quilt the project, doing outline quilting around each pieced block and each appliqued piece.

9. Trim to the finished size and bind the project. Add loops for hanging if desired.

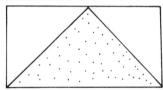

Border Rectangle Diagram

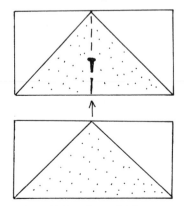

Border Piecing Diagram

Canadian Geese Diagram

Variation 1

Canadian Geese

To turn your flying geese into Canadian geese, follow the basic project directions, but use the dotted lines on the goose pattern pieces to guide you in coloring the goose (Figures 178–178a). Add white in the areas indicated by the Canadian Geese Diagram. Use white fabric appliqued onto the black fabric goose applique, or use white fabric paint on the black goose applique. Complete the project as directed.

Project 17
The Pond

Project Diagram
Finished size: 35" × 25"

About the Project

This project and the two that follow it use irregular block combinations. We tend to think of block quilts as containing many blocks of the same size and shape. Irregular block quilts are becoming an increasingly popular contemporary variation on the old-time block design.

Keep in mind the possibility of using the patterns as suggested in the project or one of its variations, but use color to suggest a different season or time of day—autumn or nighttime, for instance.

Materials

Center background block—15½″ × 15½″ (blue)

Two large left and right background rectangles—10½″ × 25½″ (lavender)

Four small top and bottom background rectangles—8″ × 5½″

Batting—39″ × 29″

Backing rectangle—39″ × 29″

½ yard fabric for cattails (light brown calico)

½ yard fabric for grasses (light green calico)

½ yard fabric for water ripple (light blue)

Assorted fabric scraps for remaining appliques

Thread to match applique fabrics

Quilting thread

Quilt binding to match (approximately 4 yards)

Color Suggestions for Project 17

Background for cattails—lavender

Background for flowers—green

Background for ducks (stream)—light blue

Background for stream, waterlilies—blue

Ducks—light brown

Flowers—pink (calico)

Leaves of flowers—light green (calico)

Cattails—light brown (calico)

Leaves of cattails—light green (calico)

Water lilies—white

Leaves of water lilies—dark green (calico)

Directions

1. Mark a ¼″ seam allowance on each side of each of the background blocks and rectangles. This means that when your blocks and rectangles are pieced together, their measurements will be:

Center background block: 15″ × 15″

Large background rectangles: 10″ × 25″ each

Small background rectangles: 7½″ × 5″

2. You will be appliquing each block separately and using a number of patterns from other projects. Photocopy or trace the patterns for the following:

Tulip and leaf from **Project 2: The Folk Tree** (Figures 42 and 36)

Cattail and grass blade from **Project 6: Gulls on the Water** (Figures 84–85)

Duck from **Project 3: Animal Town** (Figure 51)

3. Mark and cut your fabric for the appliques from the above patterns. You will need:

7 tulips: 4 from tulip fabric and 3 from water lily fabric

20 leaves: 8 from leaf fabric and 12 from water lily fabric

6 cattails at varying lengths from 18″ to 14″ high *(Note: You will need to extend the pattern from the bottom for the cattails and the grass blades.)*

8 grass blades at varying lengths from 18″ to 14″

2 ducks *(Note: When marking fabric for the ducks, leave off the legs to make swimming ducks.)*

4. Trace, mark and cut out the water lily (Figures 42, 36 and 179).

5. Trace the pattern pieces for the water ripple (Figures 183–184) that goes diagonally across the center block. Tape the two pieces together to make a template. Cut the water ripple from a single piece of fabric using the template you have made.

6. Applique the water ripple to the center background block. Sew together the petals and lily pad of each water lily using the Water Lily Diagram as a guide. Applique the finished water lilies in place on the center block.

7. Applique the cattails and grass blades to the two large background rectangles.

8. Applique a tulip and two leaves on each small background rectangle.

9. Join all of the background blocks and rectangles together.

10. Quilt the project, doing outline quilting around each appliqued piece.

11. Trim to the finished size and bind the project, adding loops for hanging if desired.

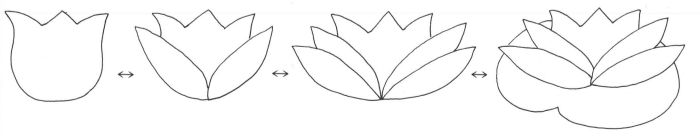

Water Lily Diagram

Variation 1

Songbirds by the Pond

How often have your seen a red-winged blackbird as it perched impossibly on the tip of a slender reed? Use the bird from **Project 1: The Animal Tree** (Figure 16) in black with a swatch of red along the wing to suggest a blackbird. Follow the basic project directions, but use four water lilies (See Steps 4 and 6 above) in the small background rectangles. Instead of water lilies in the center block, substitute the long-stemmed tulip (Figure 191), bird on a branch (Figure 188) and three-leafed twig (Figure 189). Then complete the project as directed.

Variation 2

Baby Ducks

For a spring scene, follow the basic project directions, substituting four baby ducks (Figure 180) for one of the adult ducks and the frog from **Project 9: Night in the Forest** (Figure 120) for the water lilies. Use Figure 17 for the butterfly.

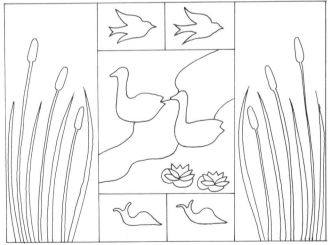

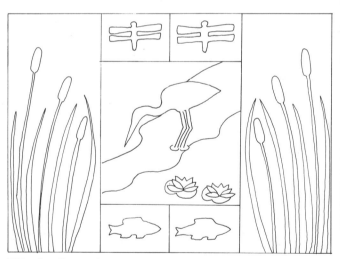

Variation 3

Swans a-Swimming

Follow the basic project directions, but substitute swallows (Figure 182) for the tulips at the top and snails (Figure 181) for the tulips at the bottom. Use two water lilies (See Steps 4 and 6 under Project 17 "The Pond.") instead of three and substitute the swans (Figure 186) for the ducks.

Variation 4

Heron in the Pond

Follow the basic project directions, but substitute the heron (Figure 187) for the ducks, the dragonflies (Figure 18) for the tulips at the top, the fish (Figure 185) for the tulips at the bottom, and use two water lilies (See Steps 4 and 6 under Project 17 "The Pond.") instead of three. You might want to use embroidery to add the suggestion of water rings around the immersed legs of the heron.

Variation 5

American Eagle

Follow the basic project directions, but use the star and the heart from **Project 2: The Folk Tree** (Figures 46 and 45). Replace the large left and right background rectangles with red calico and white strips 2½″ × 25½″. Mark the strips with a ¼″ seam allowance before sewing so that their sewn measurement will be 2″ × 25″ each. Applique two navy blue rectangles 6″ × 7½″ (does not include seam allowance) with red calico hearts and sew in place on the strips. Applique red calico stars to alternating white and navy small background rectangles. Divide the center block into four squares or eight triangles. Alternate in white and blue and applique with a red calico eagle (Figure 190).

Bird Diagram

Project 18

La Paloma

Project Diagram
Finished size: 25" × 20"

About the Project

Whether it is *molas* from the Kuna Indians of Panama, *arpilleras* by Chilean needlewomen or colorful embroidery from Mexico, American quilters are more attracted than ever before to the needlework of their Spanish-speaking neighbors to the south.

The dove forms the main subject of this project that has been inspired by several different styles of needle art. Follow the color suggestions offered here or use warm colors of your own choosing—reds, golds, greens and browns. Solid colors, rather than tiny, old-fashioned calicos, will give your wall hanging a more authentic feel.

Materials

Large, assorted fabric scraps, mostly solid colors, for background blocks, appliques and pieced geometric shapes
Batting—29″ × 24″
Backing rectangle—29″ × 24″

Thread to match applique fabrics
Quilting thread
Quilt binding to match applique fabrics (approximately 4 yards)

Color Suggestions for Project 18

Goat—red
Background for goat—light green
Dove—yellow
Background for dove—orange
Woman with basket—magenta
Background for woman—medium blue
Lizards—light green
Background for lizards—dark green

Star—red
Background for star—light green
Dark triangles and bars—red
White triangles and bar with crosses—magenta
Dotted bars—yellow
Lined bar—light green
Top white bar—dark green
Lower white bar—orange

Directions

1. Photocopy or trace the patterns for the girl carrying a bundle on her head (Figure 193), the lizard (Figure 192) and the short fabric strip (Figure 194). You will need one girl, two lizards (each facing a different direction) and ten short strips. Mark and cut out fabric.

2. Mark and cut out the following background blocks, iron and set aside:
Two 10½″ × 10½″ blocks (one for the goat and one for the dove)
One 5½″ × 10½″ block (for the girl)
One 15½″ × 5½″ block (for the lizards)
One 5½″ × 5½″ block (for the star)

3. Mark a ¼″ seam allowance all the way around each block.

4. Trace the patterns from the following projects. Mark and cut out fabric for: One large goat from **Project 8: Down on the Farm** (Figure 103), One flying dove from **Project 10: Noah's Ark** (Figure 124), One star from **Project 2: The Folk Tree**

(Figure 46), Six large and twenty small border triangles from **Project 16: Flying Geese** (Figures 176–177). (Note: the colors of the triangles should alternate as in the Project Diagram.)

5. Applique each piece to its appropriate block, turning under each piece's outer edges.

6. Piece together a pinwheel from eight of the small triangles.

7. Piece a triangle strip from the remaining triangles. See the Triangle Strip Diagram.

8. Piece together a row of ten short fabric strips.

9. Sew together all of the pieced strips or rows and all of the appliqued background blocks.

10. Quilt the project, doing outline quilting around each pieced block and around each appliqued piece.

11. Trim to the finished size and bind the project, adding loops for hanging if desired.

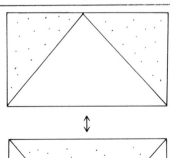

Triangle Strip Diagram

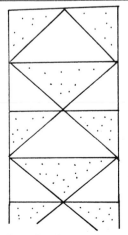

Strip Piecing Diagram

Project 19

The Shore

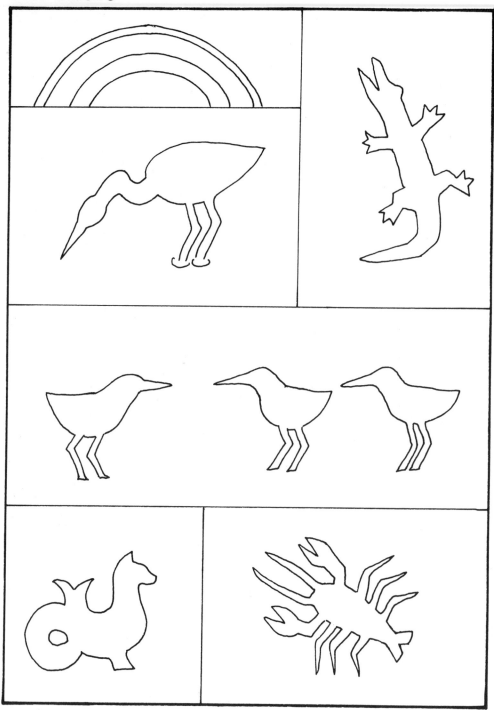

Project Diagram
Finished size: 25" × 35"

About the Project

A visit to the seashore always yields new sightings of marine birds and animals. Commemorate a trip to the coastline with this project, its variation or a variation of your own. Let blues and greens predominate for a northern shoreline, pinks and oranges for a southern one.

76

Materials

⅓ yard fabric for one large background rectangle—25½″ × 10½″ (sand)

Assorted fabrics for three background rectangles—15½″ × 10½″ each (light pink, peach and light green)

Fabric for background rectangle—15½″ × 5½″ (light blue)

Fabric for background square—10½″ × 10½″ (peach)

Assorted fabric scraps for appliques

Thread to match applique fabrics

Quilting thread

Quilt binding to match (approximately 4 yards)

Color Suggestions for Project 19

Background for rainbow—light blue

Top layer of rainbow—light pink

Second layer of rainbow—dark rose

Third layer of rainbow—peach

Bottom layer of rainbow—light blue

Background for heron—light green

Heron—white

Background for alligator—peach

Alligator—light green

Background for ibis—sand

Ibis—light brown

Background for sea creature—aqua

Sea creature—peach

Background for lobster—light pink

Lobster—light green

Directions

1. Mark a ¼″ seam allowance all the way around each background block.

2. Photocopy or trace the patterns for the lizard (Figure 195), the sandpiper (Figure 196), the sea serpent (Figure 197) and the crayfish (Figure 198). Mark fabric. Be sure to mark three sandpipers with two facing one direction and one facing another. Cut out and set aside.

3. Trace the patterns from the following projects: Half circle and several moon rings from **Project 7: Wolves and the Rising Moon** (Figures 89–92), Large heron from **Project 17: The Pond** (Figure 187).

4. Mark, cut out and set aside.

5. Sew each applique to its appropriate block. See the Project Diagram. Follow the directions from **Project 7: Wolves and the Rising Moon** for sewing together the rings of the rising sun in the upper left corner rectangle (page 47).

6. Sew together the background blocks.

7. Quilt the project, doing outline quilting around each applique.

8. Trim to the finished size and bind the project, adding loops for hanging if desired.

Variation 1

Florida Shore

Florida is the home of a number of threatened species. Porpoises and pelicans especially need our help if they are to survive. Follow the basic project directions including the half circle and several moon rings (Figures 89–92) and crayfish (Figure 198), but substitute the porpoise from **Project 4: Seal Mother and Baby** (Figure 56), the scallop shell from **Project 3: Animal Town** (Figure 54), and the small fish from **Project 17: The Pond** (Figure 185). Use the exotic fish, small pelican, and crayfish (Figures 198–200) included in this project. Complete the project as directed.

Project 20
Ideas and More Ideas

As you become acquainted with the animal patterns in this book, you'll come up with all kinds of uses for them. Here are a few smaller projects that make up quickly and easily.

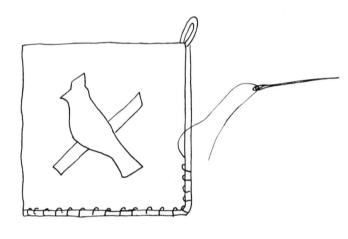

2. Placemat

Follow the directions for the potholder, but use large fabric or washable felt rectangles—18″ × 12″.

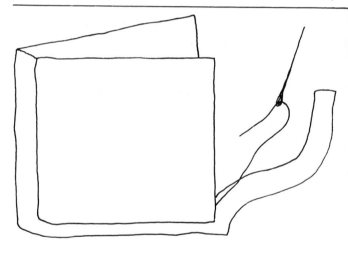

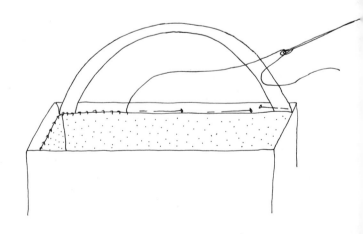

1. Potholder

Use fabric or washable felt to create an animal potholder. Trace, mark and cut out your animal applique. Turn under the edges if you are using fabric, as you machine- or hand-stitch onto an 8″ × 8″ or 9″ × 9″ fabric or felt square. Use a matching size square of batting and of backing. Whip-stitch around the edge, add a fabric loop and hide your rough whip-stitching with fabric binding.

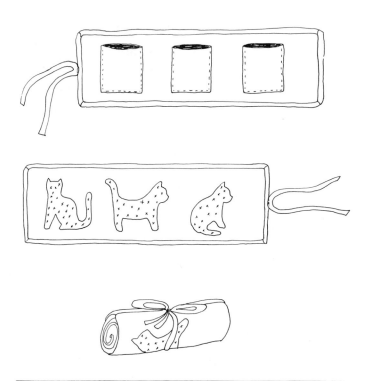

3. Tote Bag

Make an animal tote bag from two 12″ squares and one 36″ × 4″ strip of pre-quilted fabric (available at most fabric stores). With right sides together, join the strip to the squares along three sides. Turn right side out. Turn under and hem the ragged top edge. On the outside of the squares, applique the animals of your choice. Add a lining, if desired, from unquilted fabric or felt. You will need again two 12″ squares and one 36″ × 4″ strip for your lining. Sew just as you did the quilted outside of your tote, but leave the wrong side out. Turn under the top and pin the lining just inside the top of the quilted tote. Position canvas strip handles so the ends are between the lining and the quilted tote. Sew the lining in place along the top, reinforcing your stitches along the handles.

4. Sewing Organizer

An animal-appliqued sewing organizer will keep all your different kinds of quilting equipment handy. It also makes a nice gift. Cut a piece of pre-quilted fabric to 16″ × 9″. Bind the ragged edge with quilt binding all the way around. On one side applique three small pockets 3″ × 6″ each. Be careful not to let your stitches run all the way through to the opposite side. On the other side applique several animals in a row. Again, do not let your stitches show through to the pocket side of the fabric. Attach a matching ribbon long enough to tie around the organizer when it is rolled up—about 18″ long.

5. Shawl

A unique triangular animal shawl can be made from a 2½ yard piece of firmly woven plain background fabric. Fold the fabric in half and cut on the diagonal to make the basic triangle. Applique your chosen animals along the short sides of the triangle. Cut a lining from a 2½ yard piece of thin, loosely woven lining fabric. Turn under, pin and iron the three edges of each triangle. Pin together the two triangles. As you pin, you may find you have to make the lining triangle smaller so its edges will not stick out beyond the appliqued triangle. Blind stitch the two triangles together. Add fringe along the two short edges of the appliqued triangle. You will need approximately 5 yards of fringe.

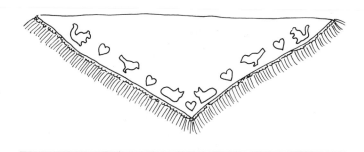

6. Clothing Appliques

Add animal appliques to the bottom of a skirt, or the top of a jumper or full-length apron. Try adding them to a skirt or apron pocket, vest and more.

7. Book Cover

Make an appliqued fabric cover for a blank book, sketch book, or photo album. Glue batting rectangles to the front and back of the book. Cut a rectangle of background fabric 2″ larger on each side than the open, flattened book. Mark the front panel of the fabric rectangle. Applique the animals in place on the part of the fabric that will be the book's cover. Position the open book on the wrong side of the appliqued rectangle. Make four clips in the fabric just to the edge of the book binding. Fold under the fabric that sticks out beyond the top and bottom of the binding and glue. Fold the corners of the fabric rectangle around the corners of the book and glue in place. Use masking tape to hold the glue in place while it dries. When dry, glue a rectangle of fabric on the inside front and back covers to hide the ragged edges of the appliqued rectangle.

Template Diagrams

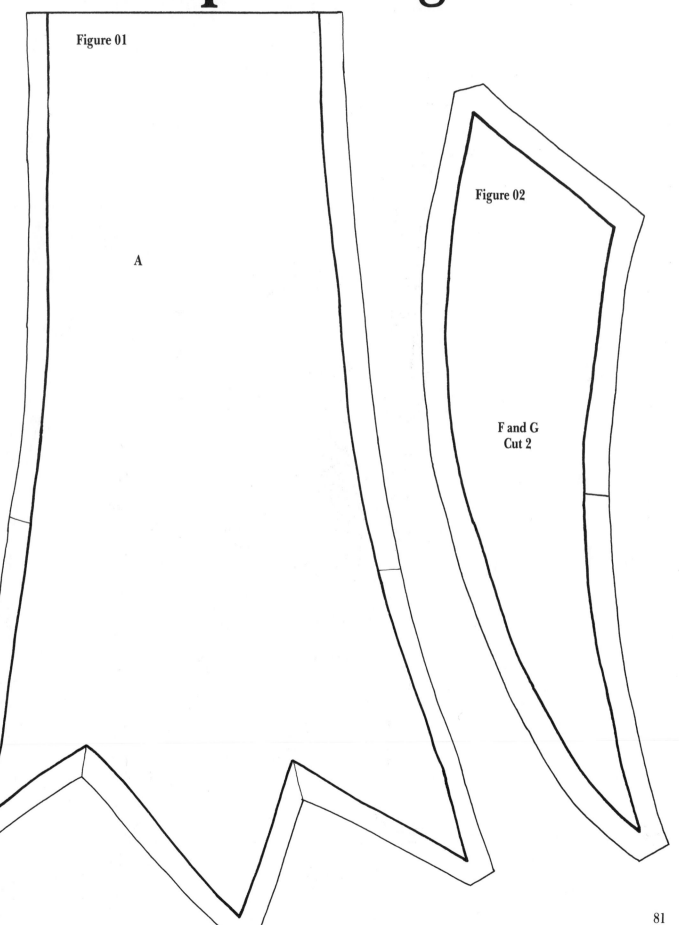

Figure 01

A

Figure 02

F and G
Cut 2

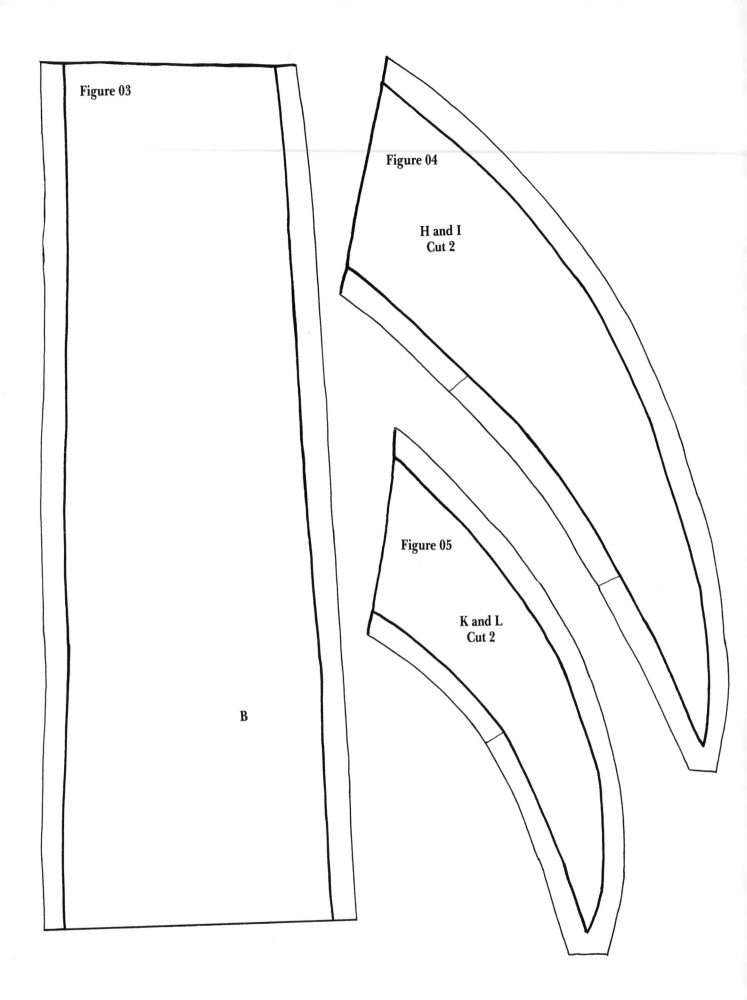

Figure 03

B

Figure 04

H and I
Cut 2

Figure 05

K and L
Cut 2

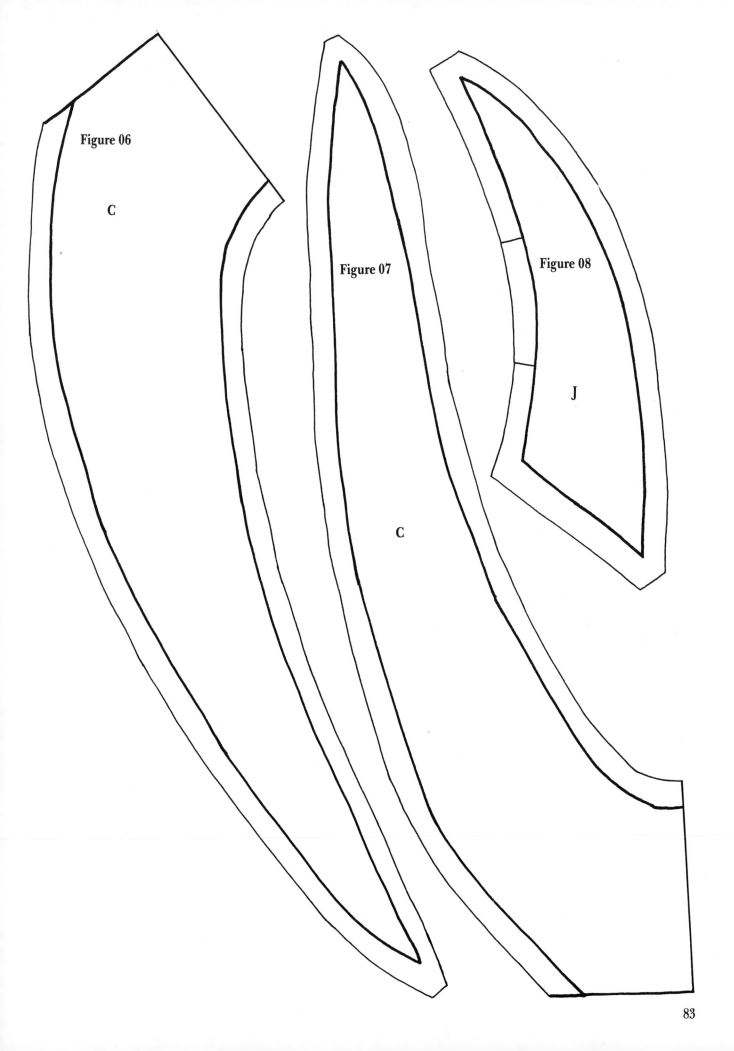

Figure 06

C

Figure 07

C

Figure 08

J

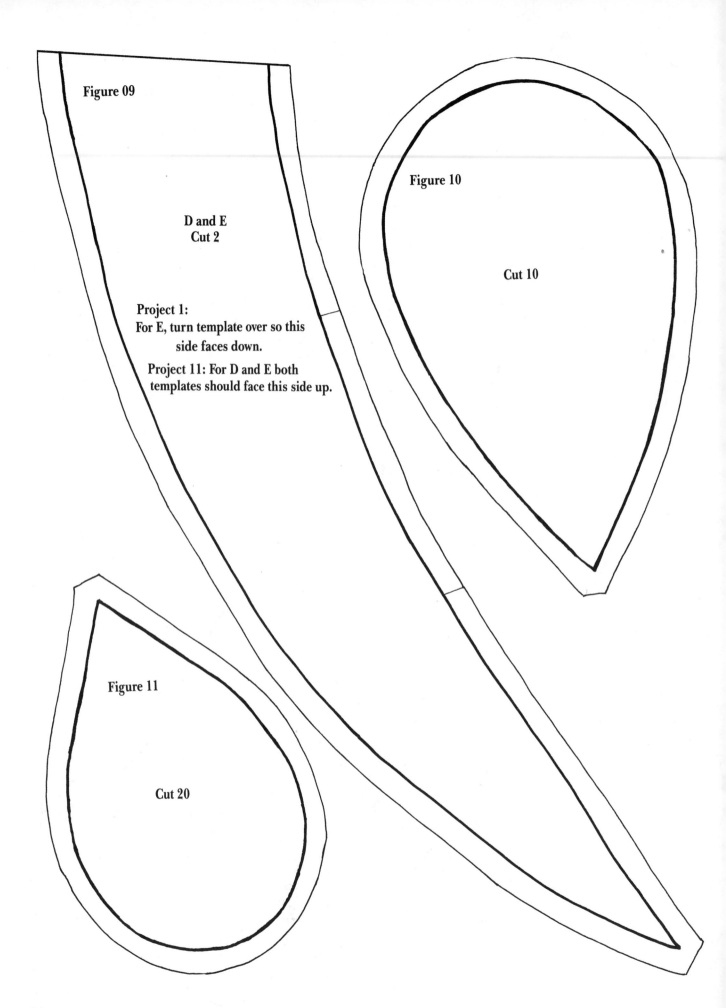

Figure 09

D and E
Cut 2

Project 1:
For E, turn template over so this
side faces down.

Project 11: For D and E both
templates should face this side up.

Figure 10

Cut 10

Figure 11

Cut 20

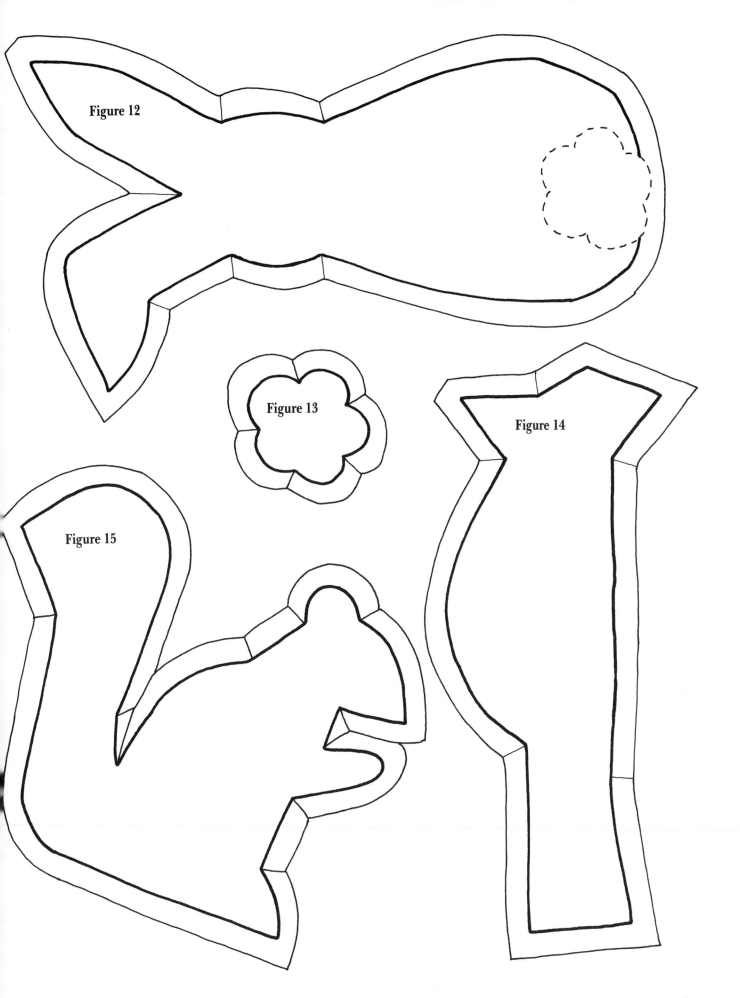

Figure 12

Figure 13

Figure 14

Figure 15

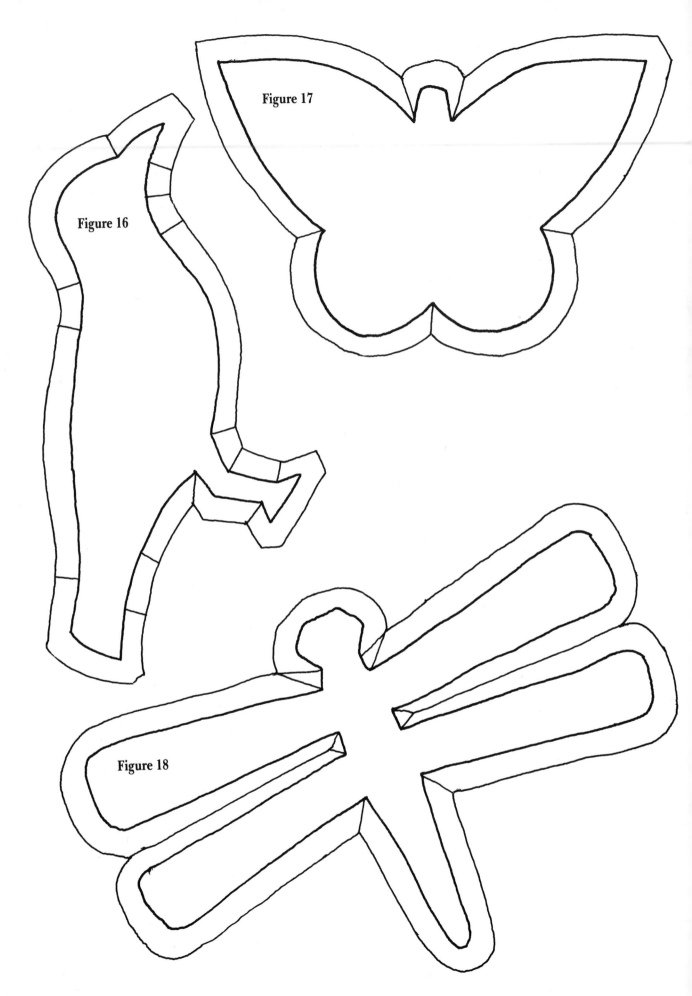

Figure 17

Figure 16

Figure 18

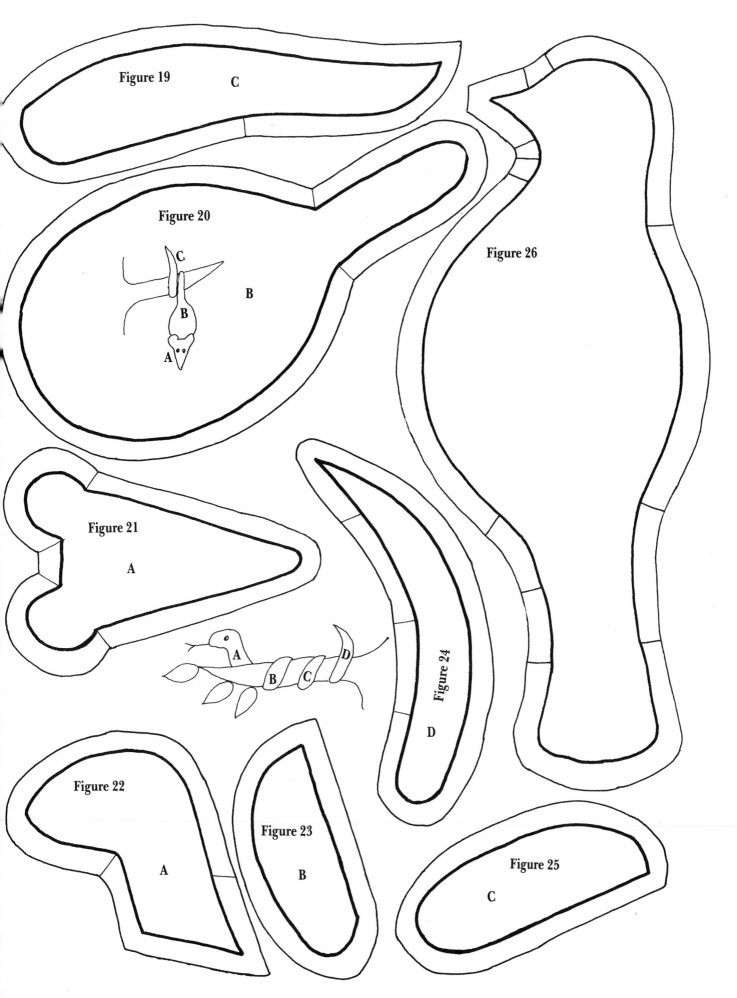

Figure 19   C

Figure 20

C

B

B

A

Figure 26

Figure 21

A

A   B   C   D

Figure 24

D

Figure 22

A

Figure 23

B

Figure 25

C

87

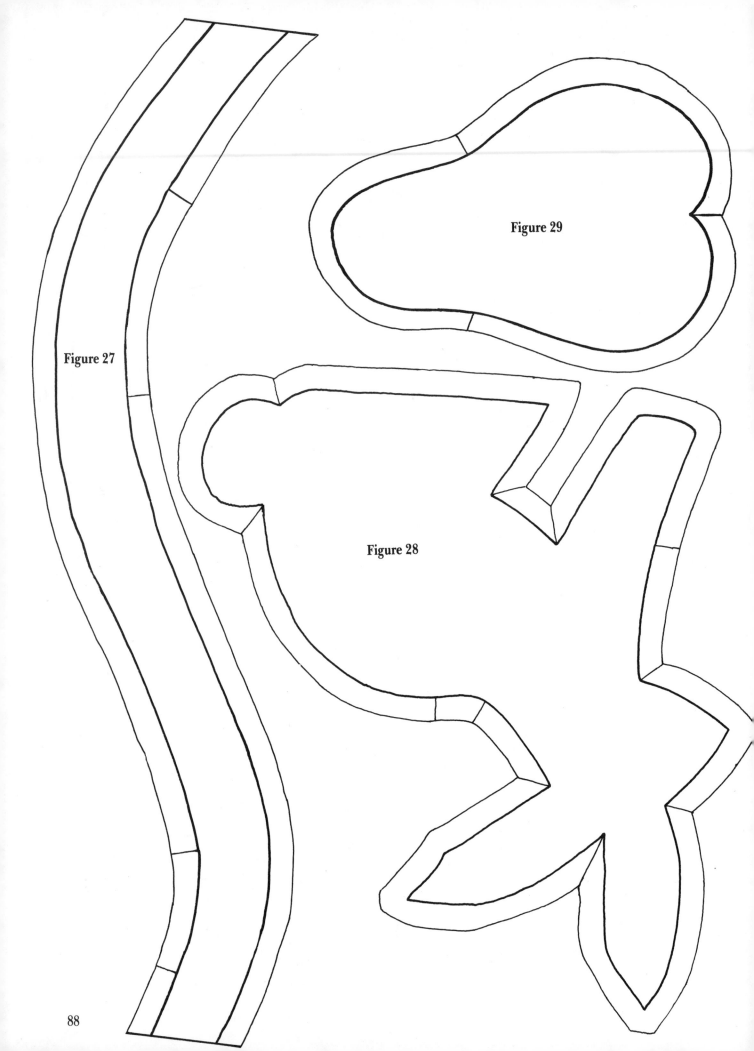

Figure 27

Figure 29

Figure 28

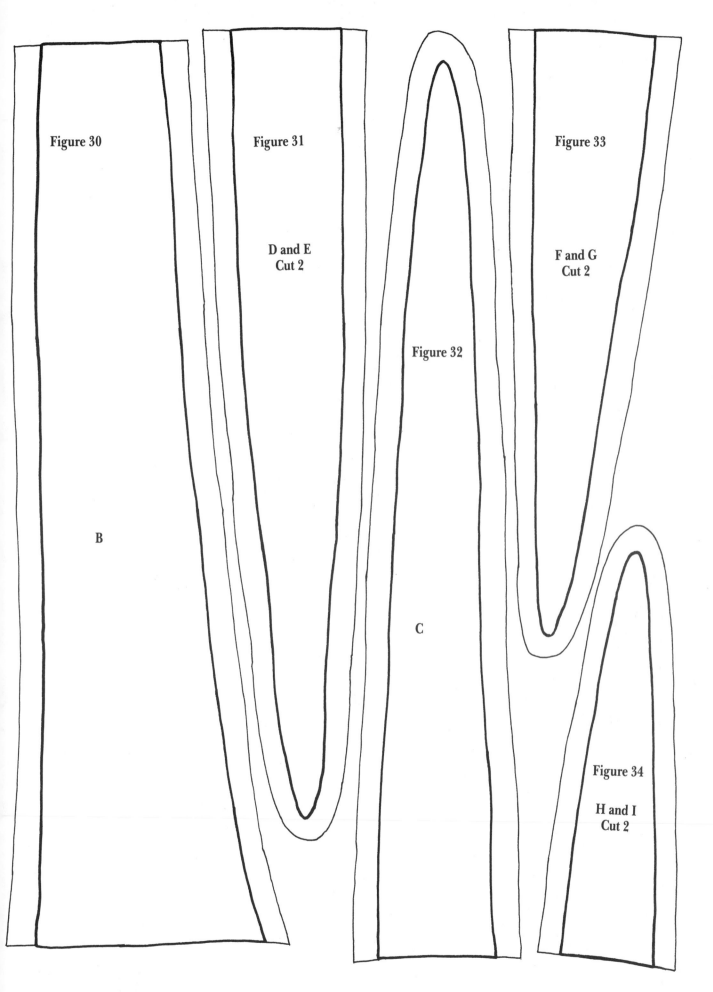

Figure 30

Figure 31

D and E
Cut 2

Figure 33

F and G
Cut 2

Figure 32

B

C

Figure 34

H and I
Cut 2

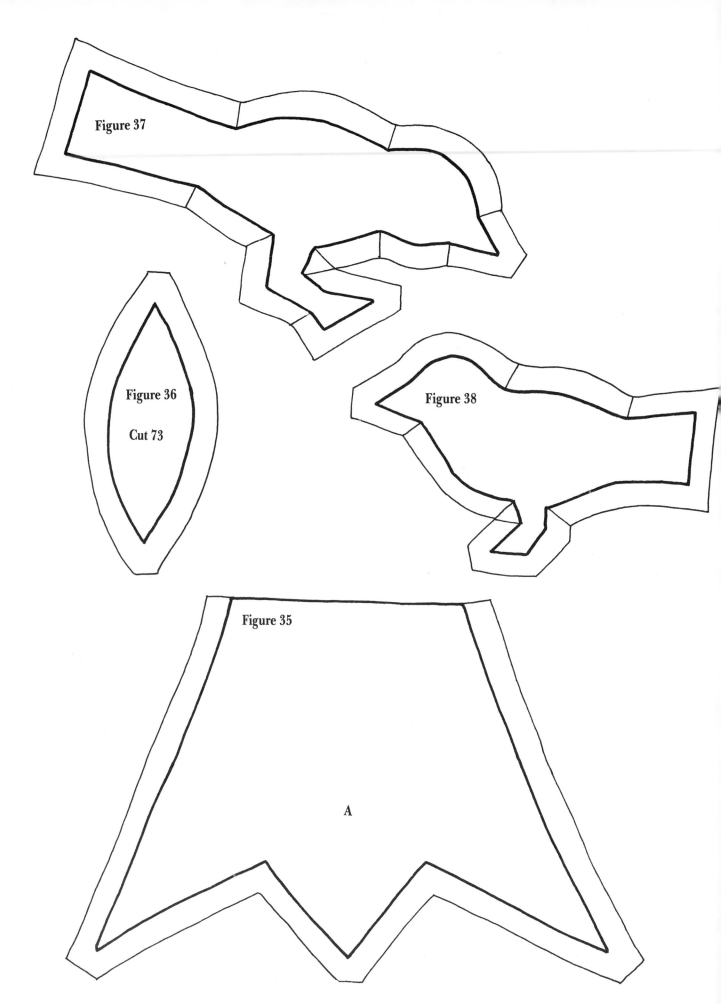

Figure 37

Figure 36

Cut 73

Figure 38

Figure 35

A

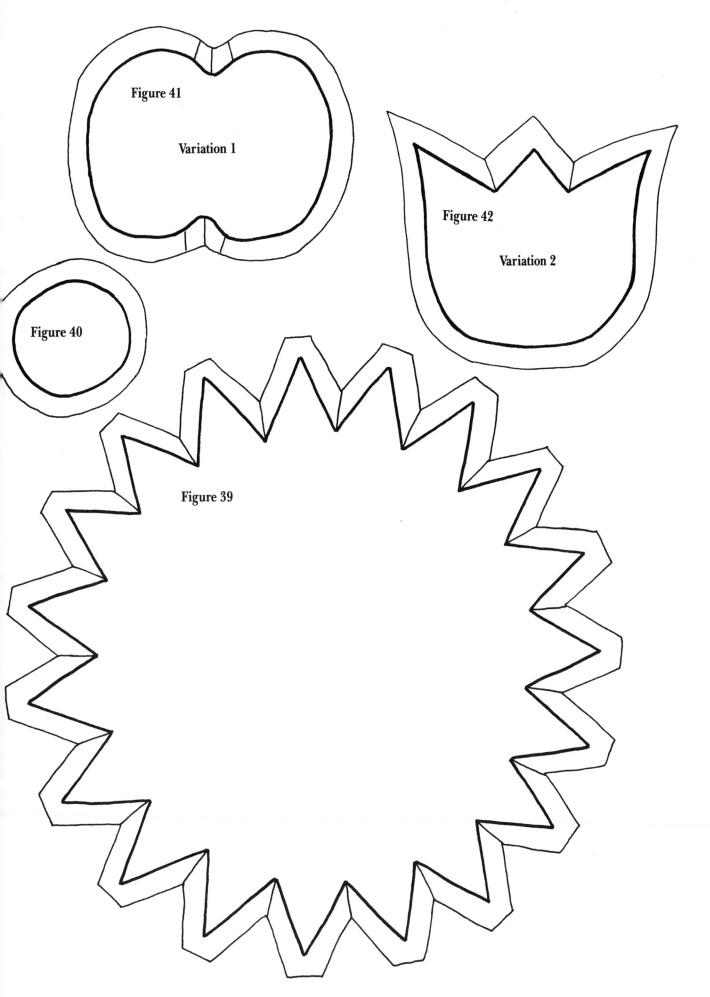

Figure 41

Variation 1

Figure 42

Variation 2

Figure 40

Figure 39

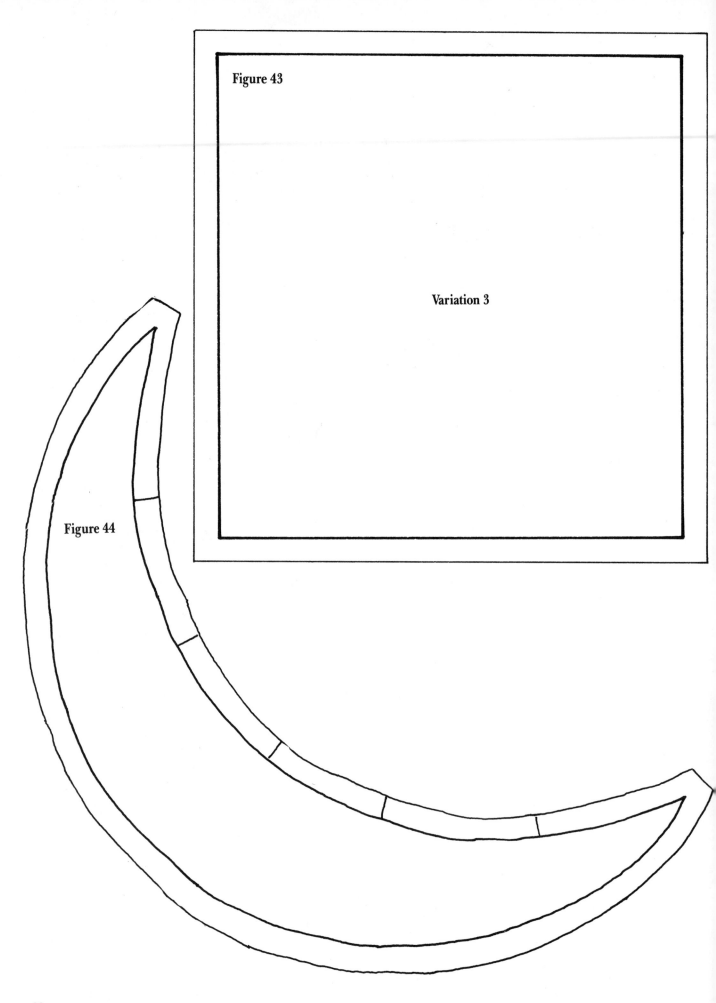

Figure 43

Variation 3

Figure 44

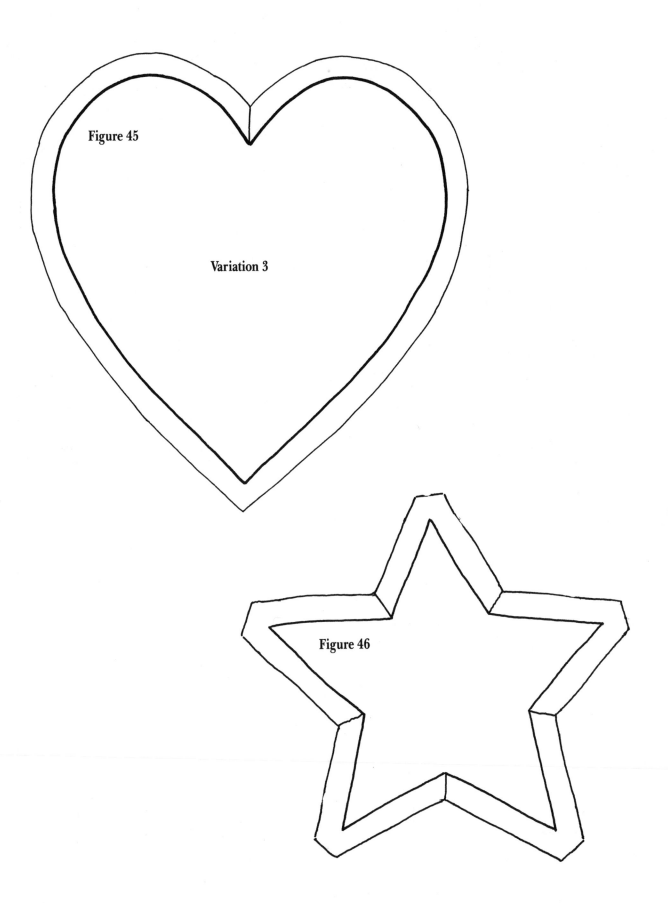

Figure 45

Variation 3

Figure 46

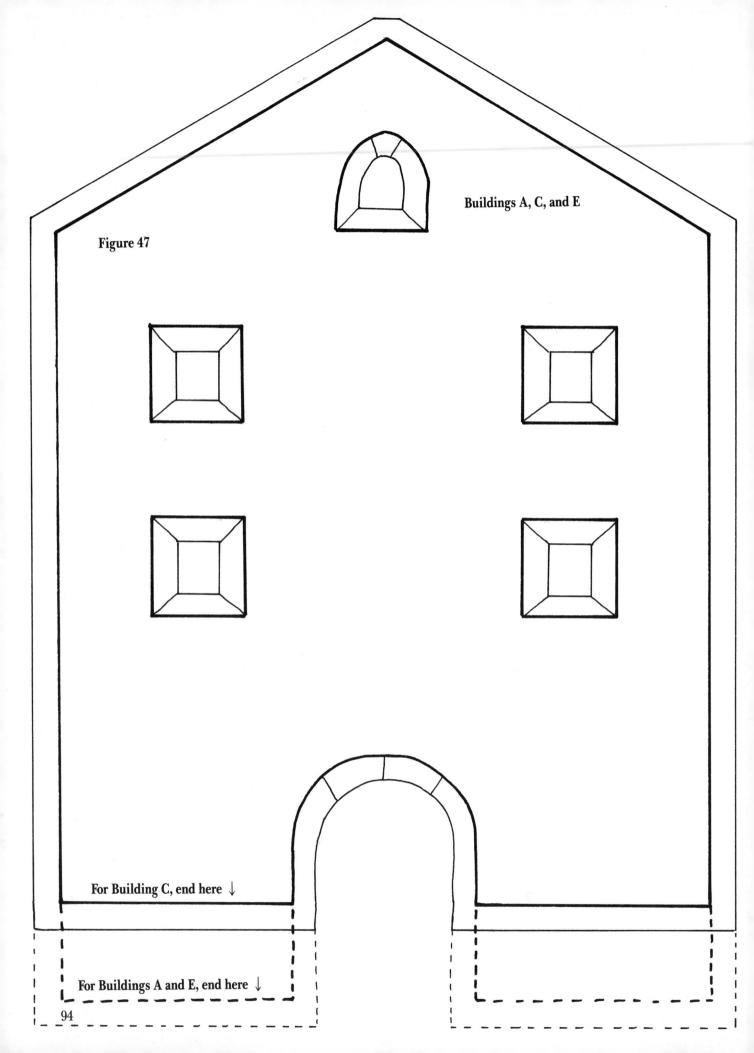

Buildings A, C, and E

Figure 47

For Building C, end here ↓

For Buildings A and E, end here ↓

94

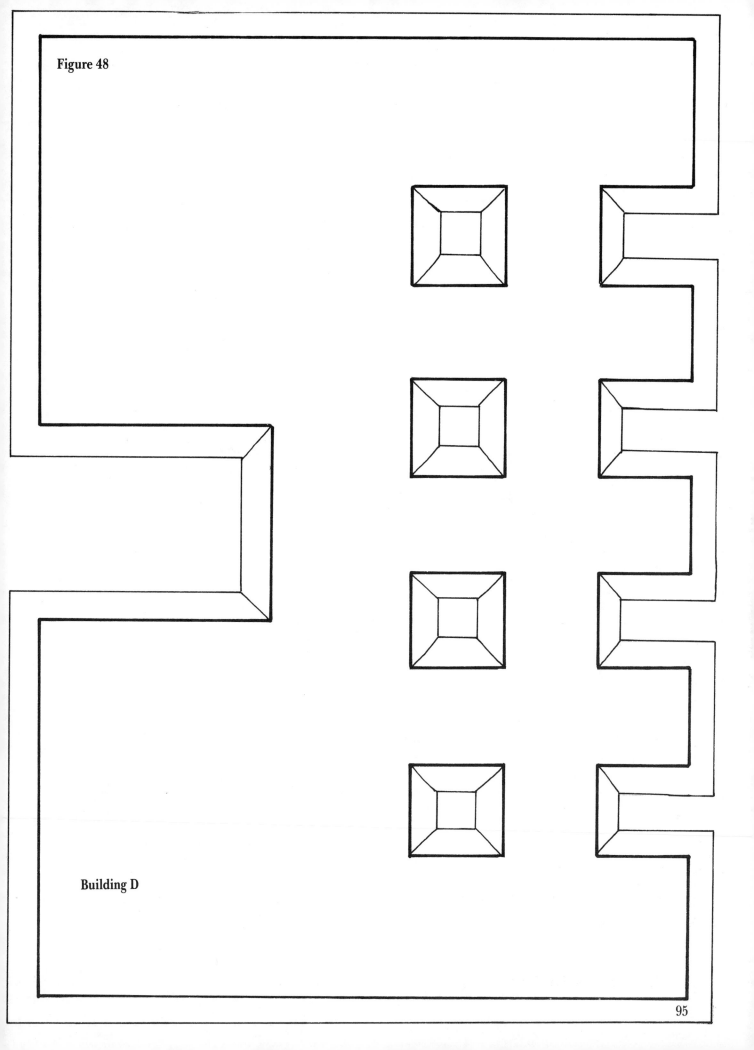

Figure 48

Building D

95

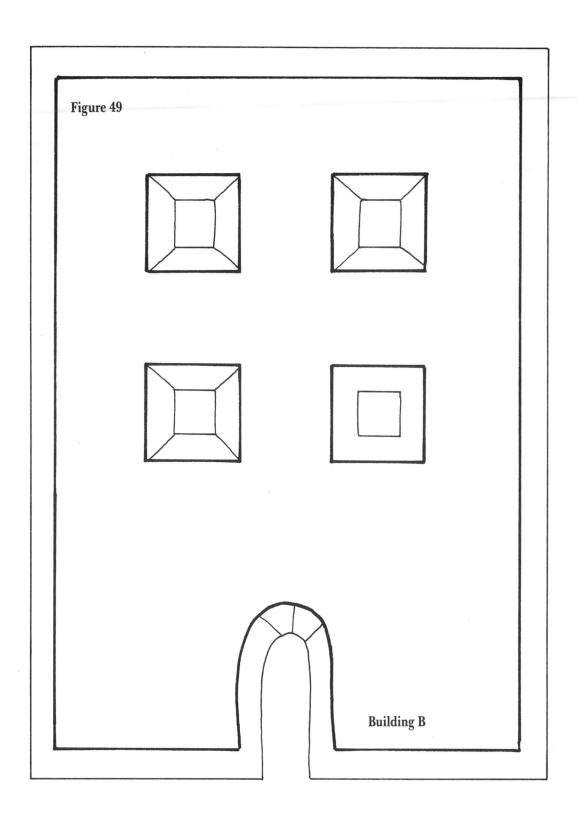

Figure 49

Building B

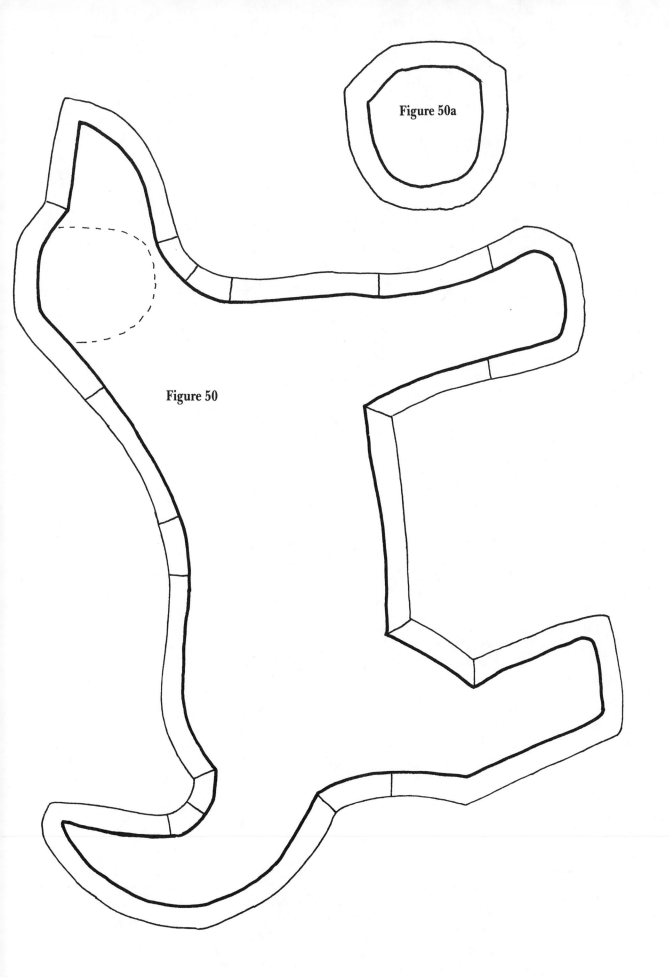

Figure 50a

Figure 50

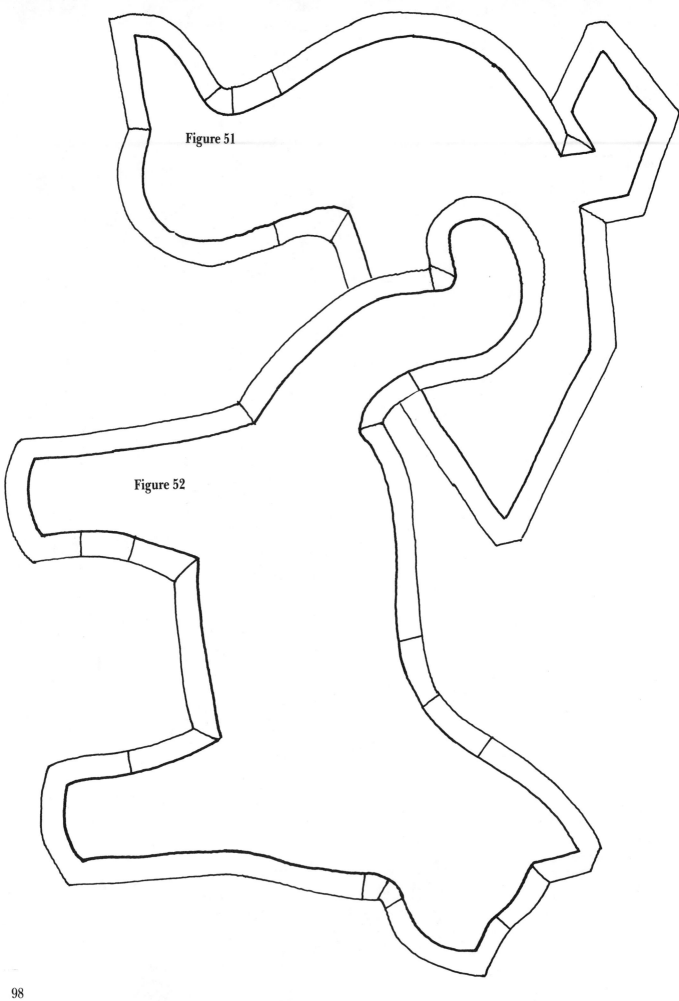

Figure 51

Figure 52

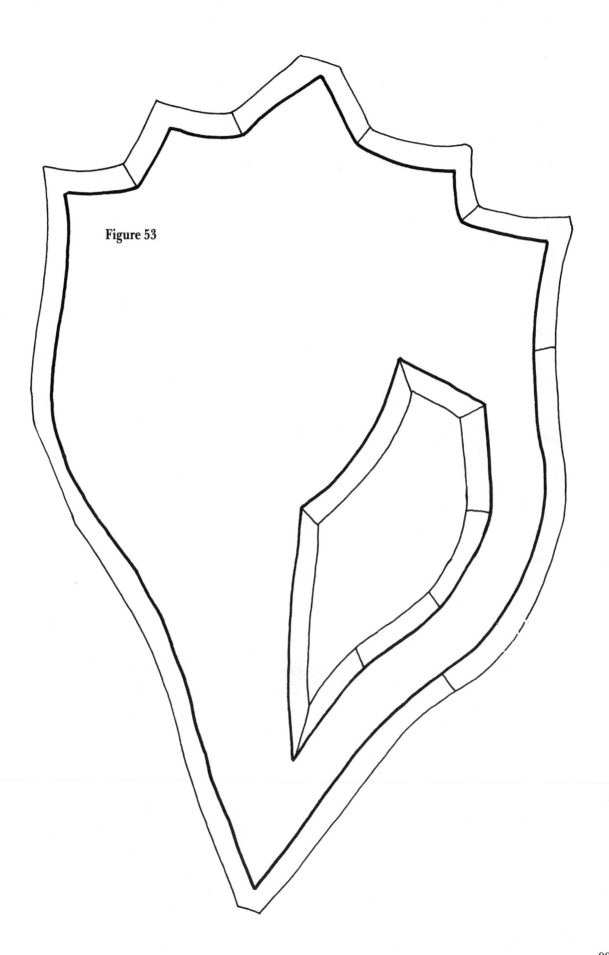

Figure 53

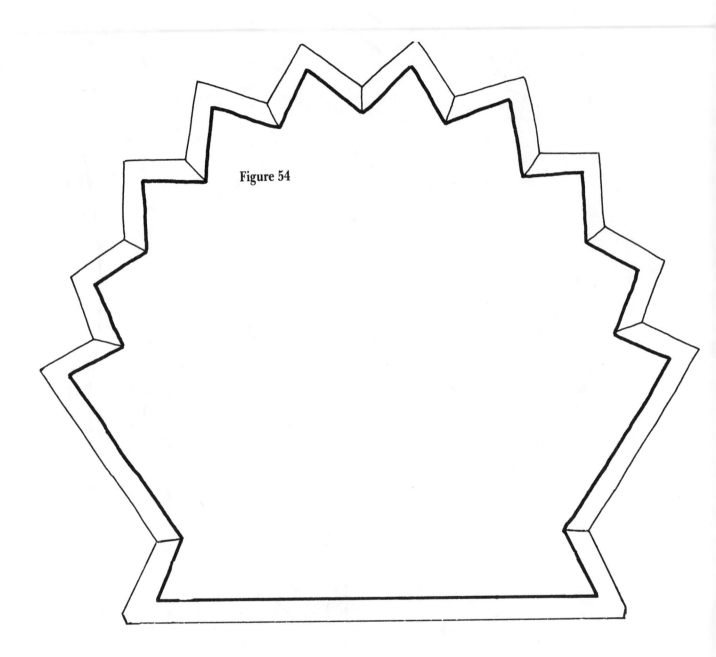

Figure 54

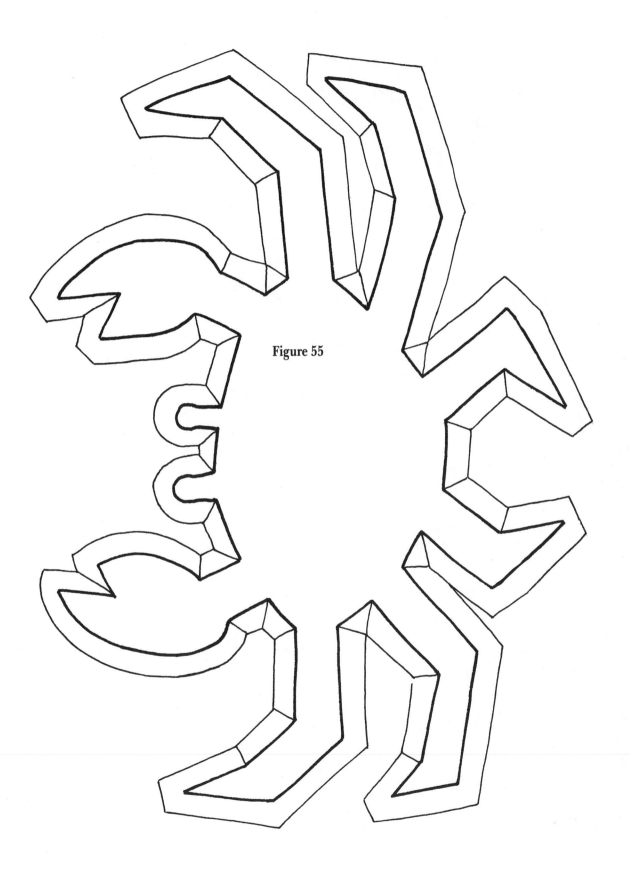

Figure 55

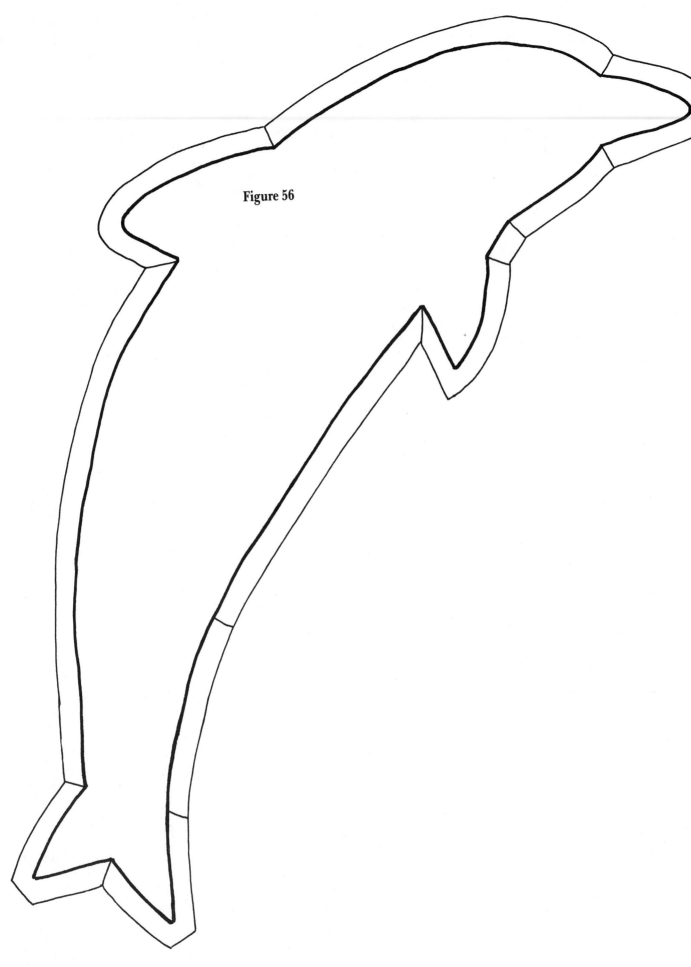

Figure 56

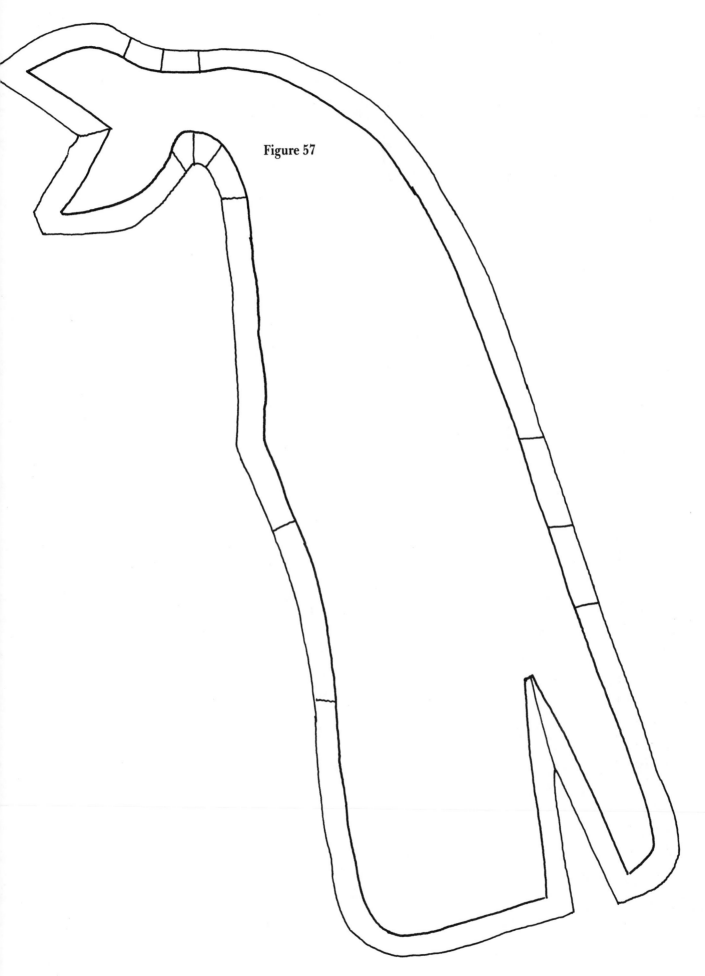

Figure 57

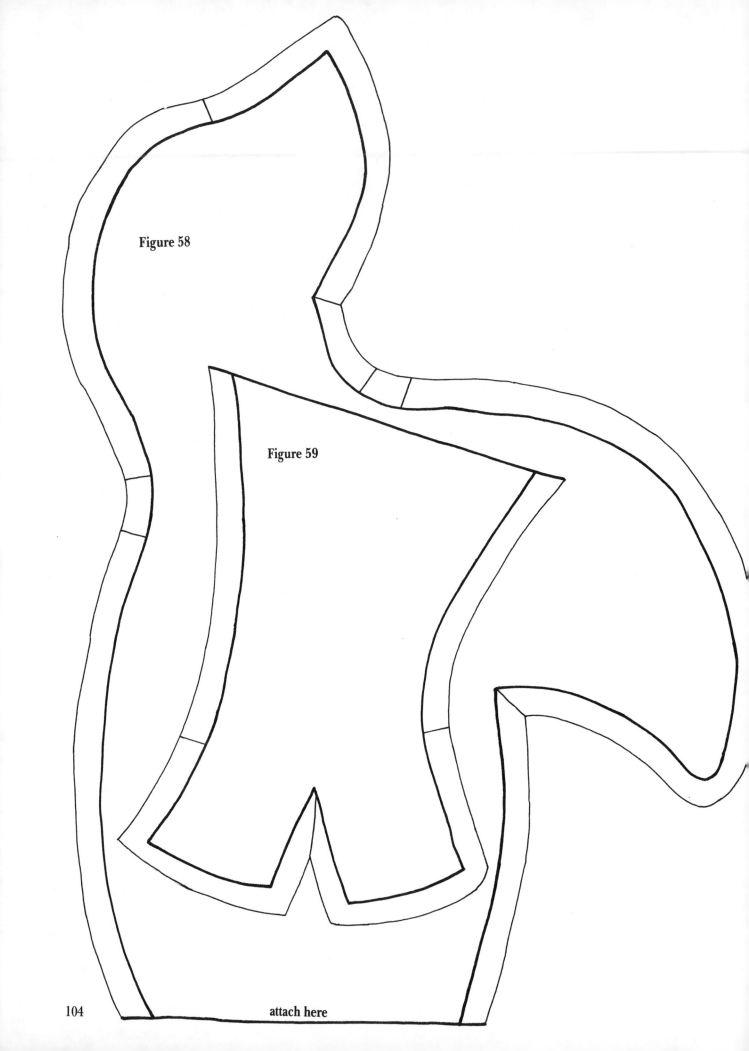

Figure 58

Figure 59

104

attach here

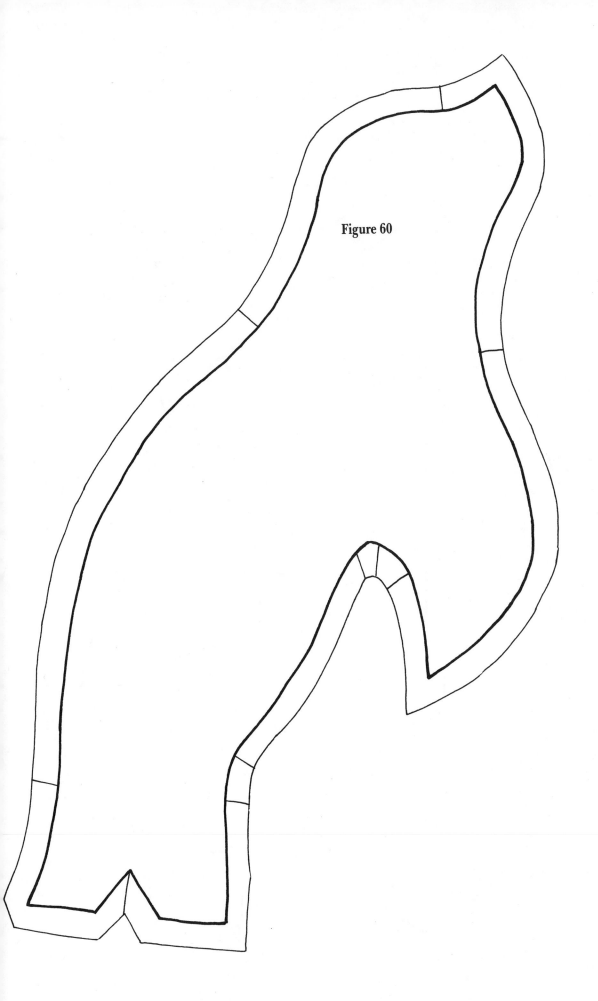

Figure 60

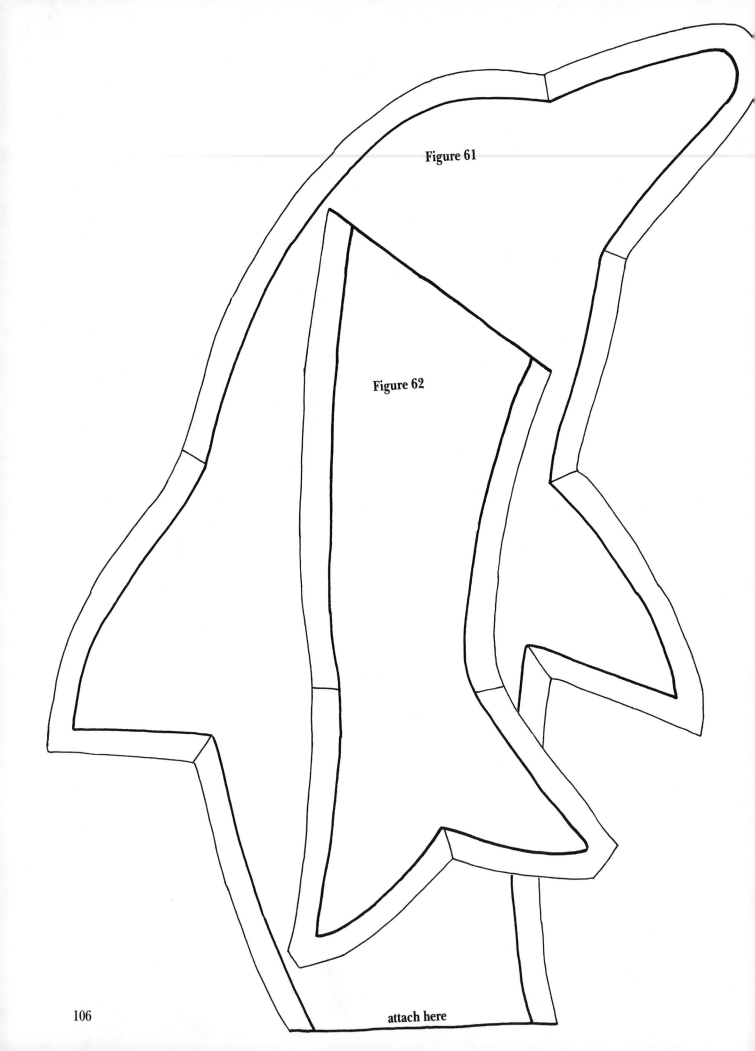

Figure 61

Figure 62

attach here

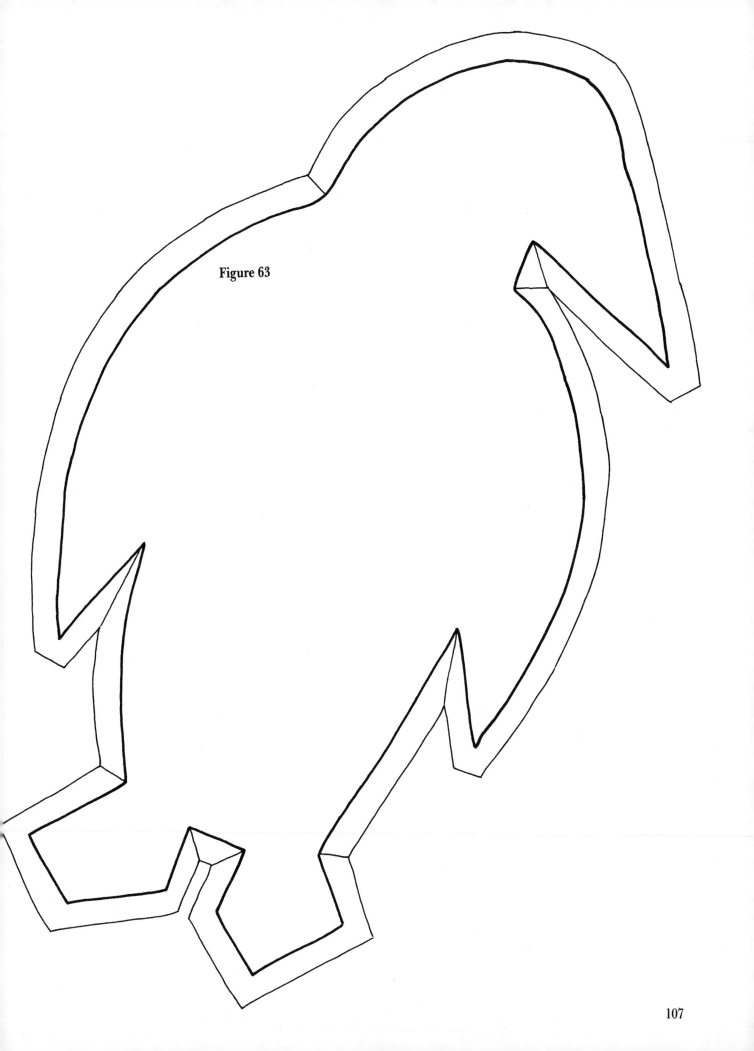

Figure 63

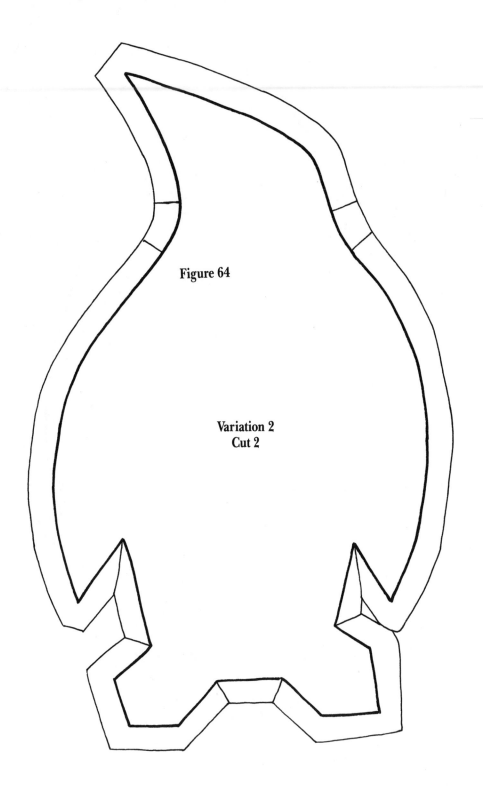

Figure 64

Variation 2
Cut 2

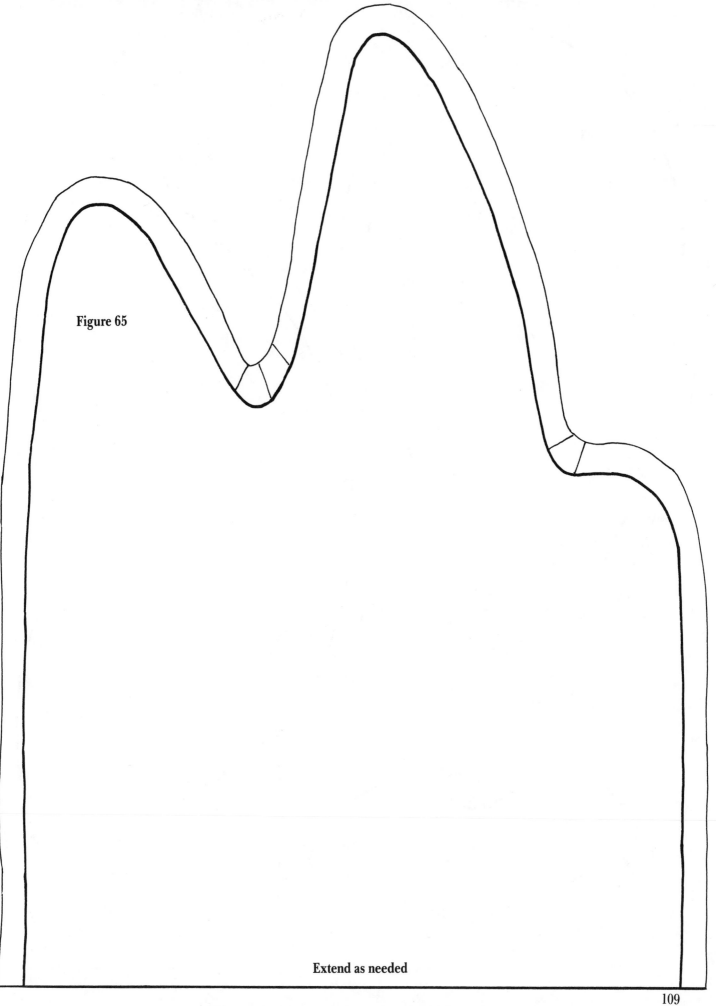

Figure 65

Extend as needed

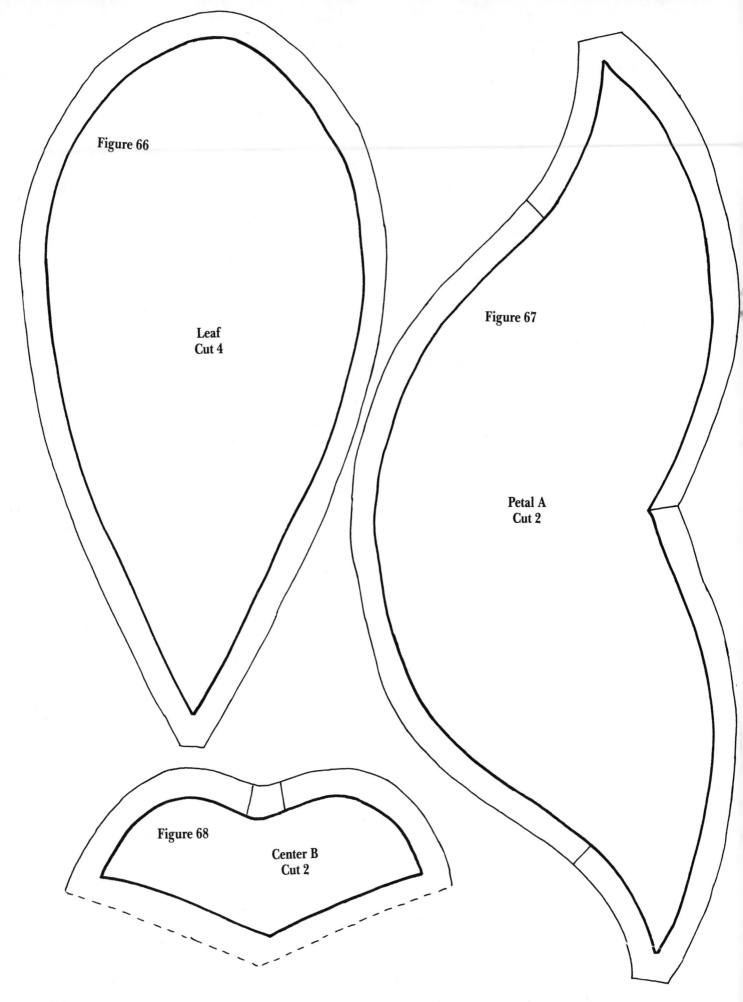

Figure 66

Leaf
Cut 4

Figure 67

Petal A
Cut 2

Figure 68

Center B
Cut 2

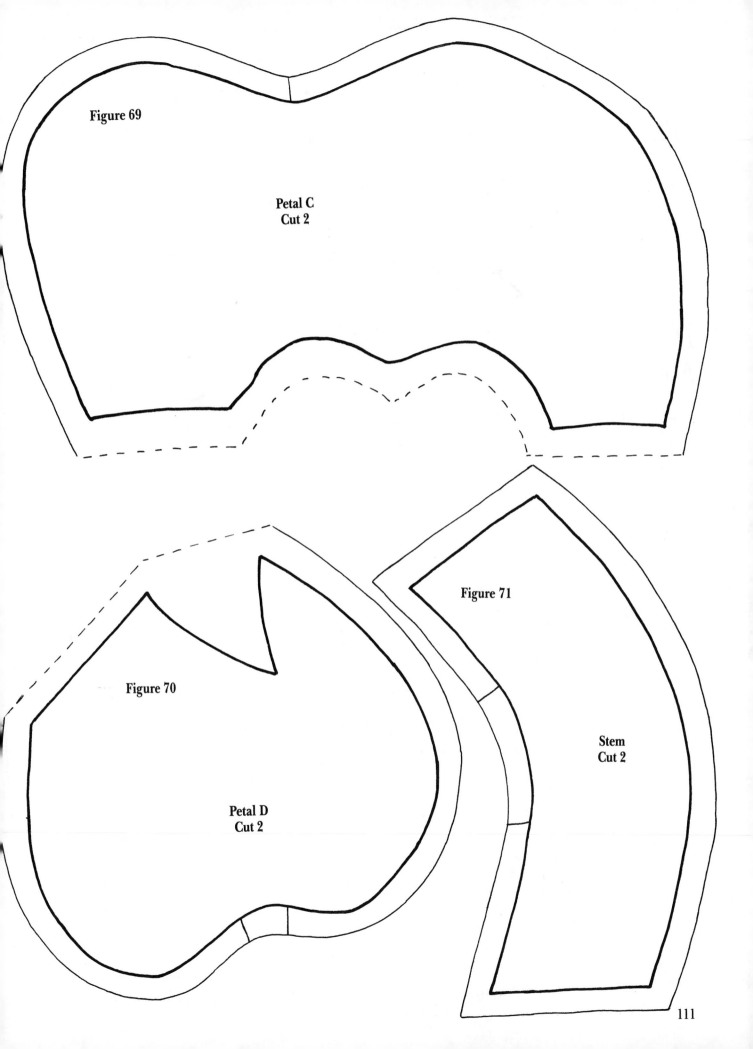

Figure 69

Petal C
Cut 2

Figure 71

Figure 70

Figure 70

Petal D
Cut 2

Stem
Cut 2

111

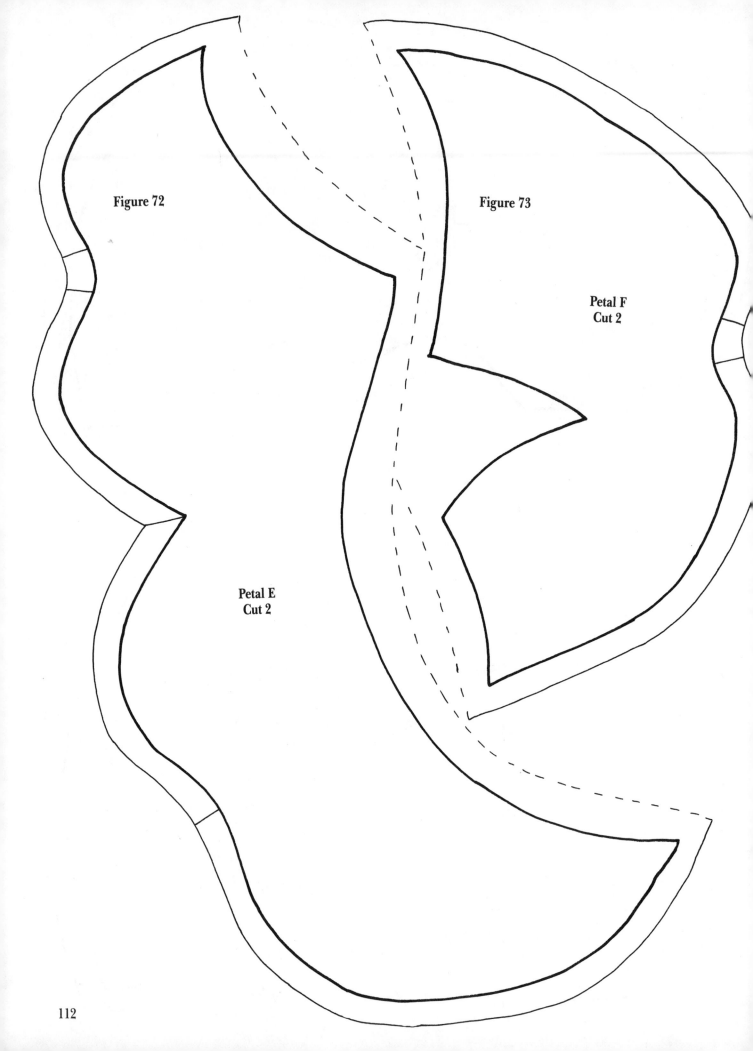

Figure 72

Figure 73

Petal F
Cut 2

Petal E
Cut 2

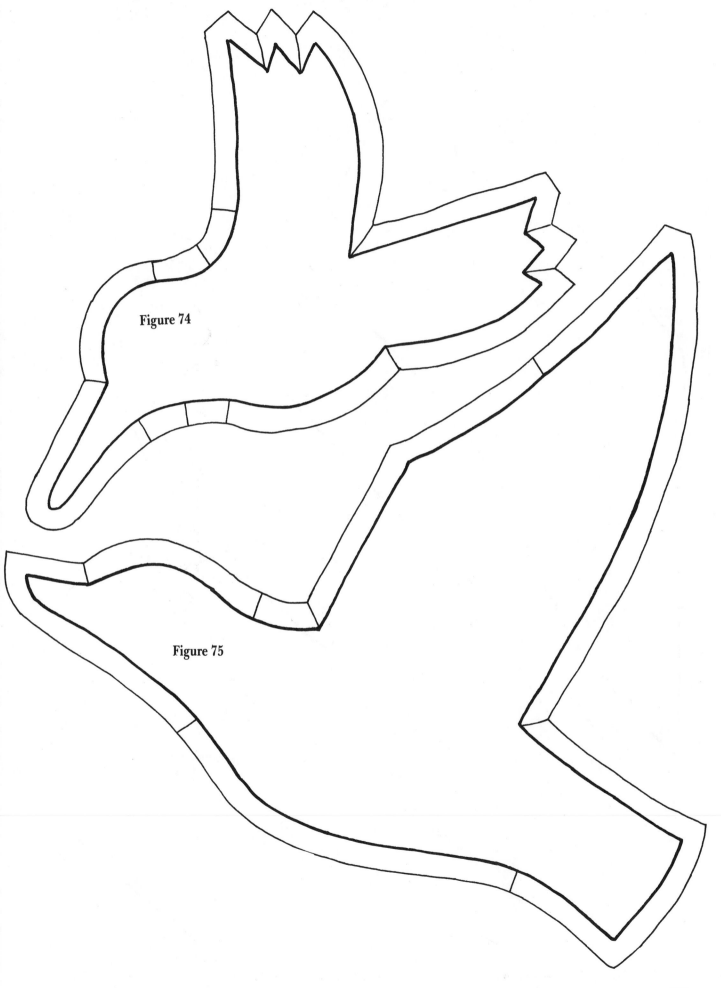

Figure 74

Figure 75

113

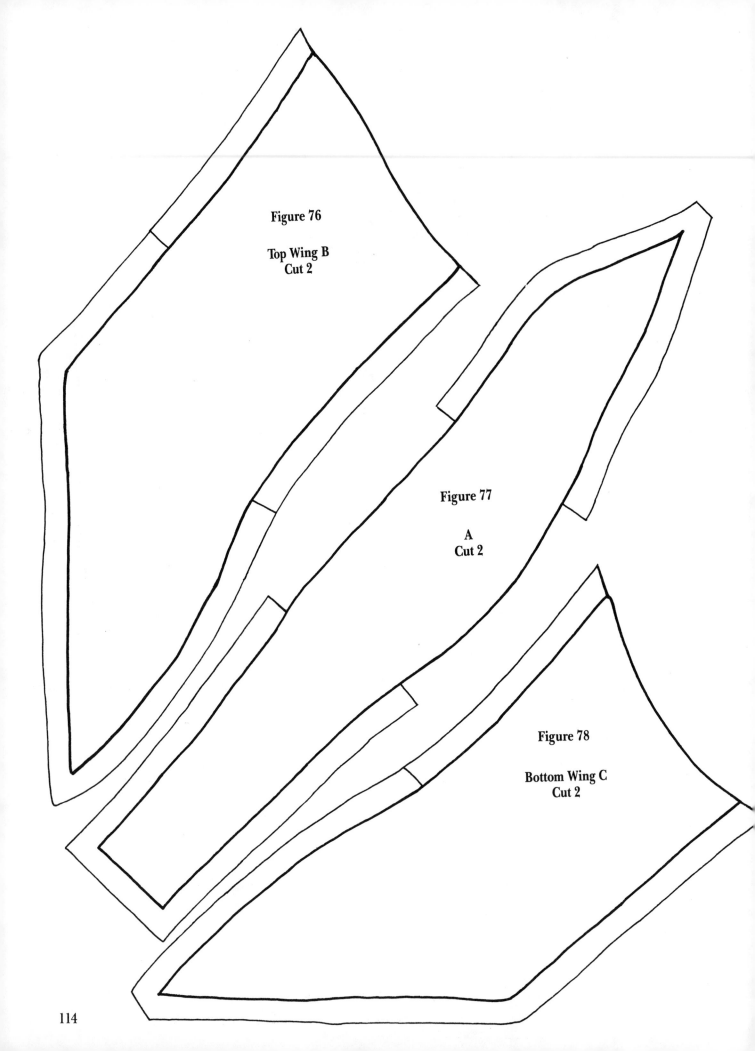

Figure 76

Top Wing B
Cut 2

Figure 77

A
Cut 2

Figure 78

Bottom Wing C
Cut 2

114

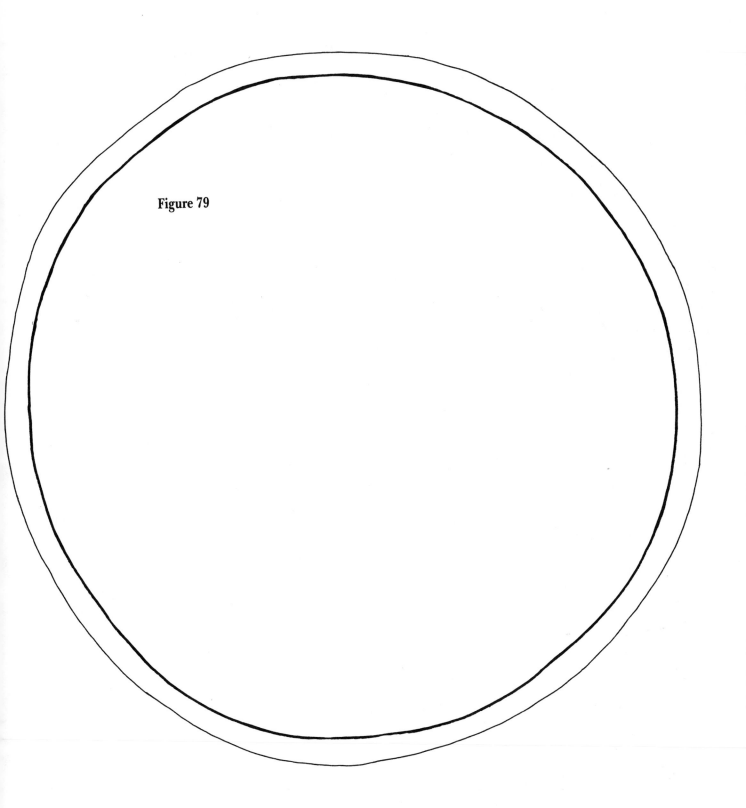

Figure 79

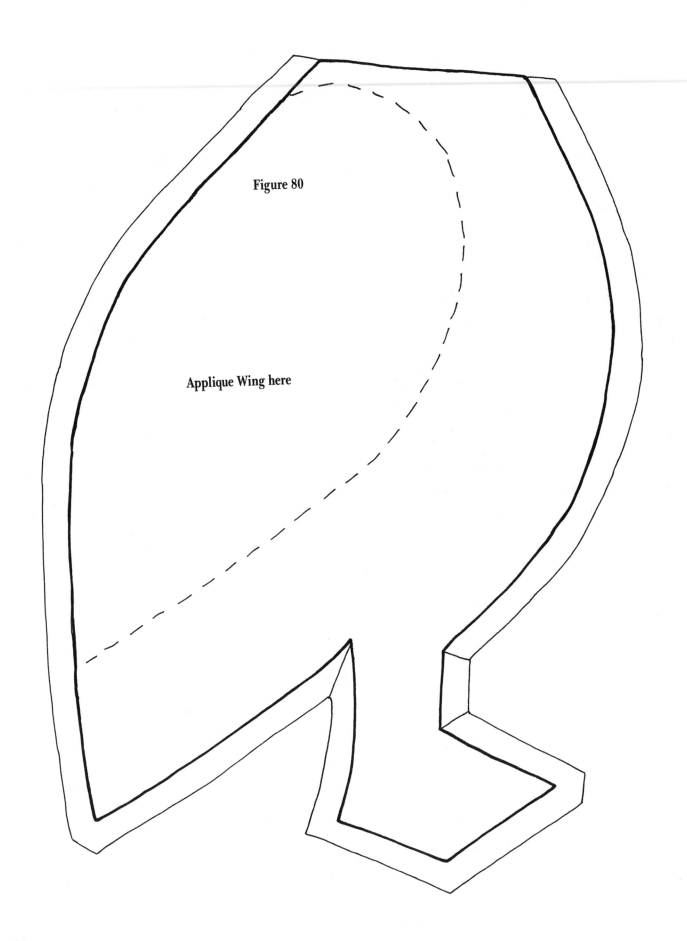

Figure 80

Applique Wing here

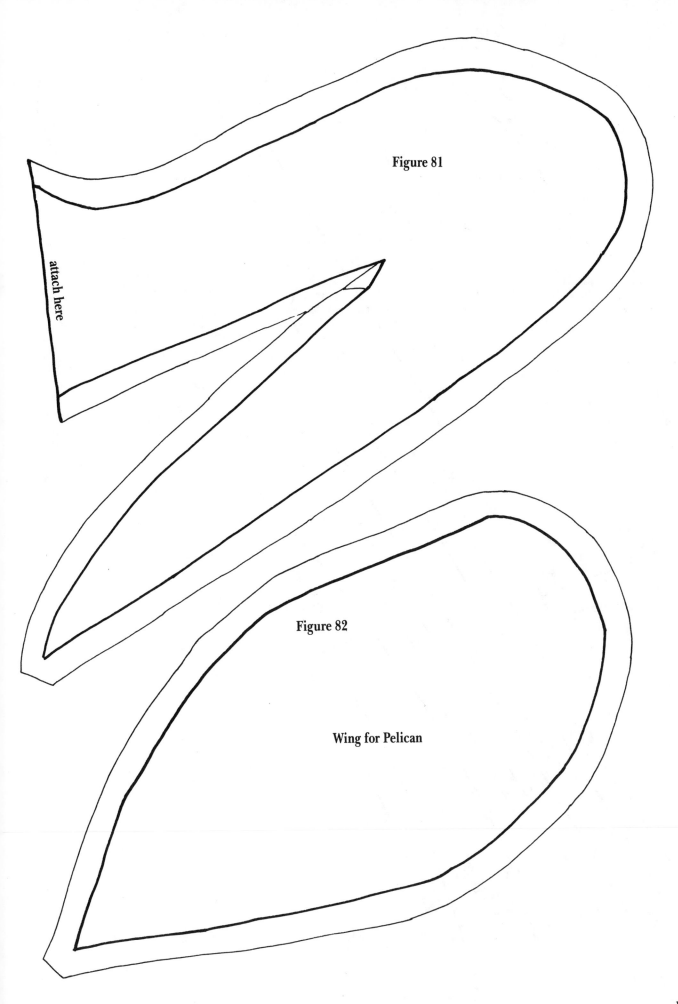

Figure 81

attach here

Figure 82

Wing for Pelican

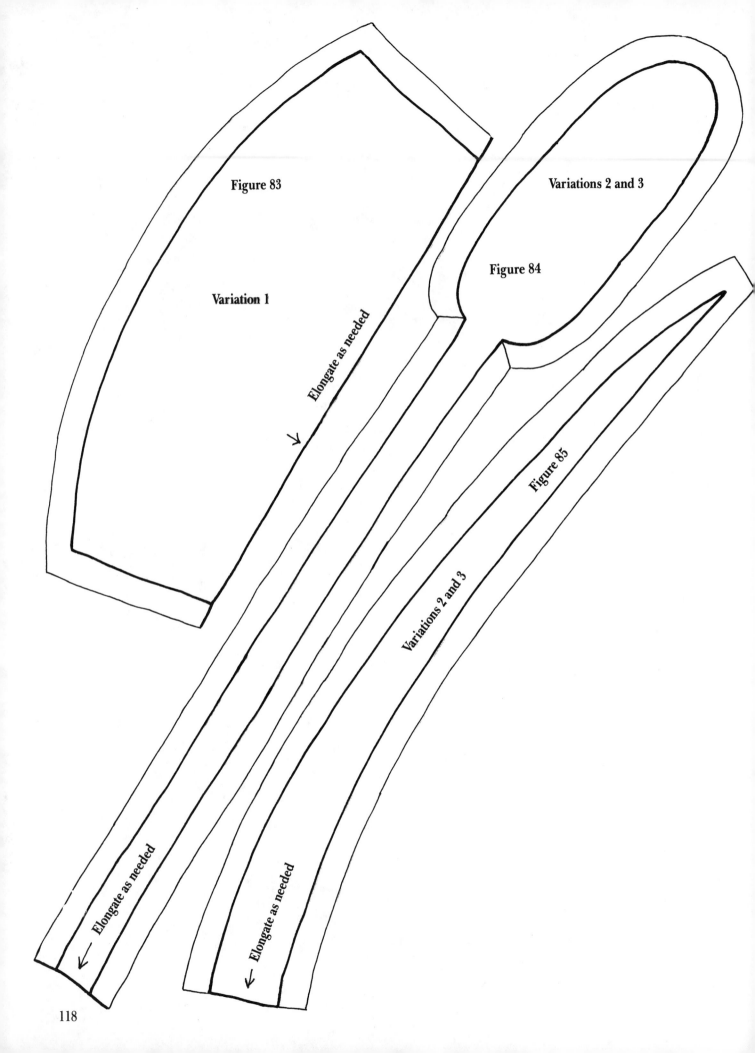

Figure 83

Variations 2 and 3

Variation 1

Figure 84

Elongate as needed

Figure 85

Variations 2 and 3

Elongate as needed

Elongate as needed

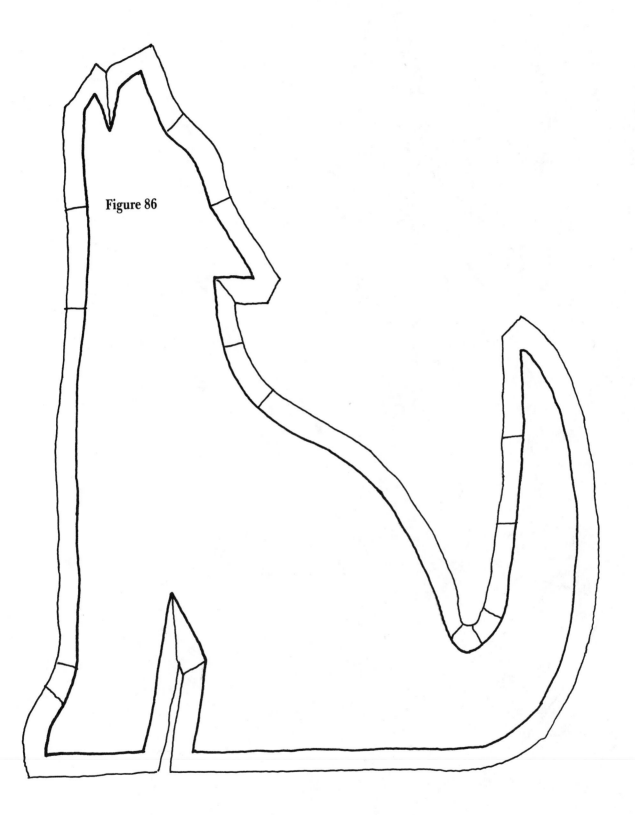

Figure 86

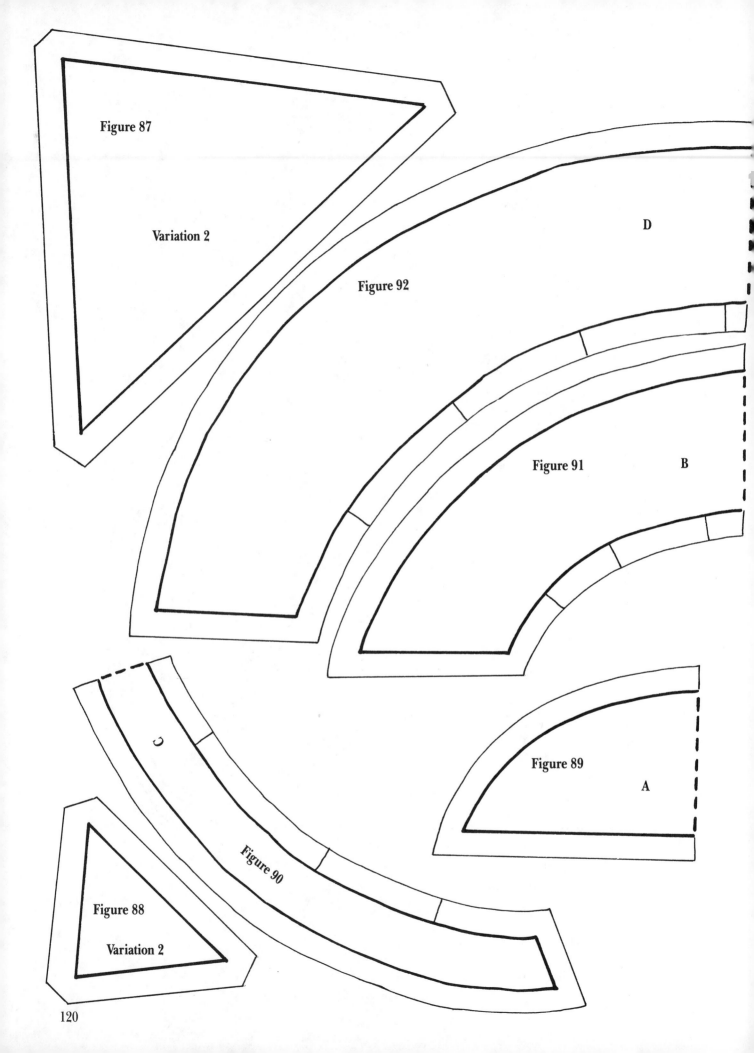

Figure 87

Variation 2

Figure 92

D

Figure 91

B

Figure 89

A

C

Figure 90

Figure 88

Variation 2

120

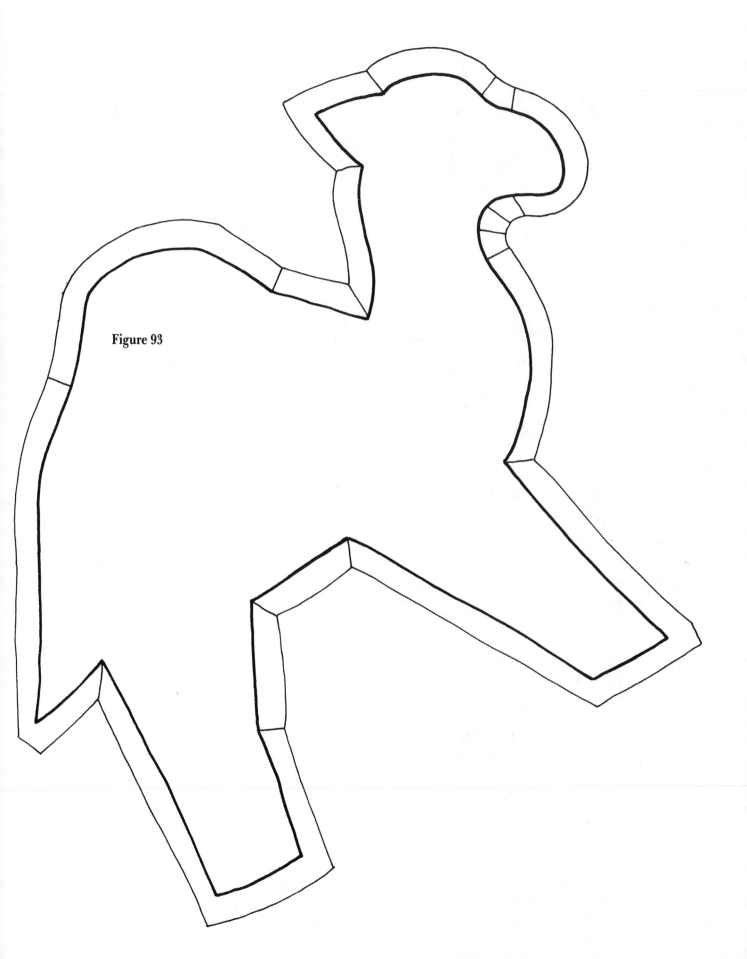

Figure 93

121

Figure 95

Figure 94

Figure 96a

Figure 96

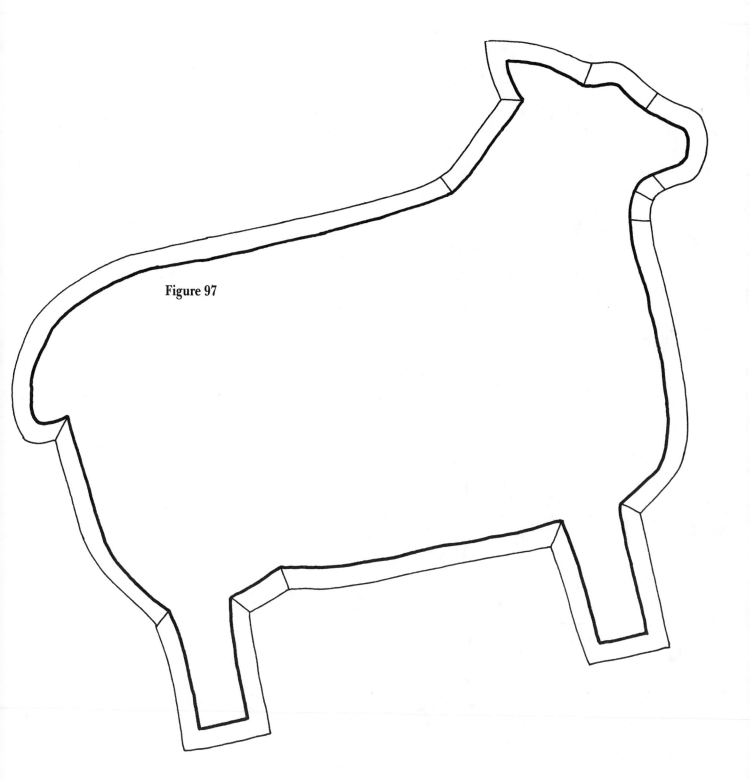

Figure 97

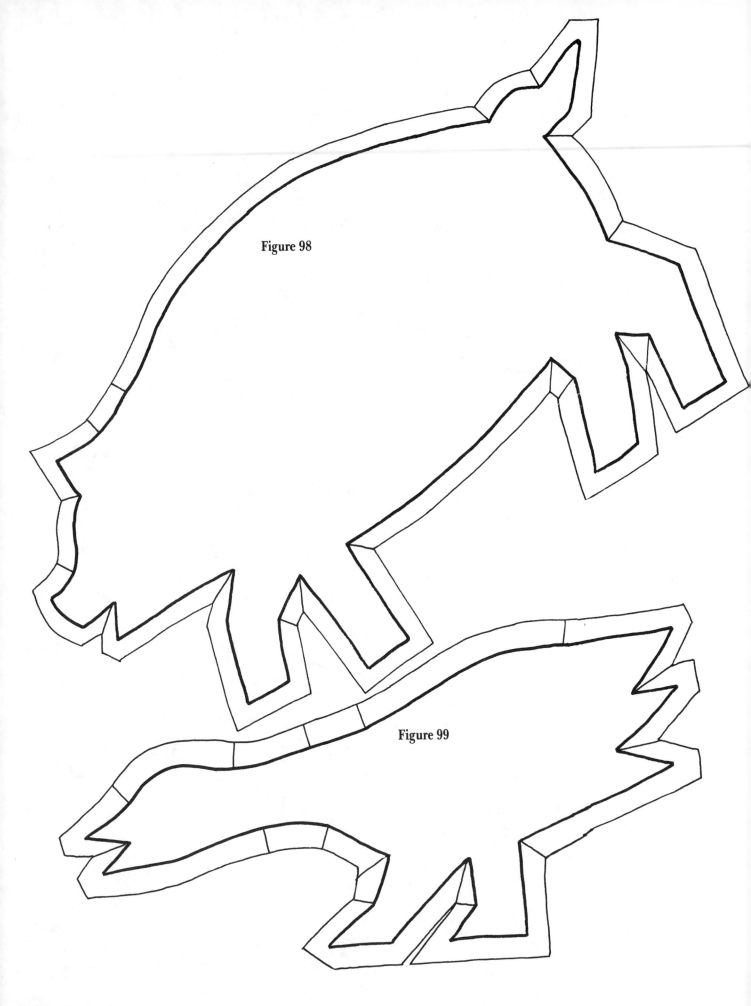

Figure 98

Figure 99

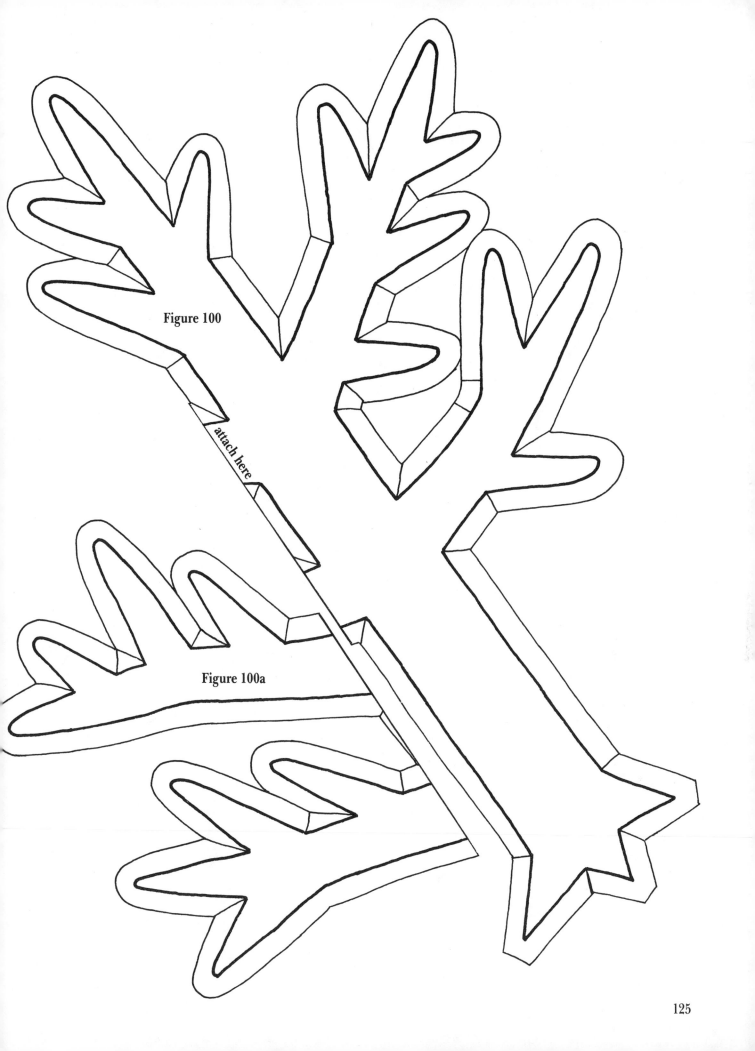

Figure 100

attach here

Figure 100a

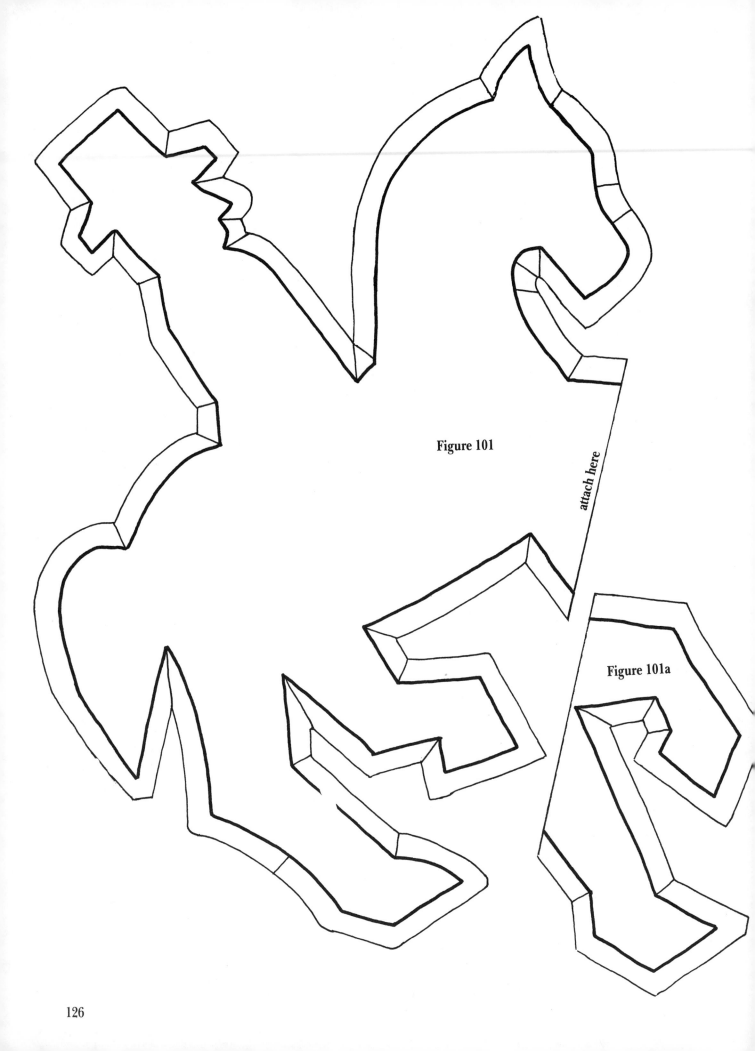

Figure 101

attach here

Figure 101a

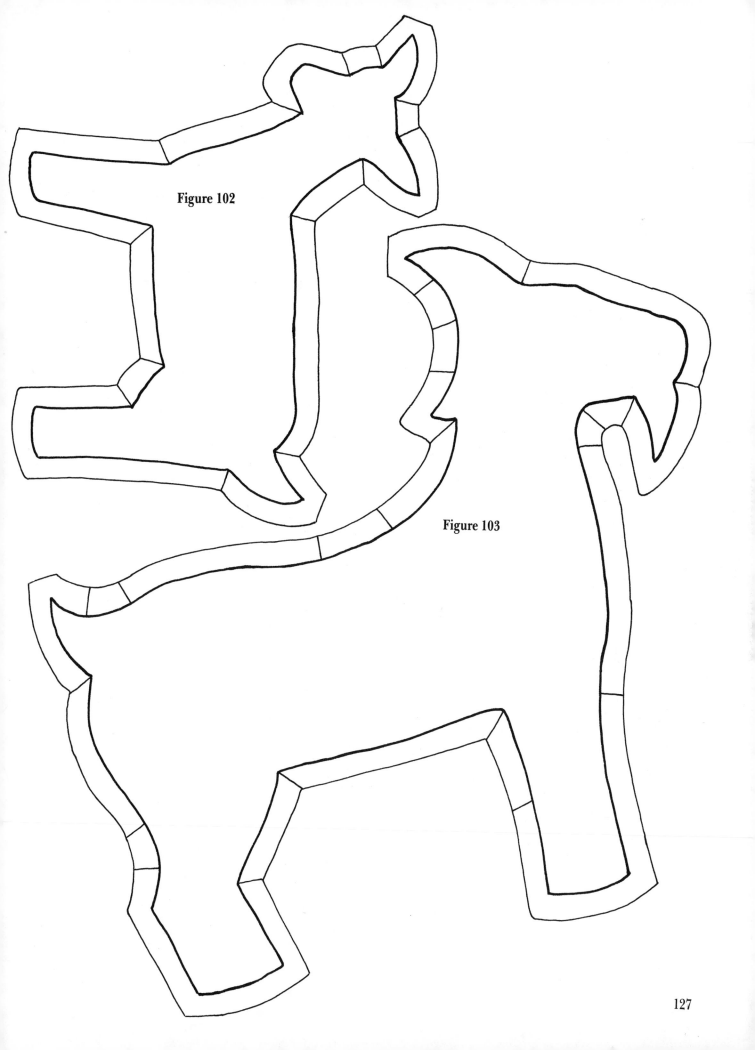

Figure 102

Figure 103

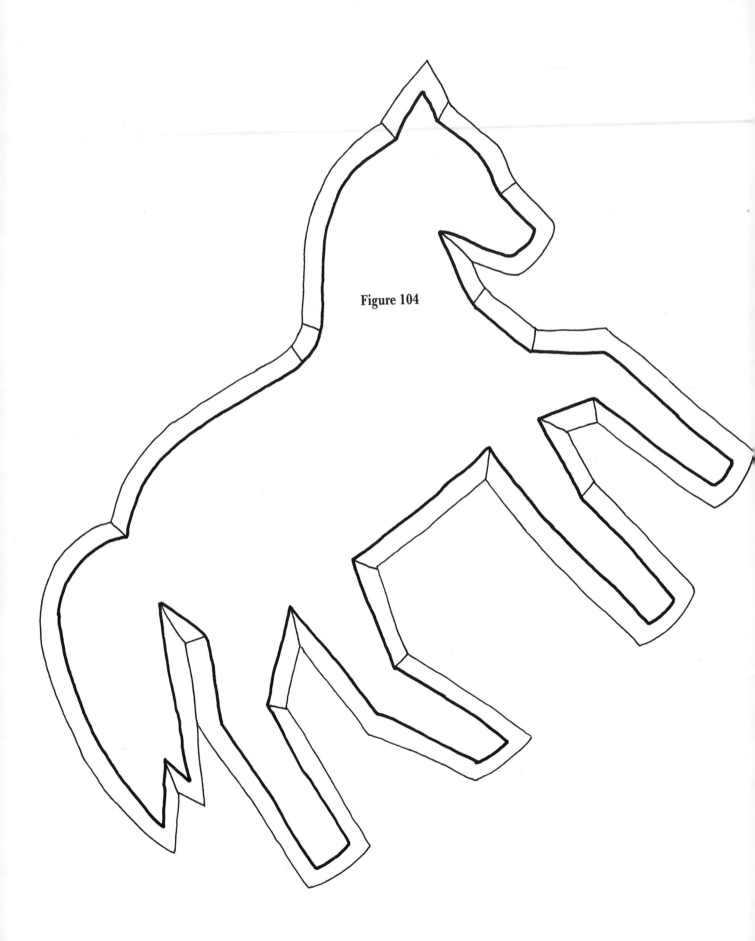

Figure 104

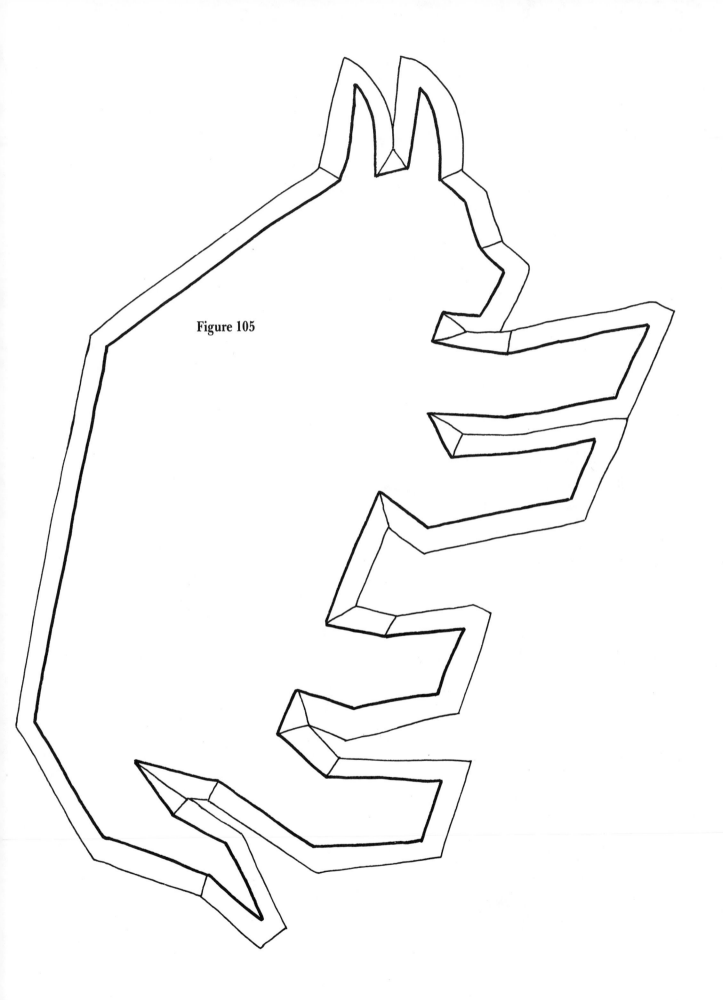

Figure 105

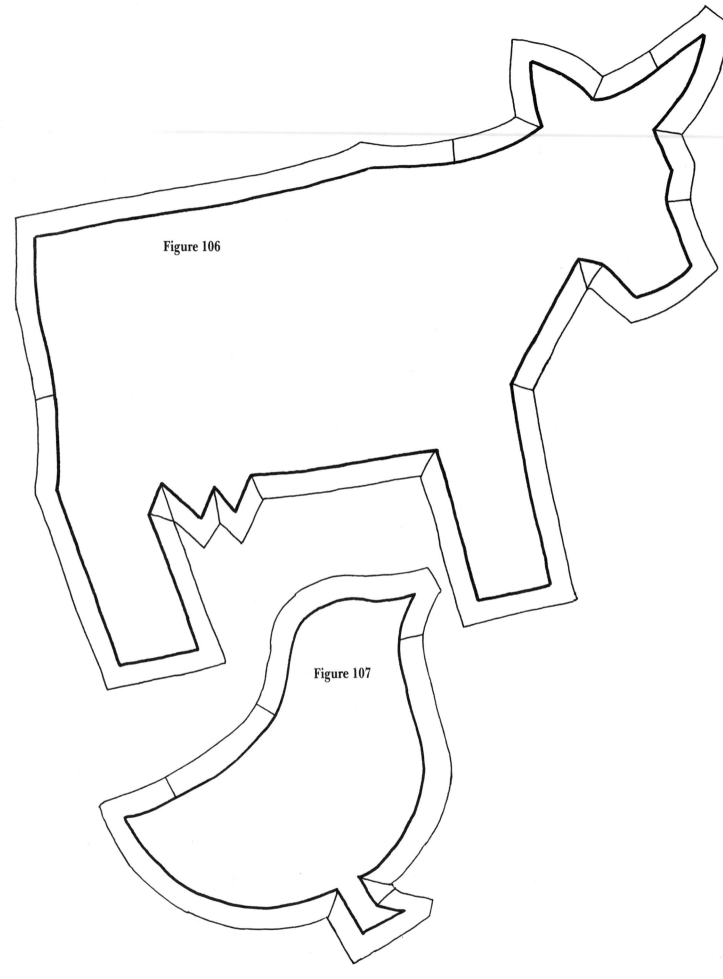

Figure 106

Figure 107

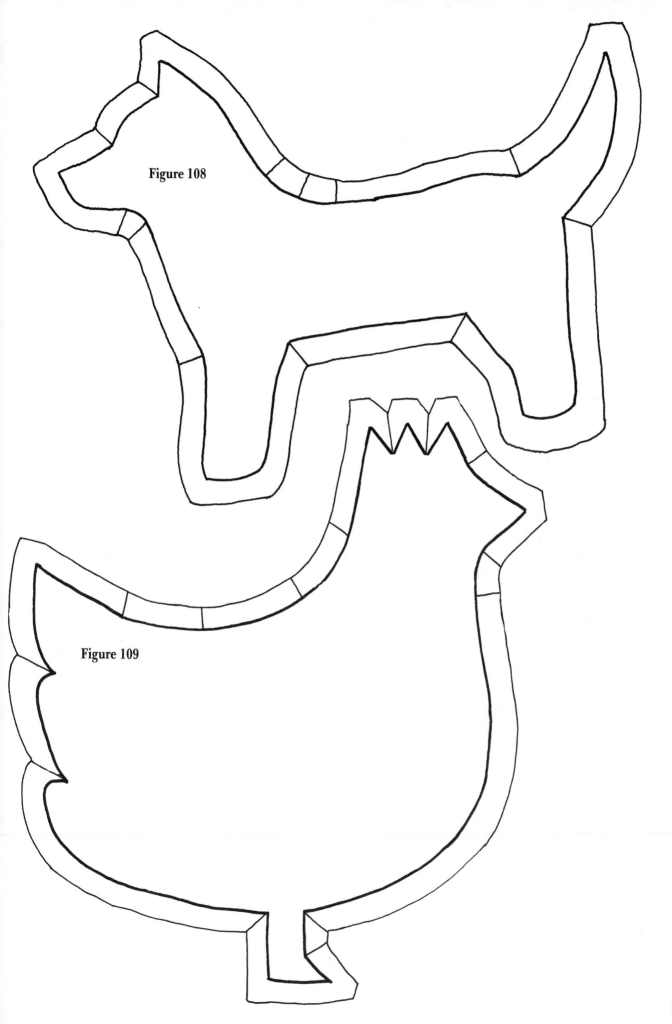

Figure 108

Figure 109

Figure 110

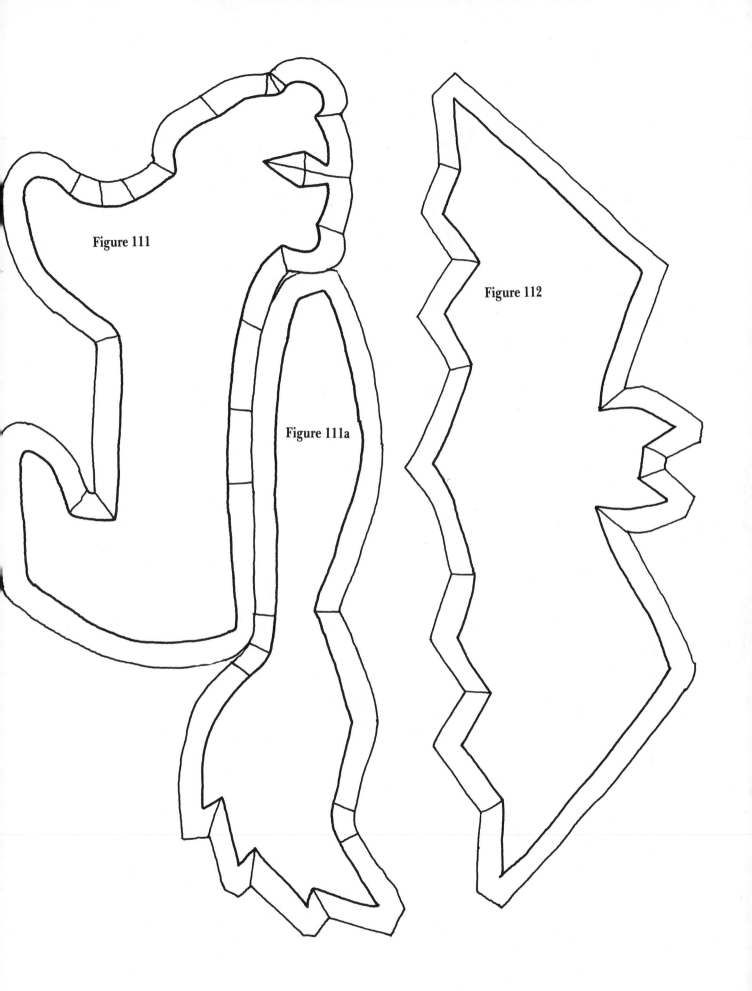

Figure 111

Figure 111a

Figure 112

Figure 113

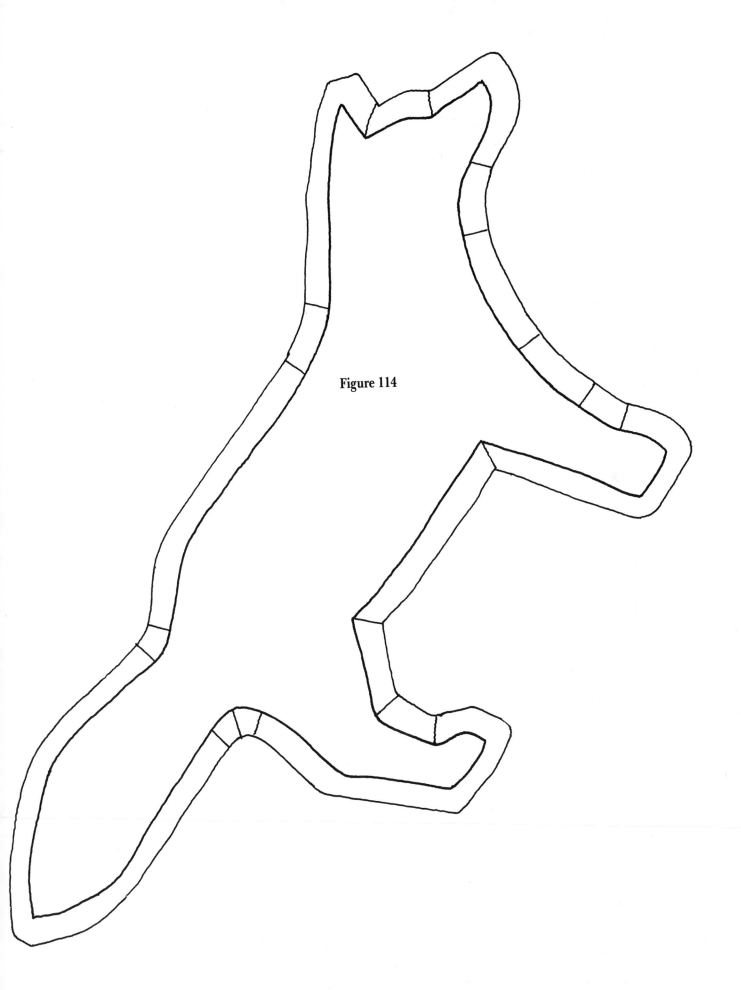

Figure 114

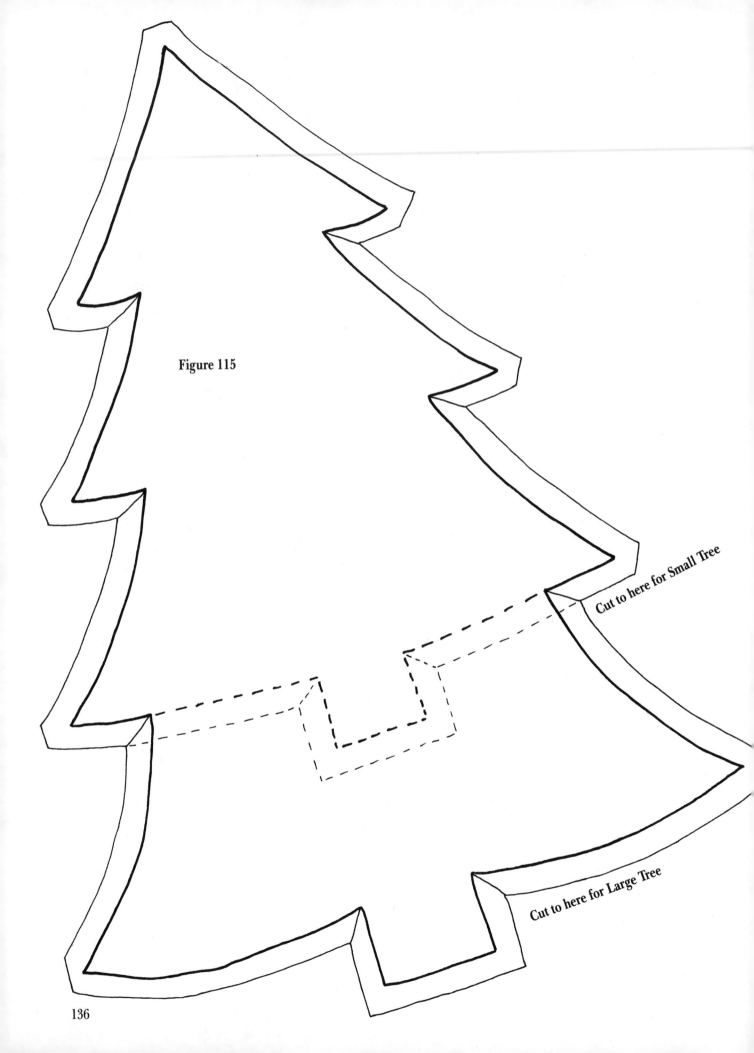

Figure 115

Cut to here for Small Tree

Cut to here for Large Tree

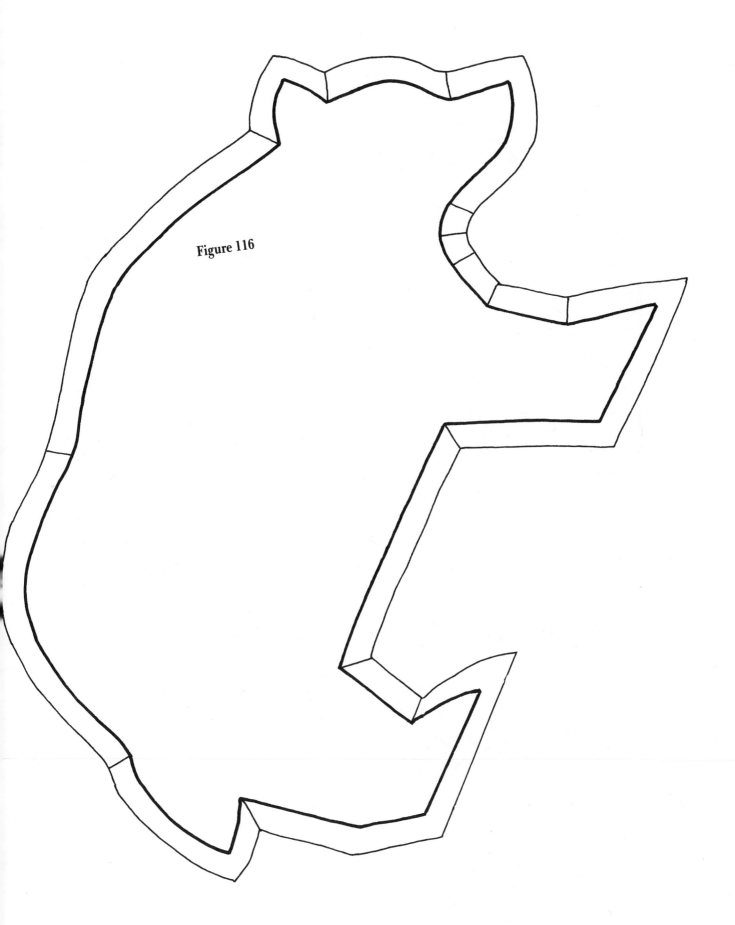

Figure 116

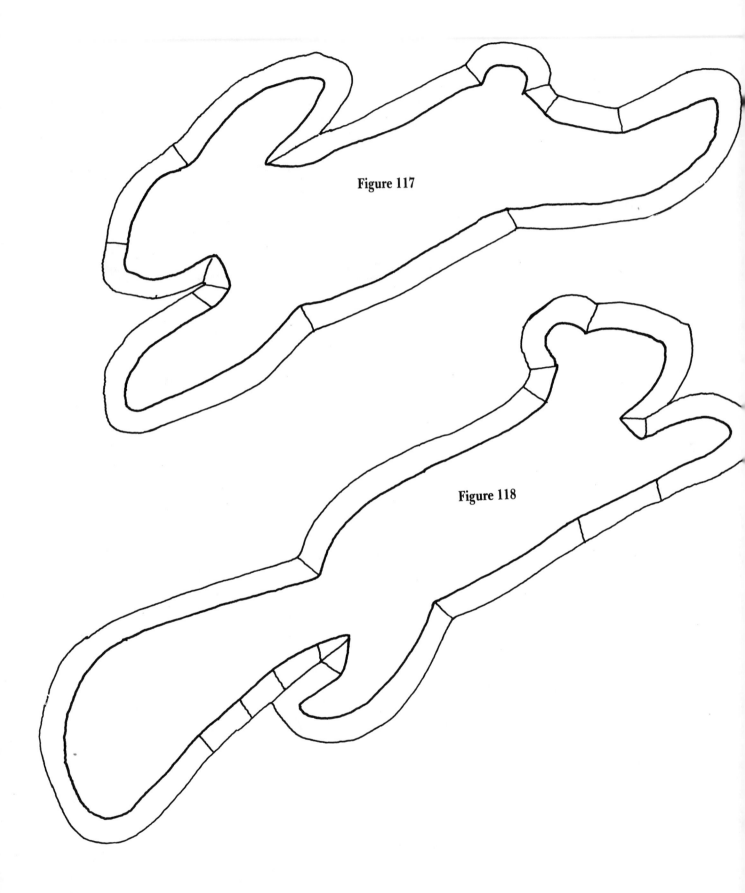

Figure 117

Figure 118

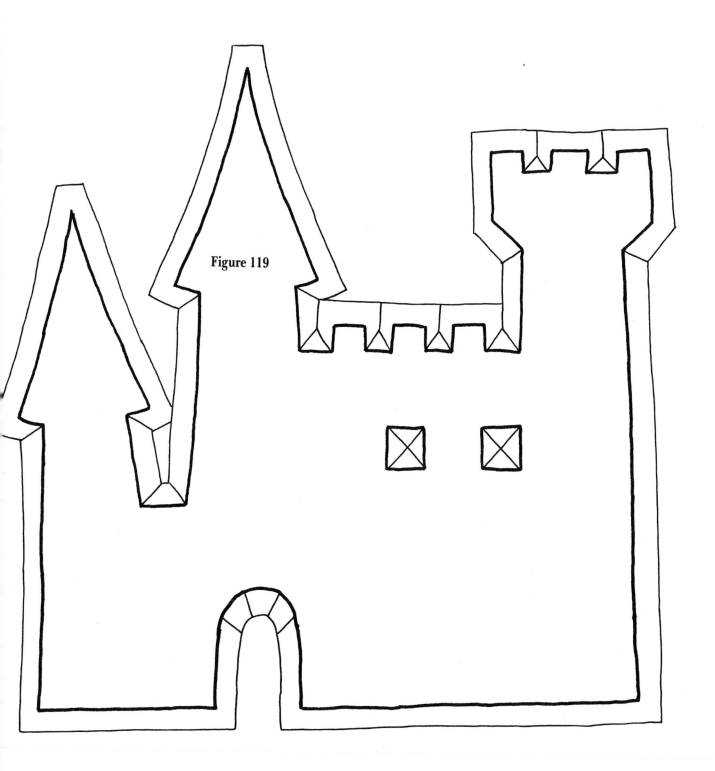

Figure 119

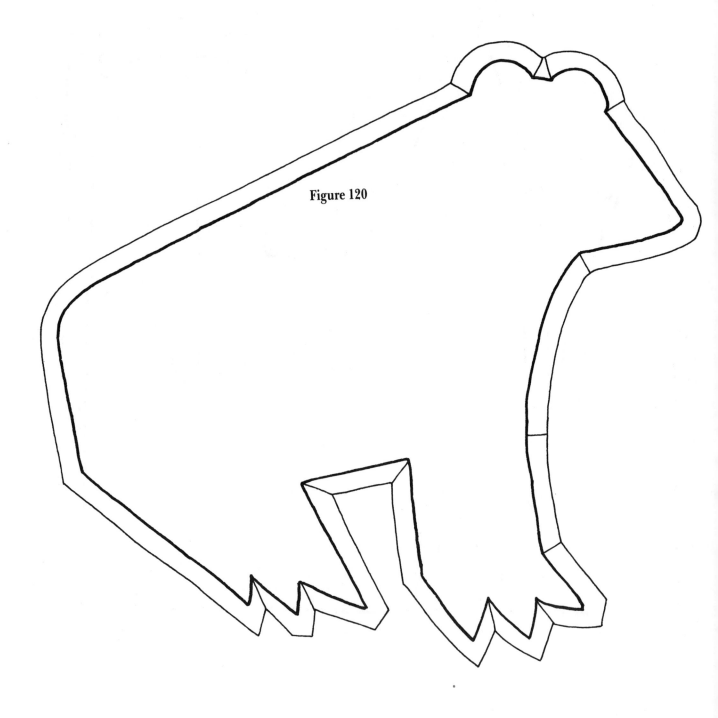

Figure 120

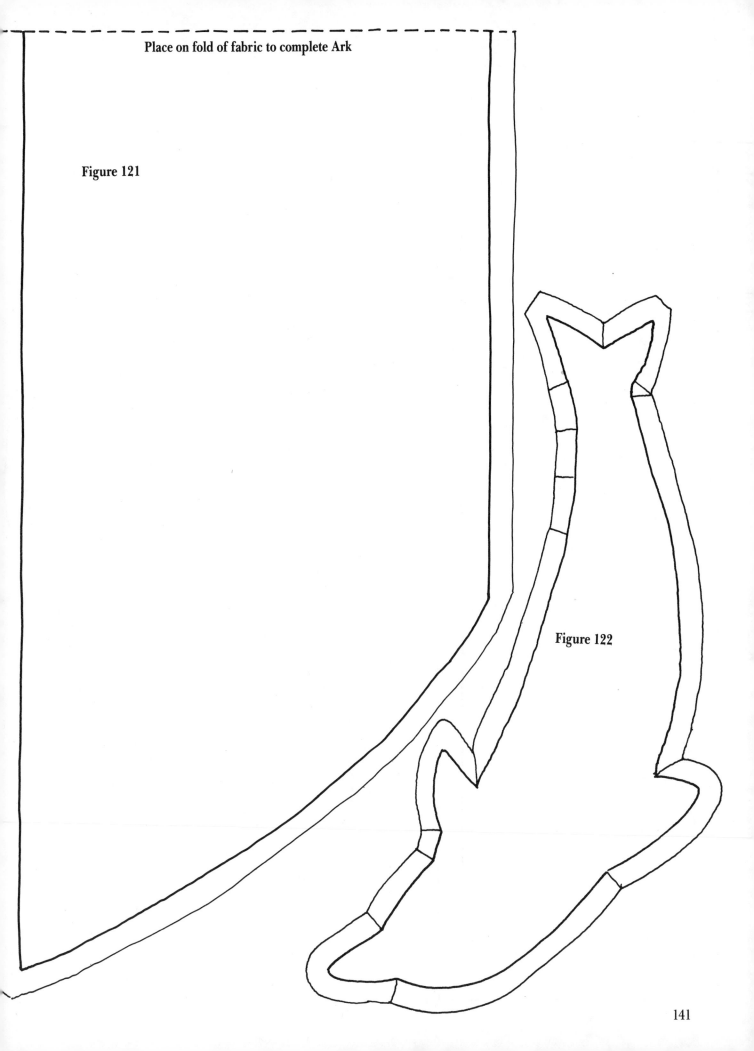

Place on fold of fabric to complete Ark

Figure 121

Figure 122

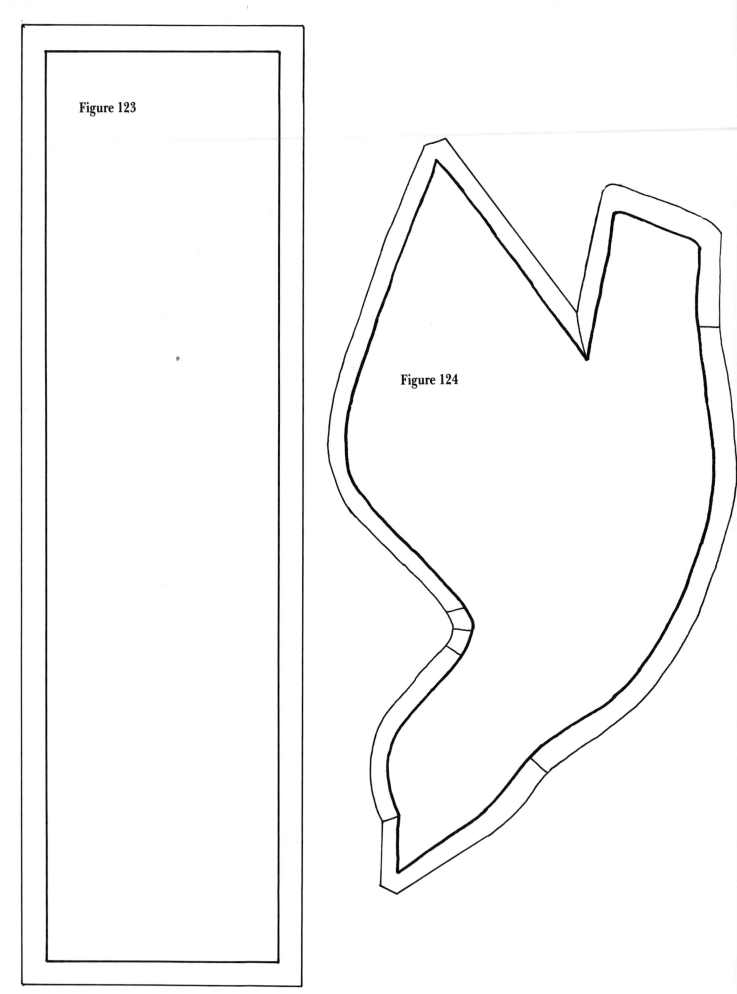

Figure 123

Figure 124

142

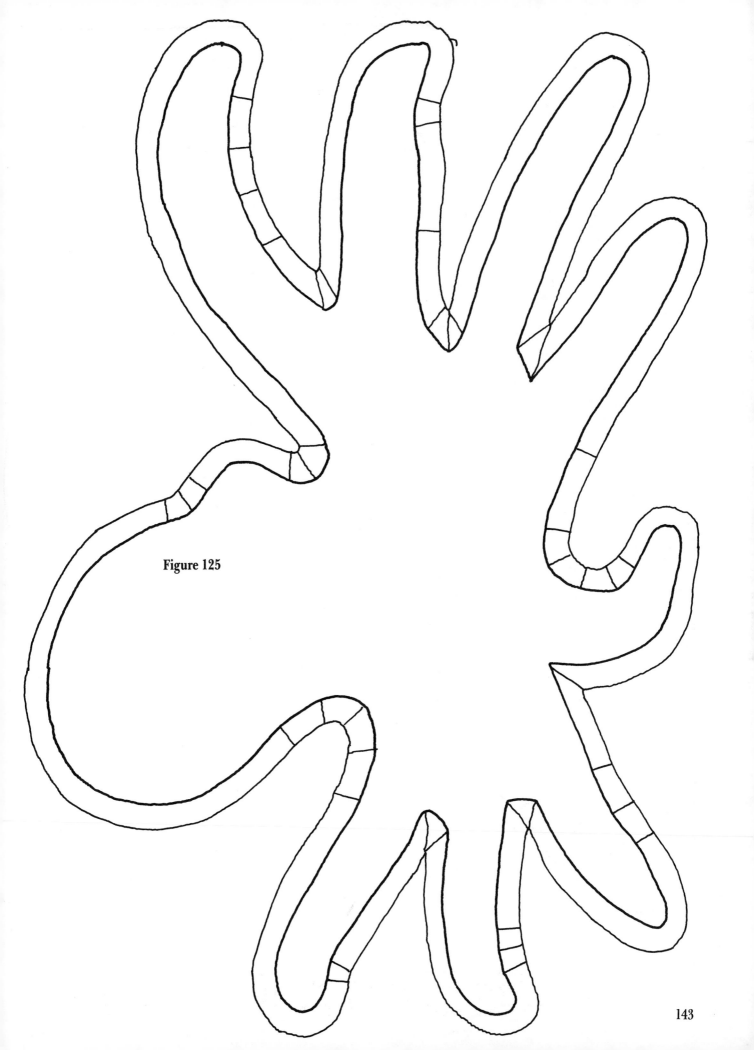

Figure 125

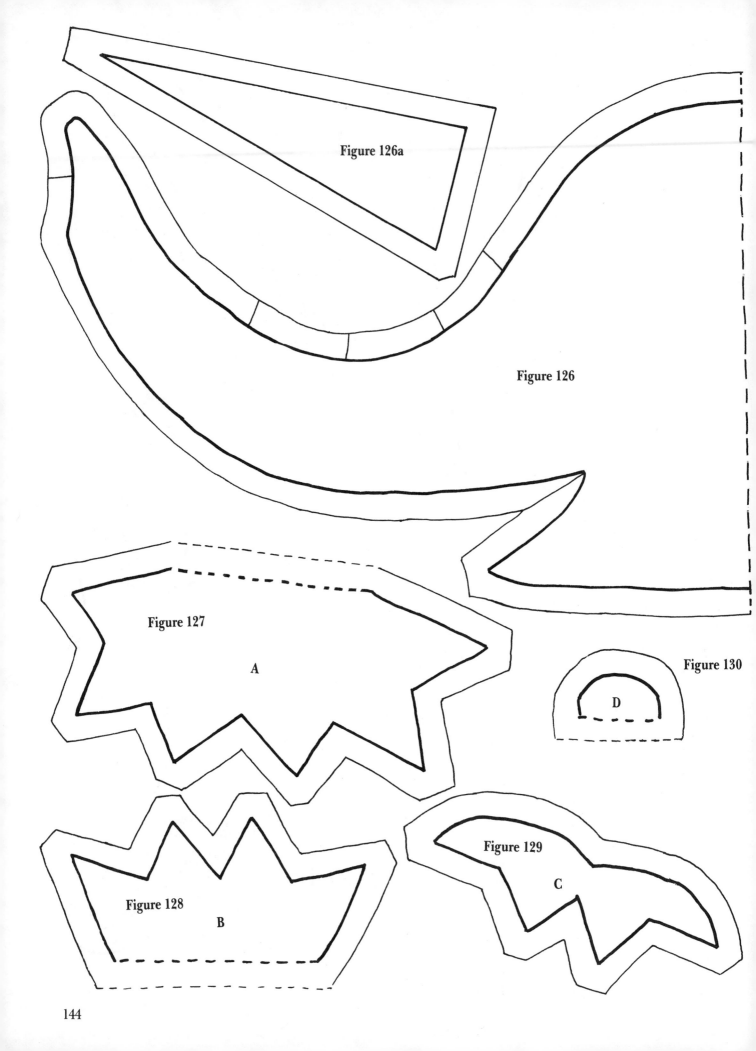

Figure 126a

Figure 126

Figure 127

A

Figure 130

D

Figure 128

B

Figure 129

C

144

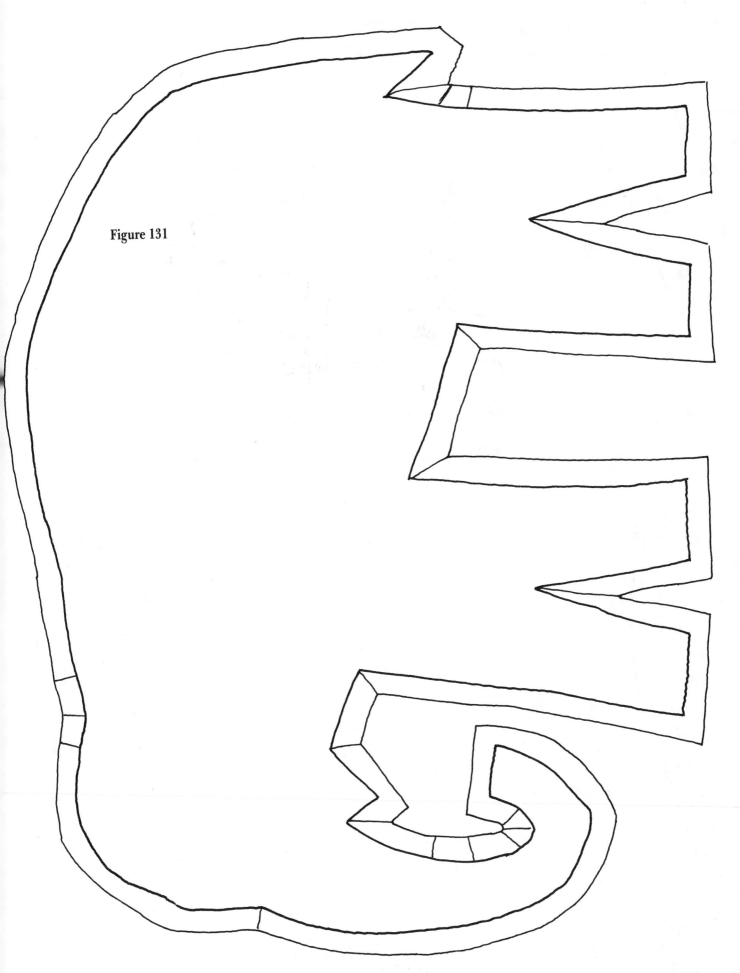

Figure 131

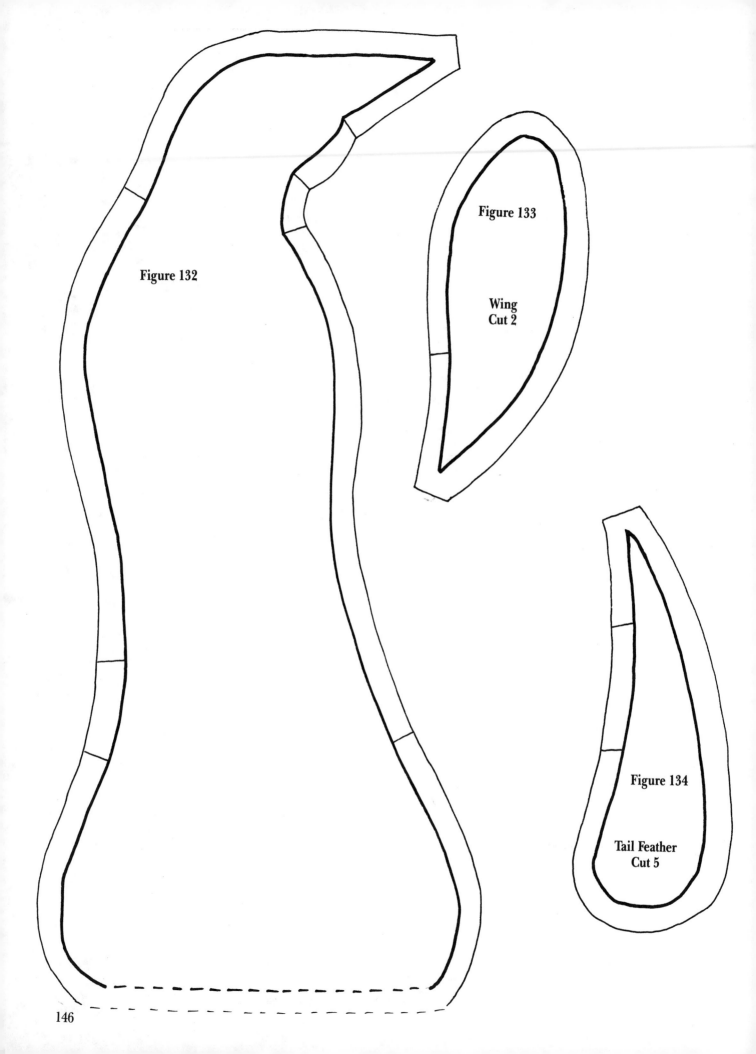

Figure 132

Figure 133

Wing
Cut 2

Figure 134

Tail Feather
Cut 5

146

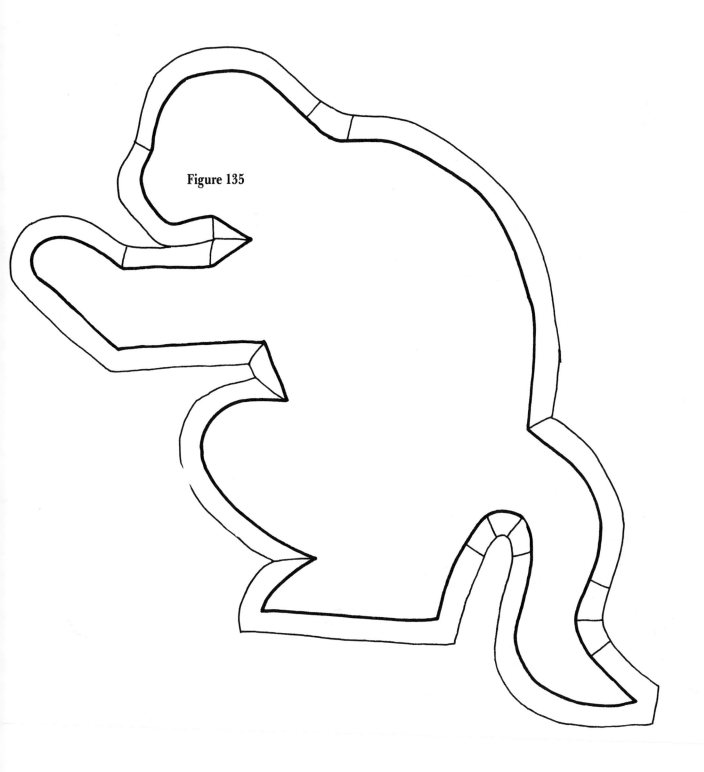

Figure 135

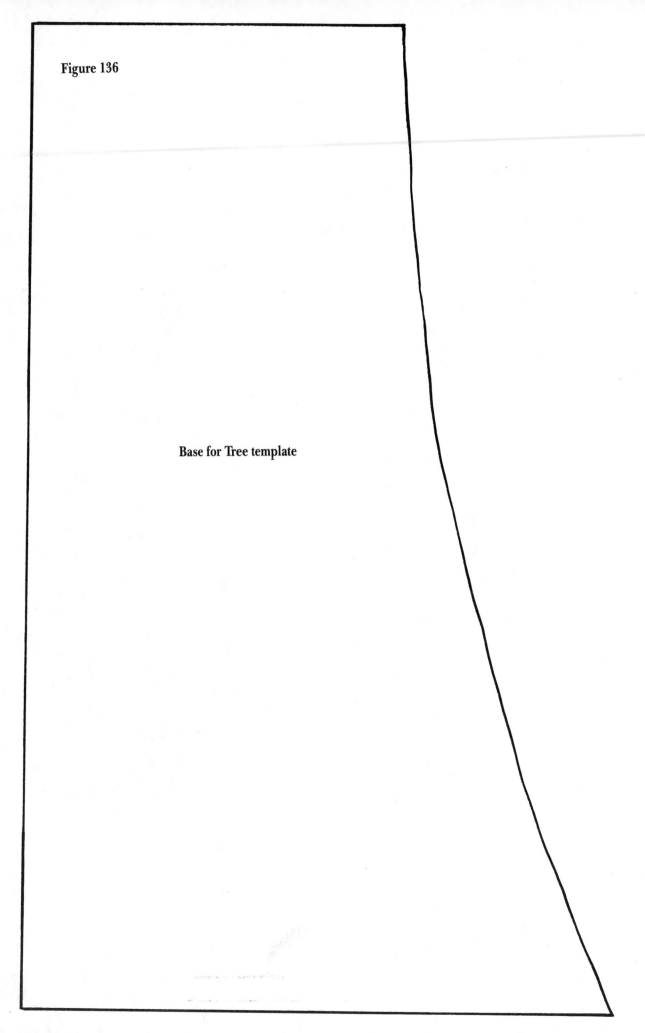

Figure 136

Base for Tree template

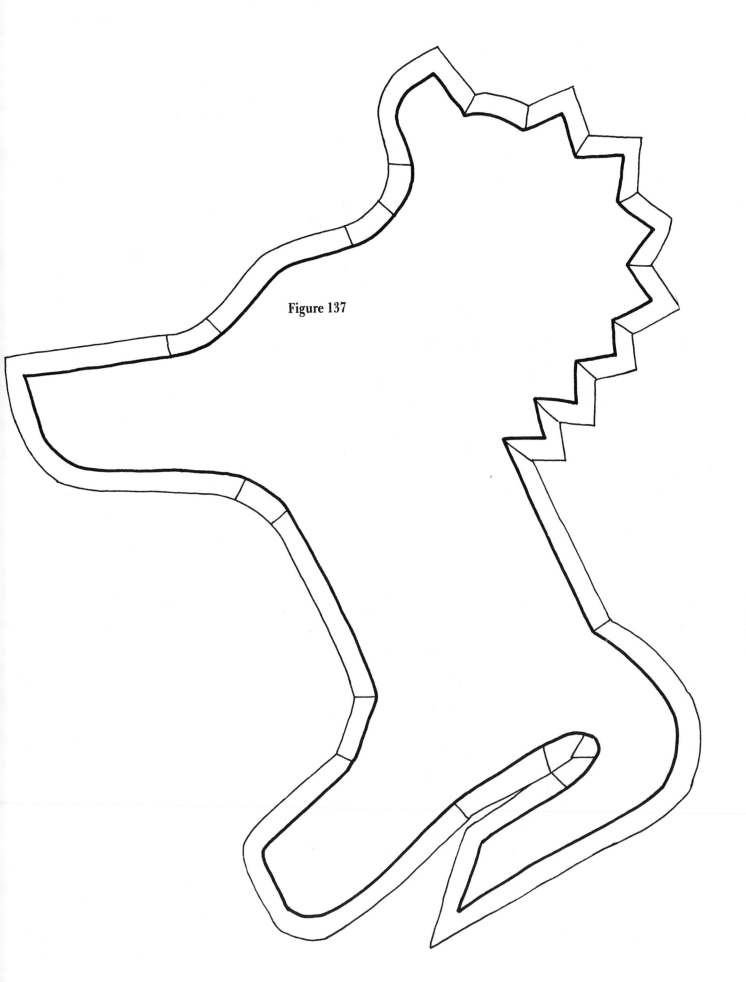

Figure 137

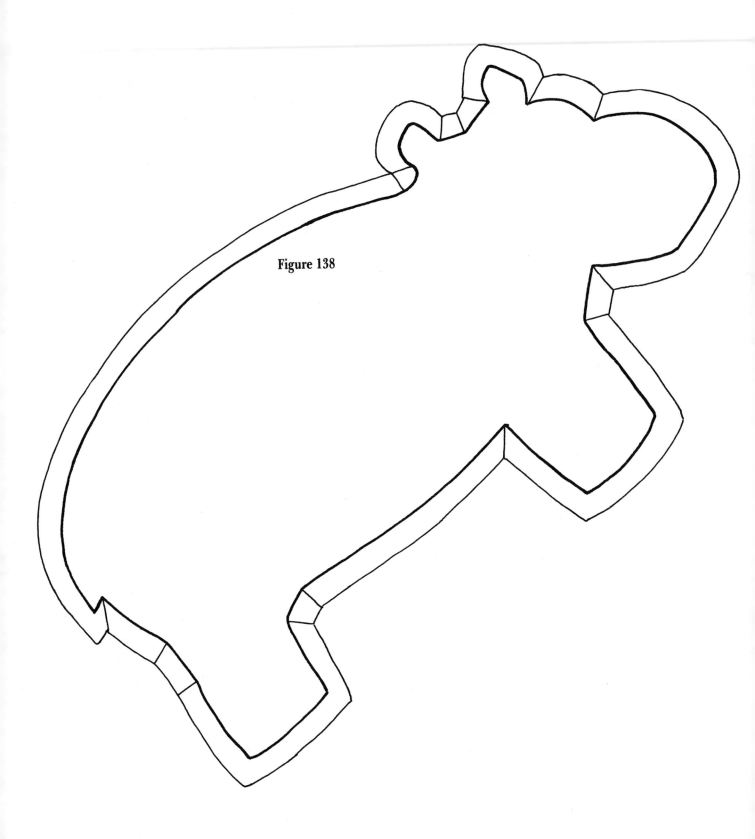

Figure 138

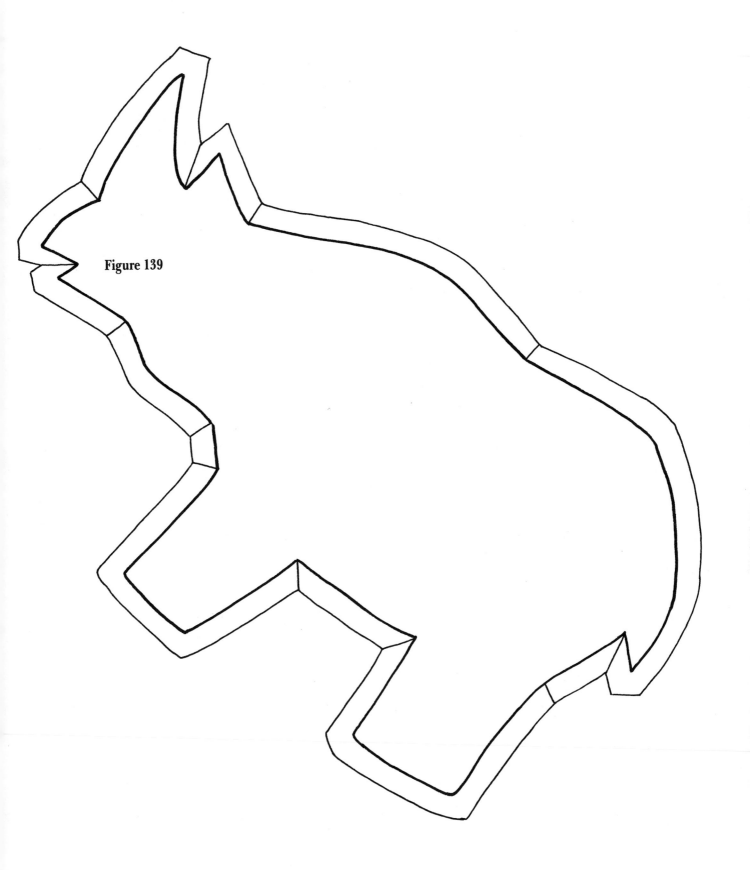

Figure 139

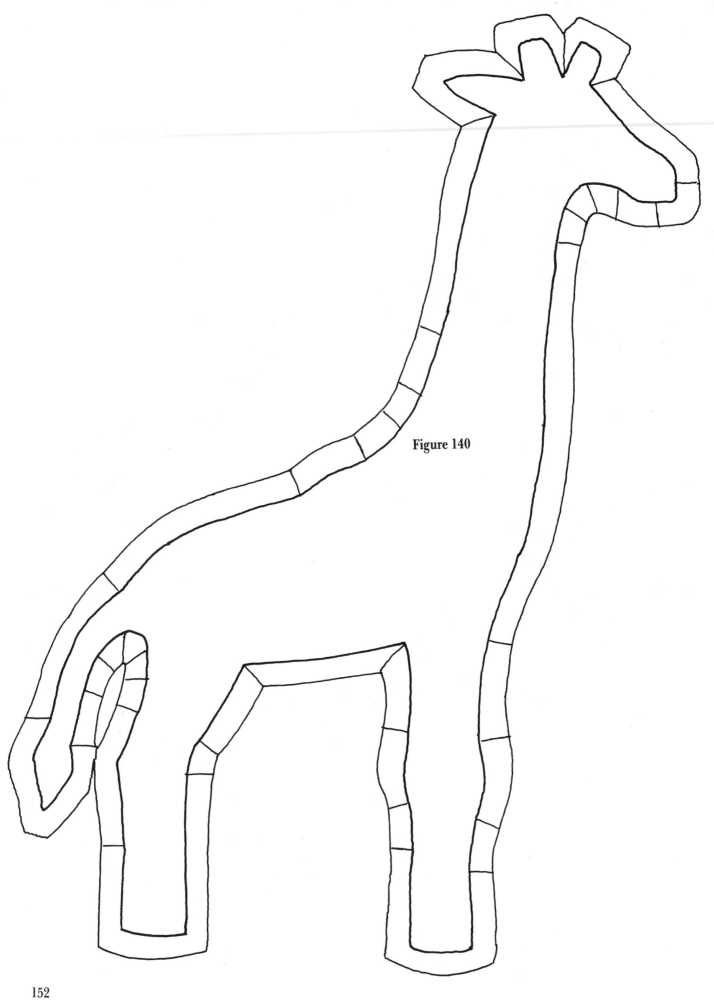

Figure 140

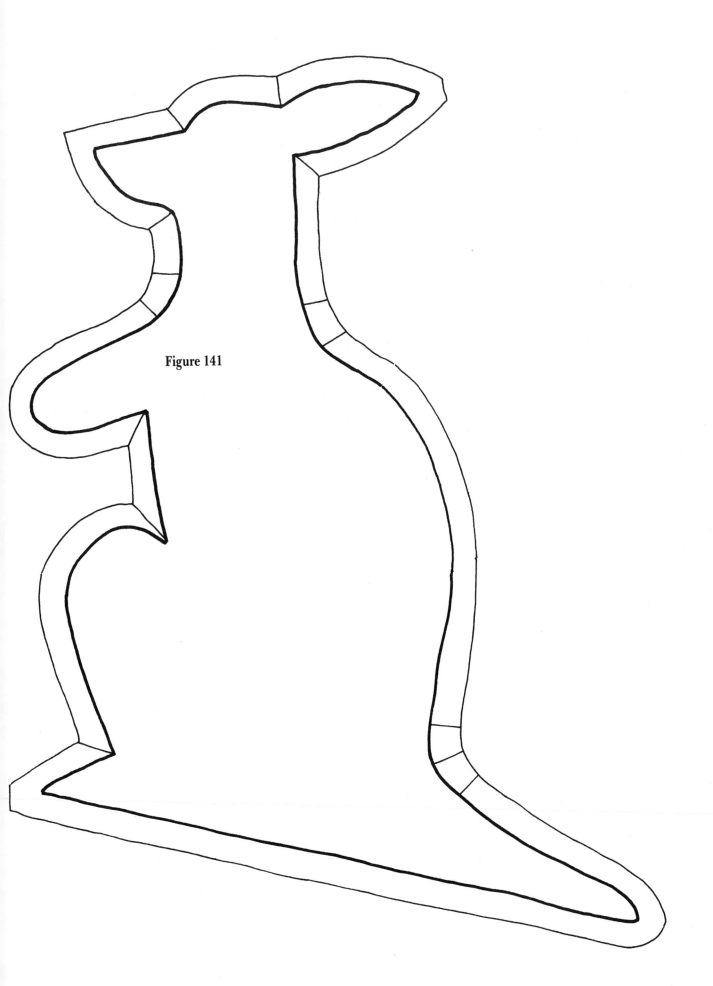

Figure 141

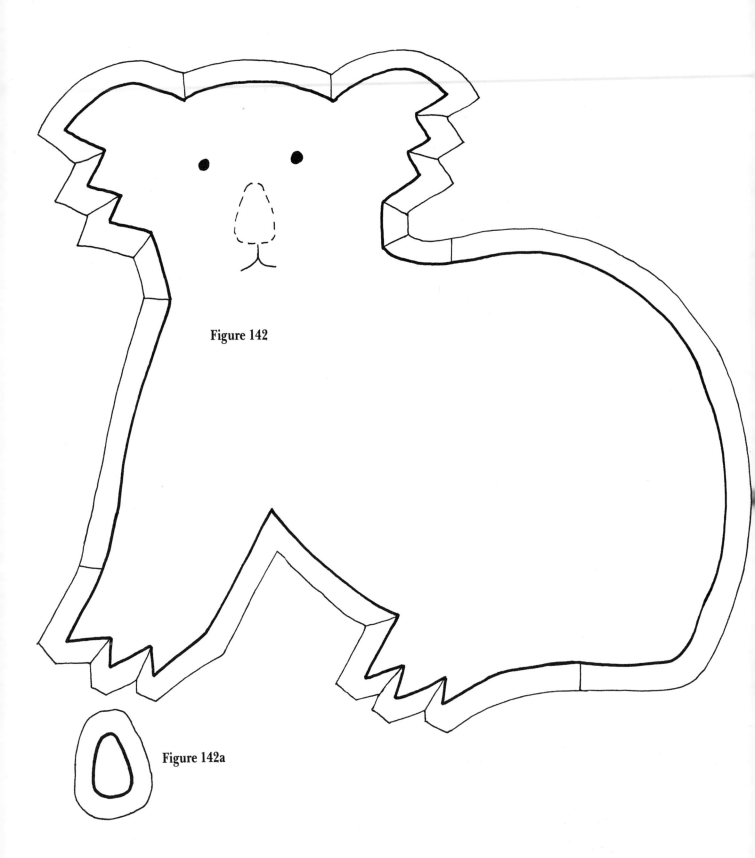

Figure 142

Figure 142a

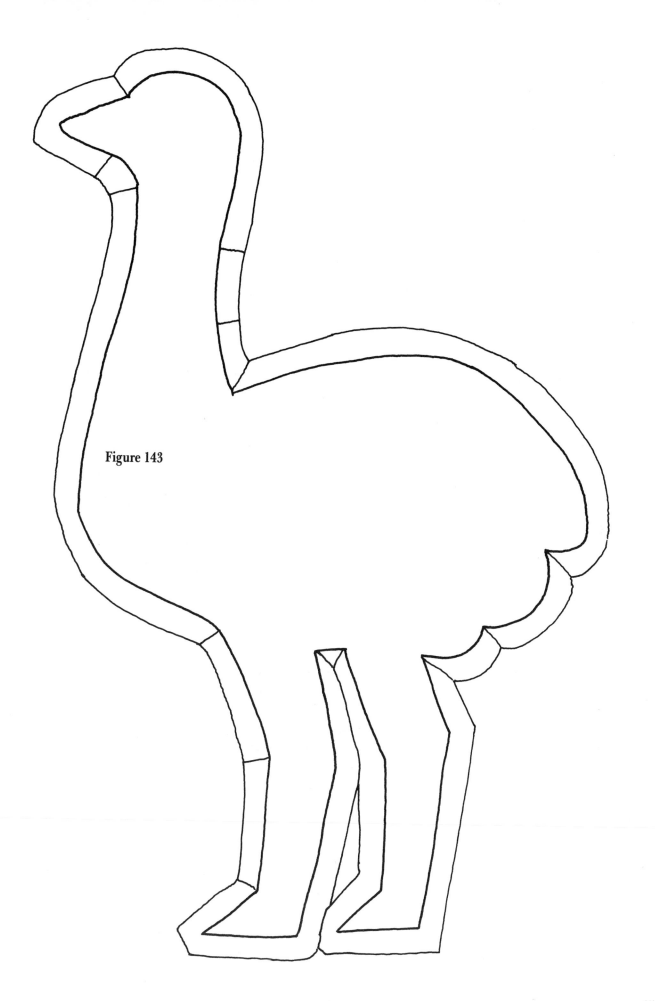

Figure 143

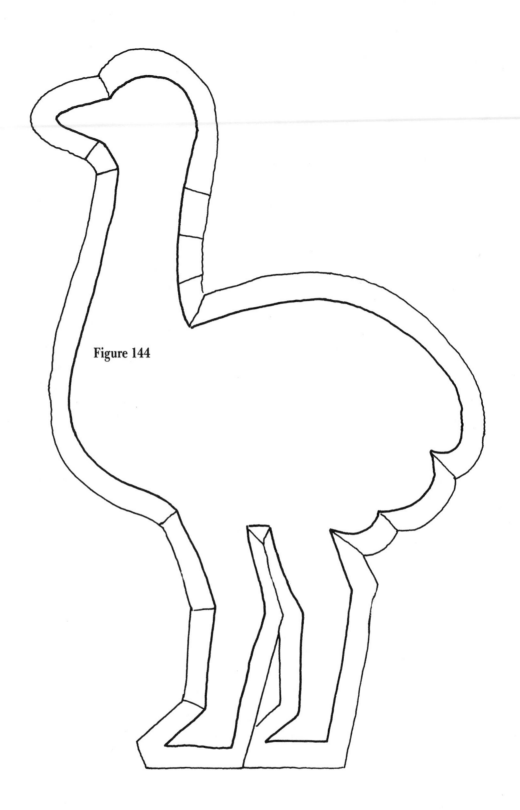

Figure 144

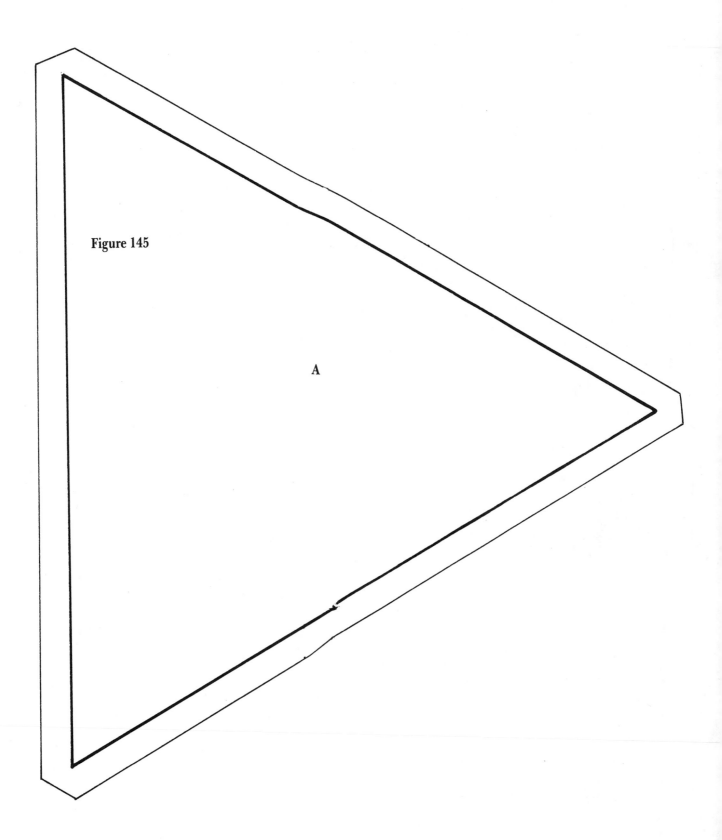

Figure 145

A

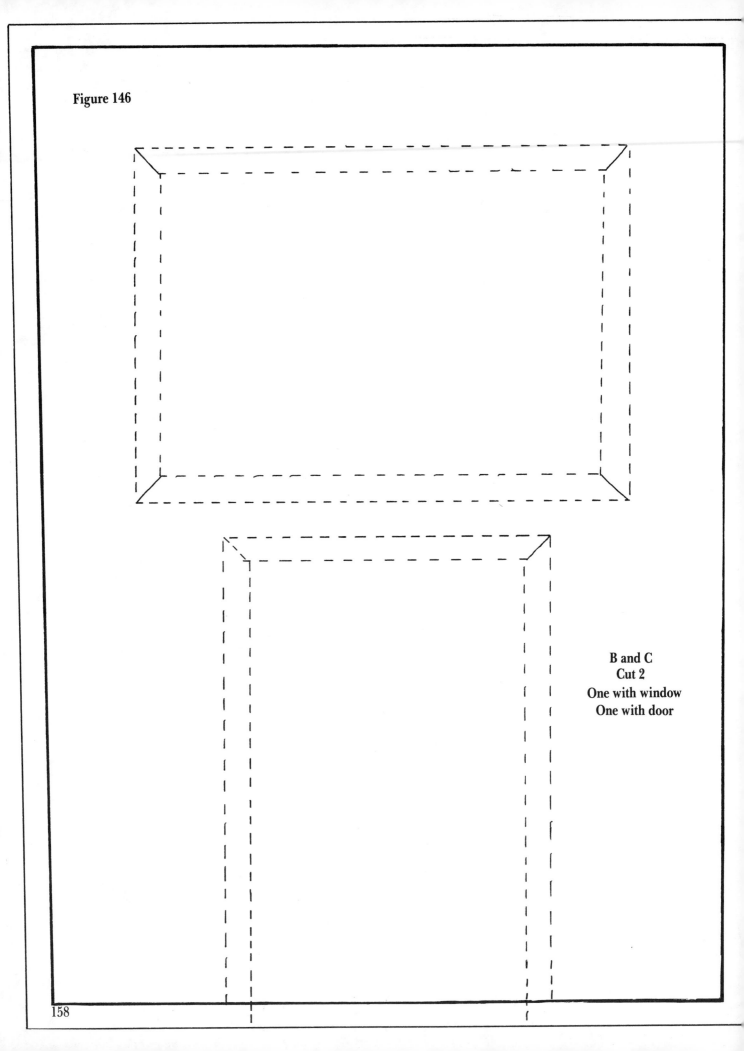

Figure 146

B and C
Cut 2
One with window
One with door

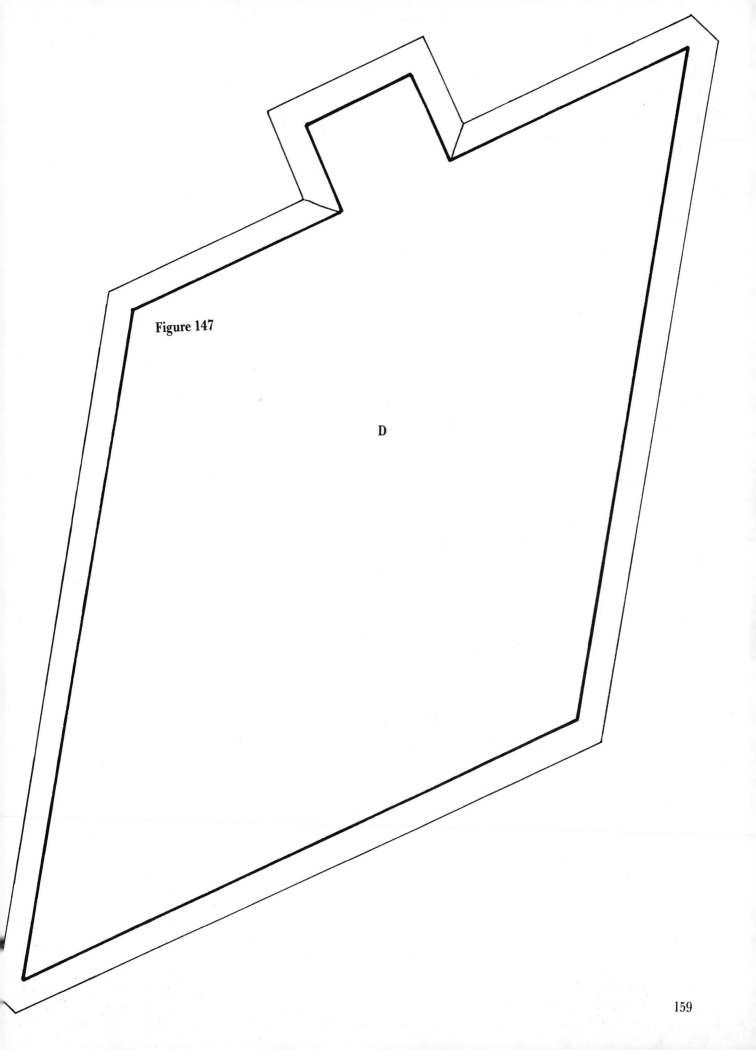

Figure 147

D

Figure 148

6½″ Square Block

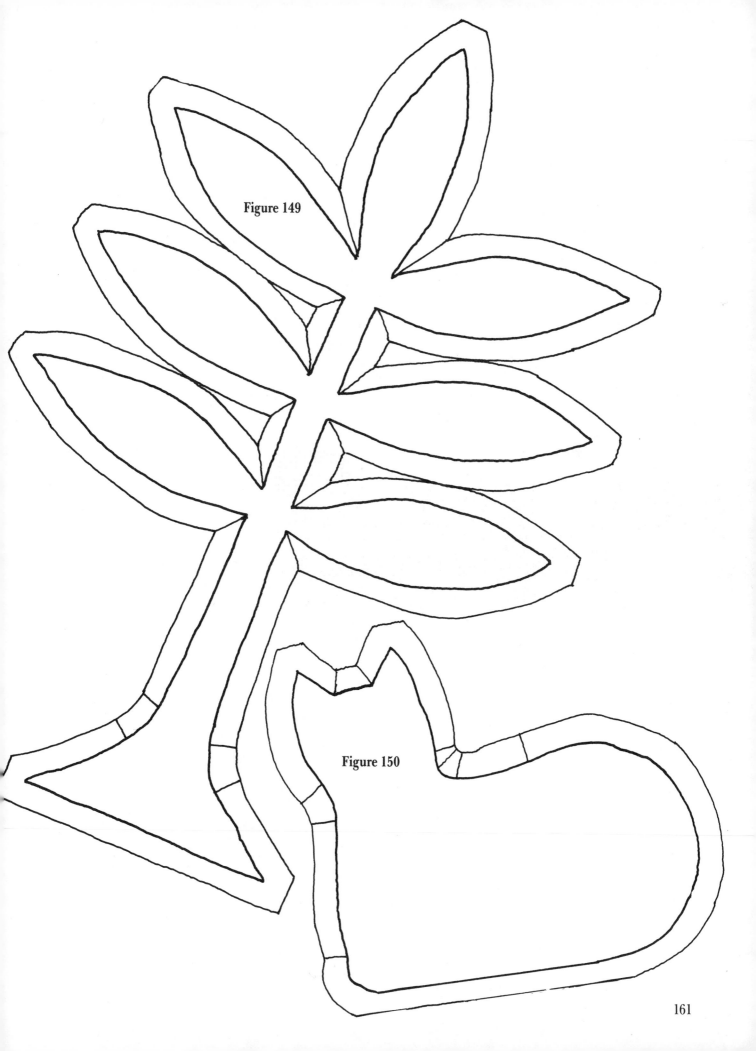

Figure 149

Figure 150

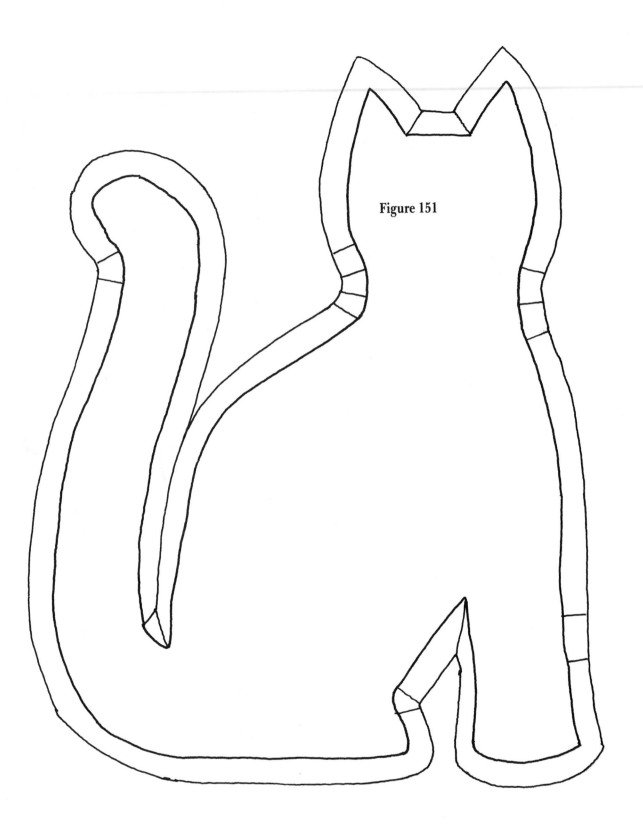

Figure 151

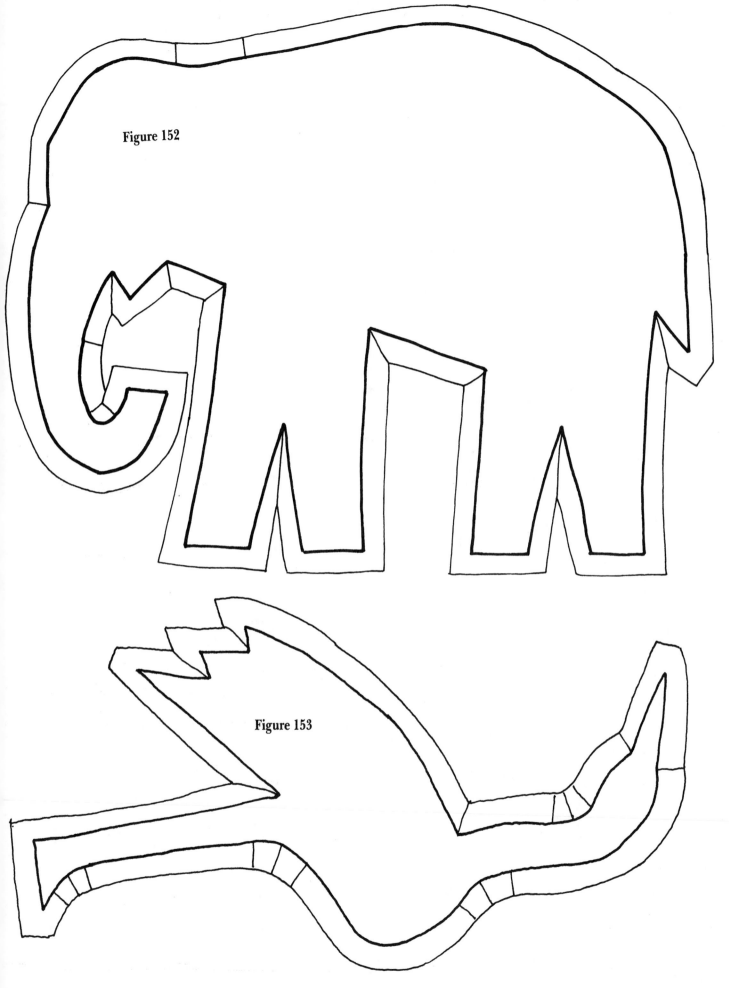

Figure 152

Figure 153

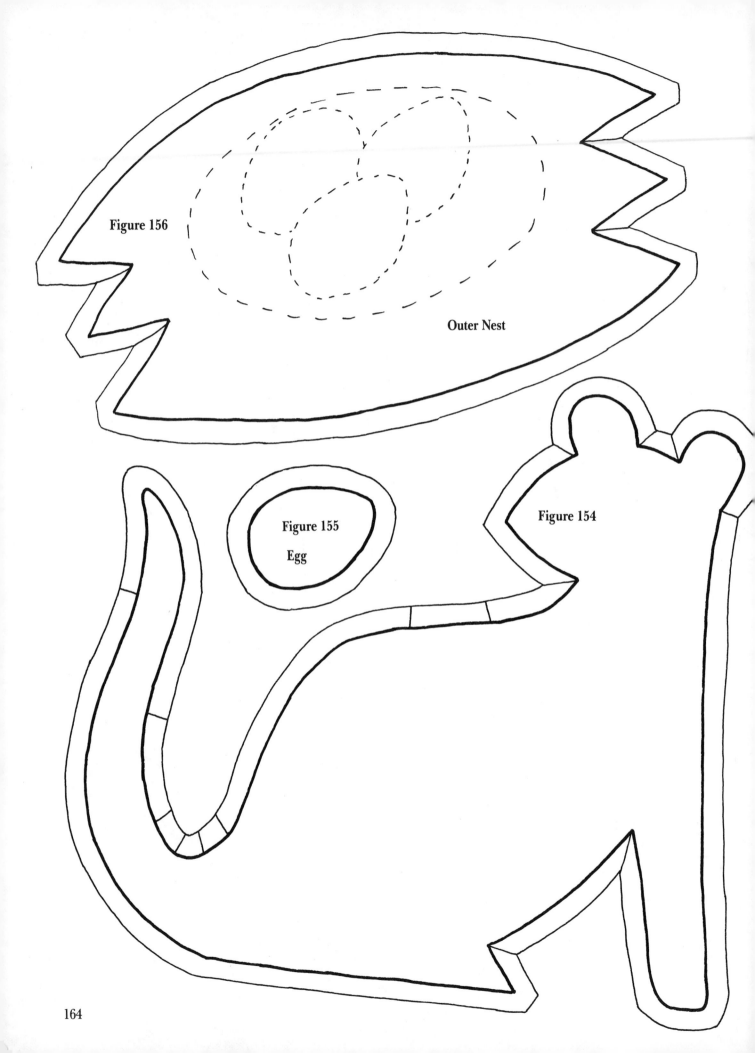

Figure 156

Outer Nest

Figure 155

Egg

Figure 154

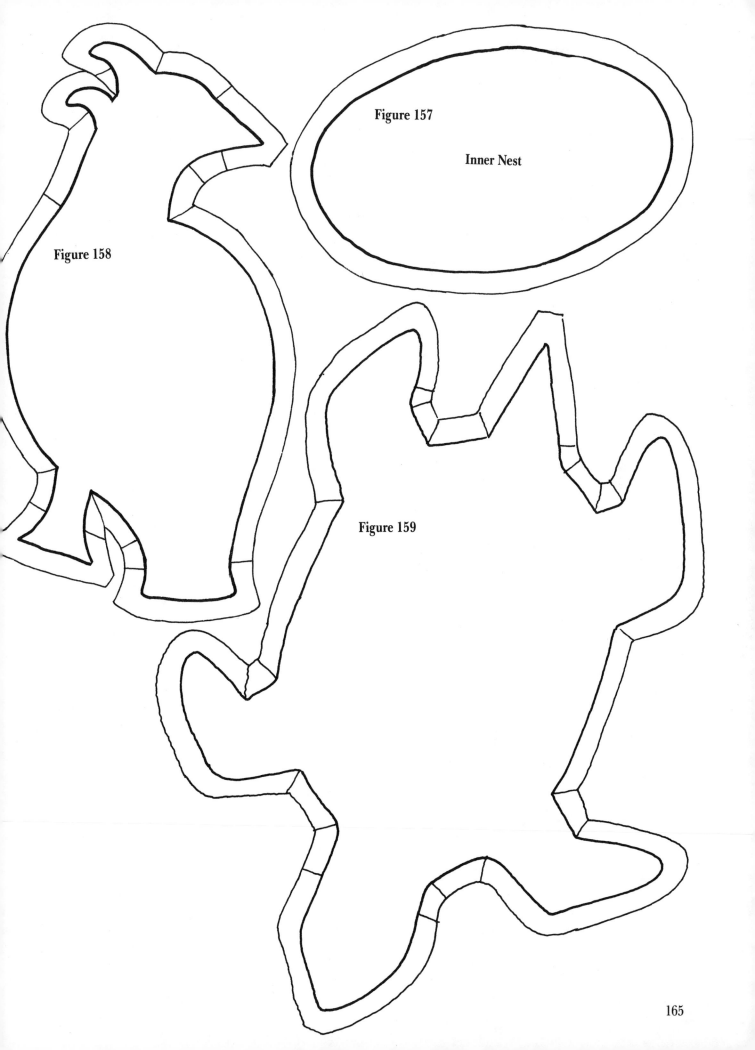

Figure 157

Inner Nest

Figure 158

Figure 159

165

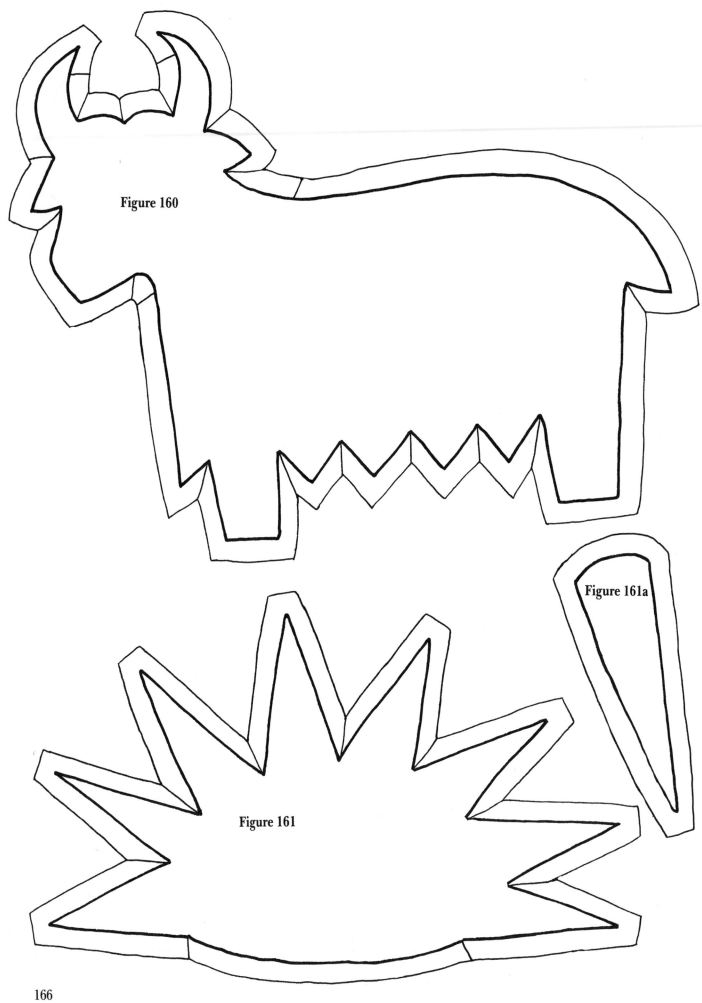

Figure 160

Figure 161a

Figure 161

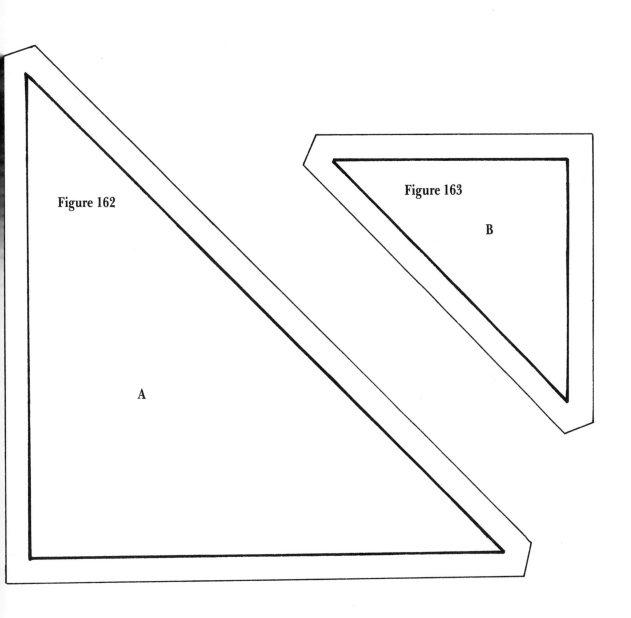

Figure 162

A

Figure 163

B

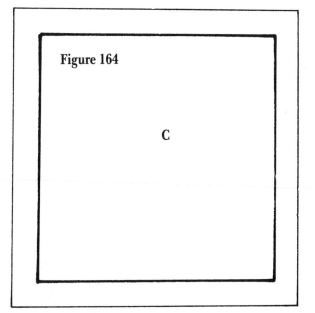

Figure 164

C

Figure 165

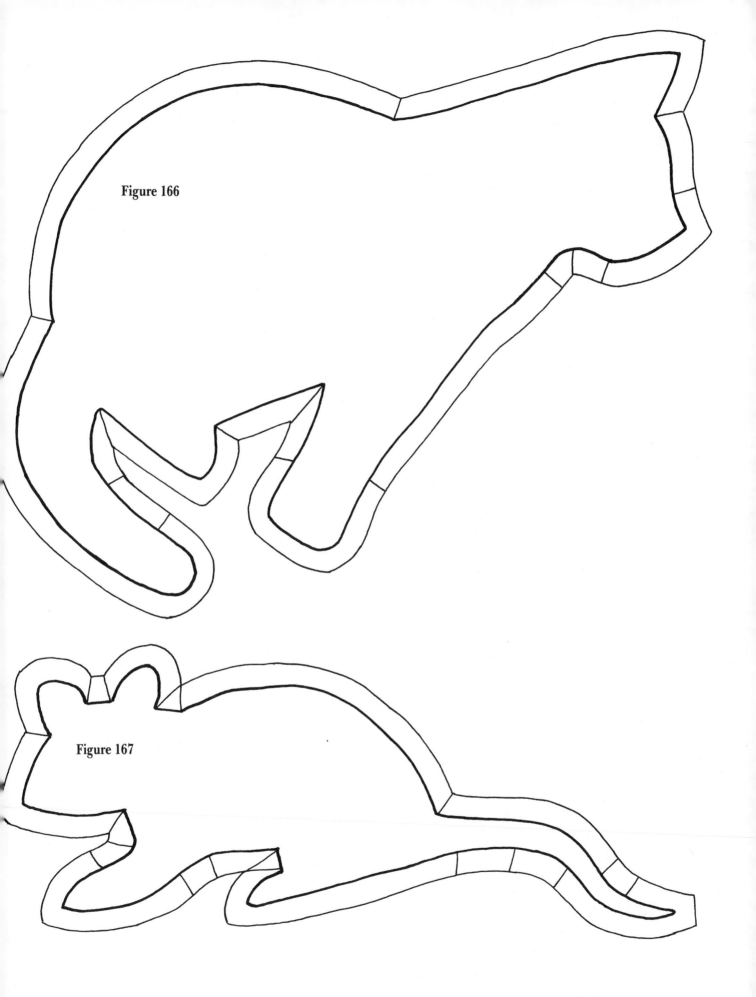

Figure 166

Figure 167

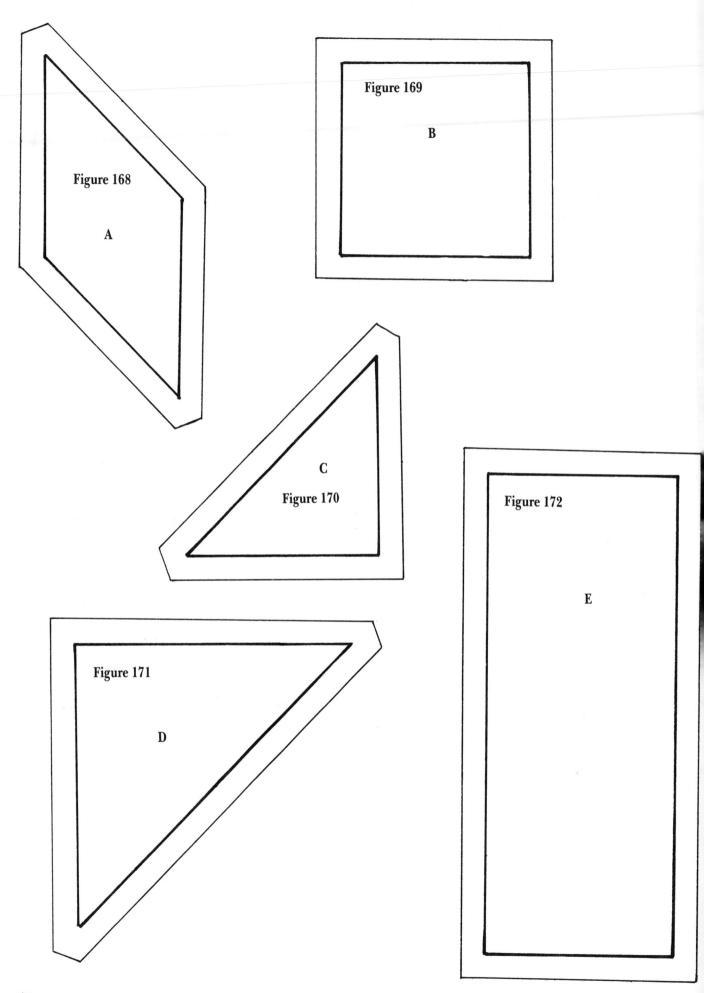

Figure 168

A

Figure 169

B

Figure 170

C

Figure 171

D

Figure 172

E

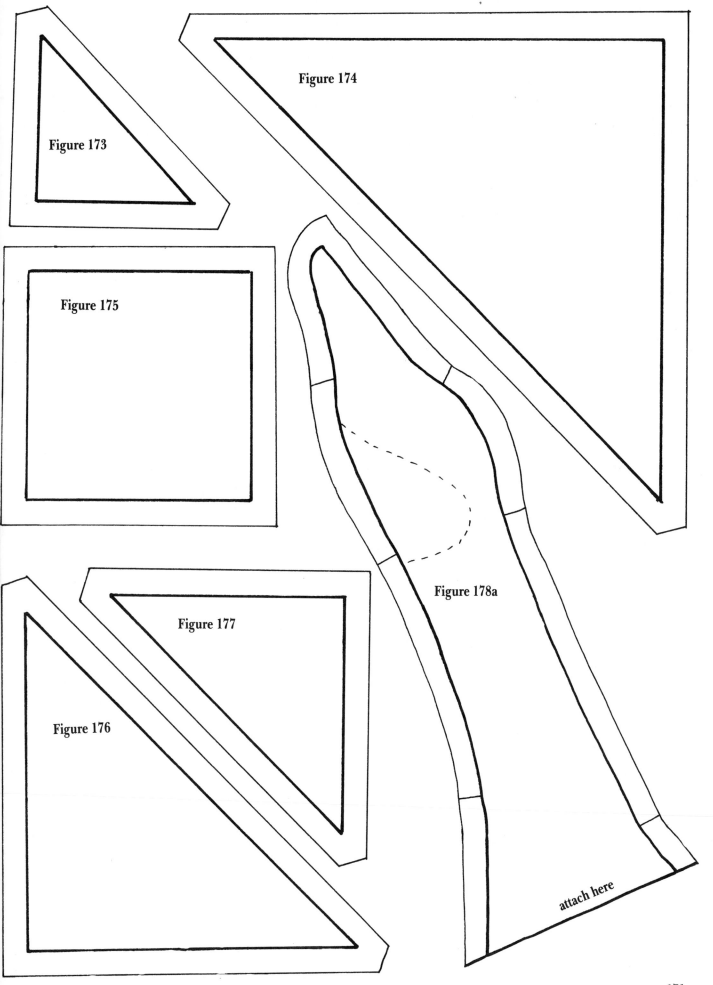

Figure 173

Figure 174

Figure 175

Figure 177

Figure 176

Figure 178a

attach here

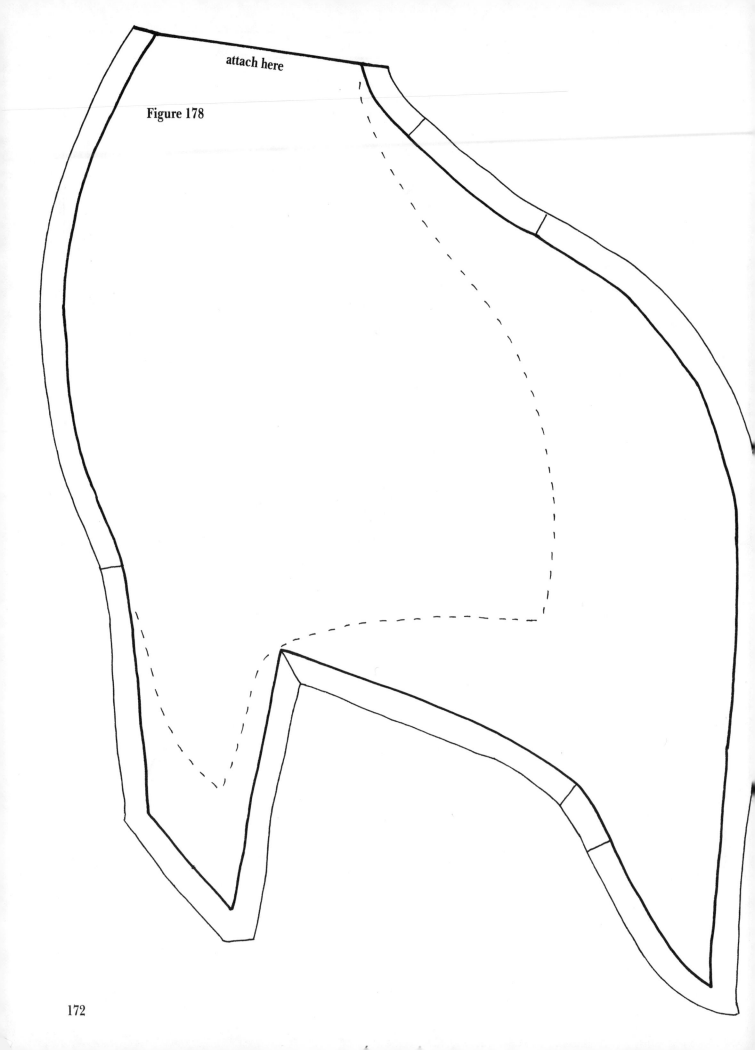

attach here

Figure 178

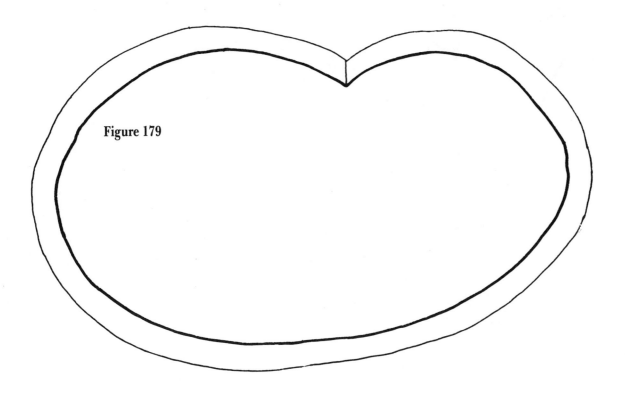

Figure 179

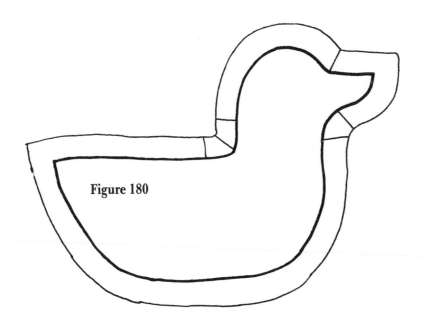

Figure 180

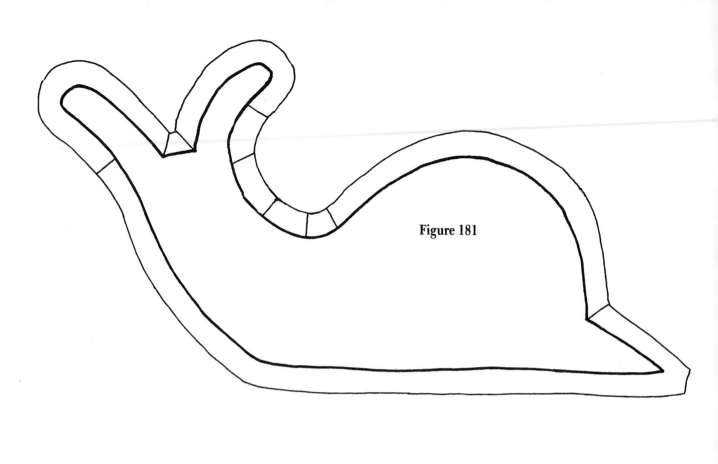

Figure 181

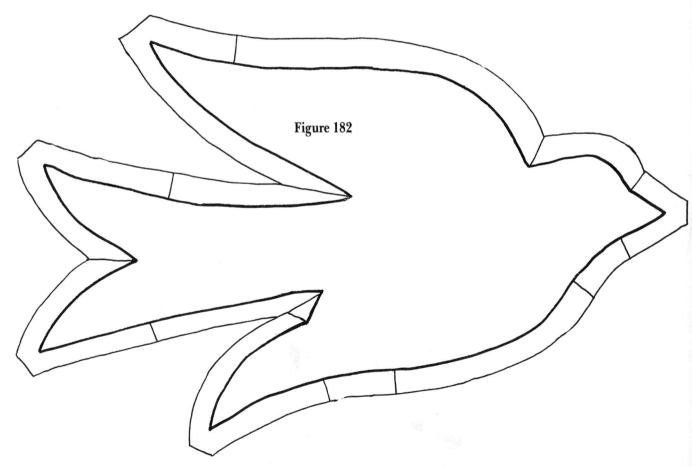

Figure 182

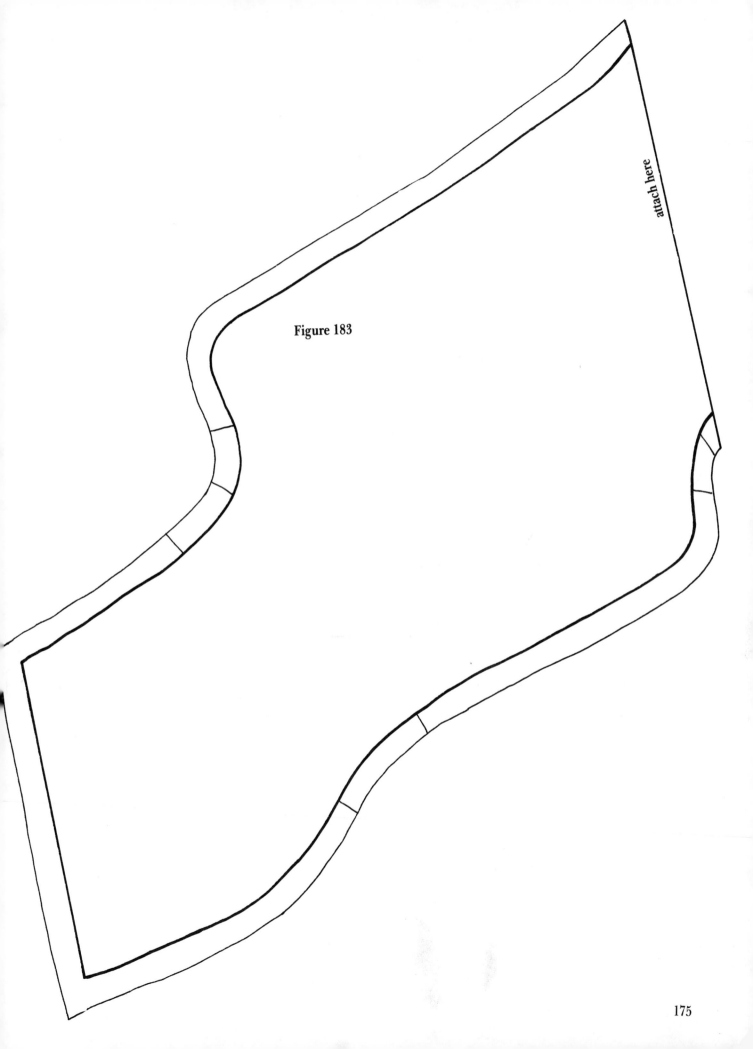

Figure 183

attach here

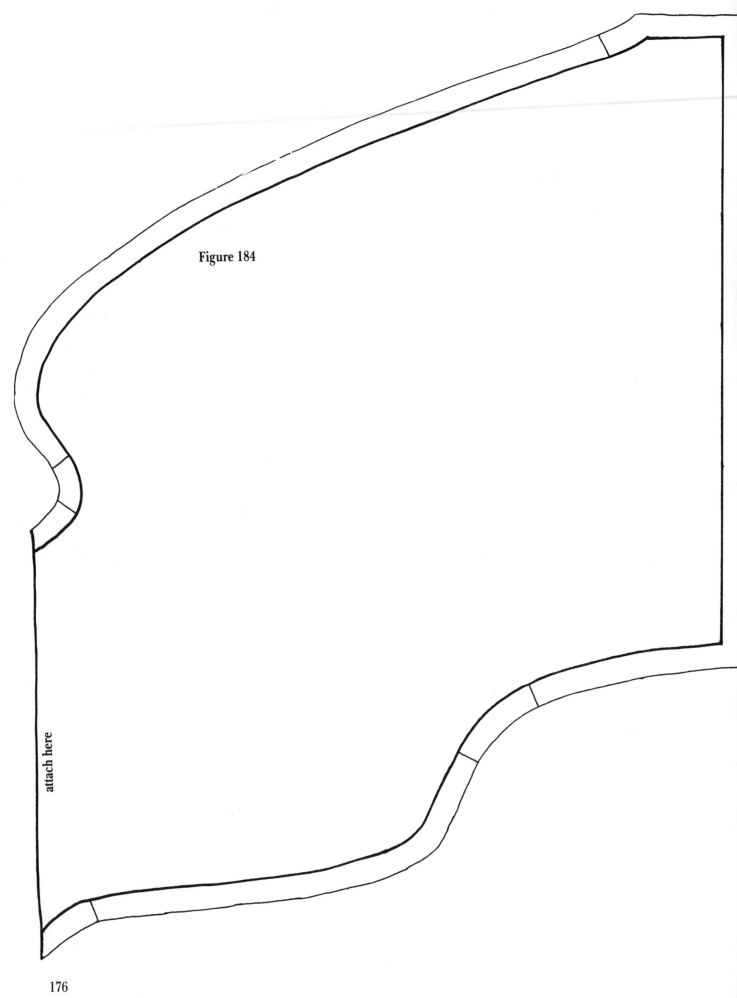

Figure 184

attach here

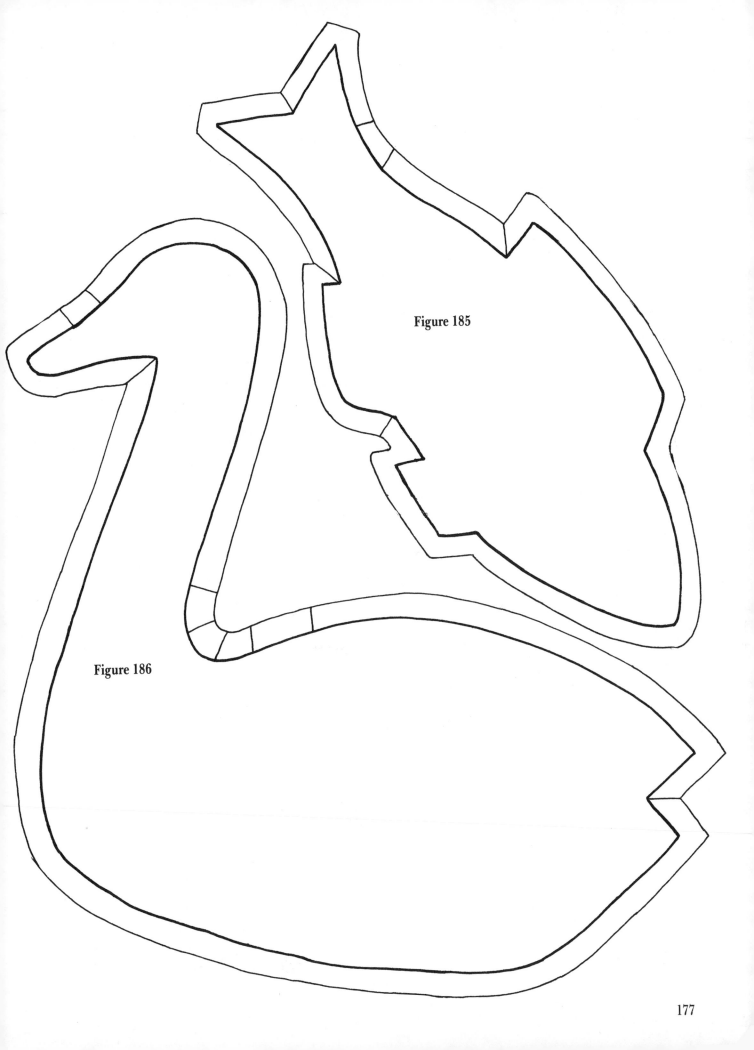

Figure 185

Figure 186

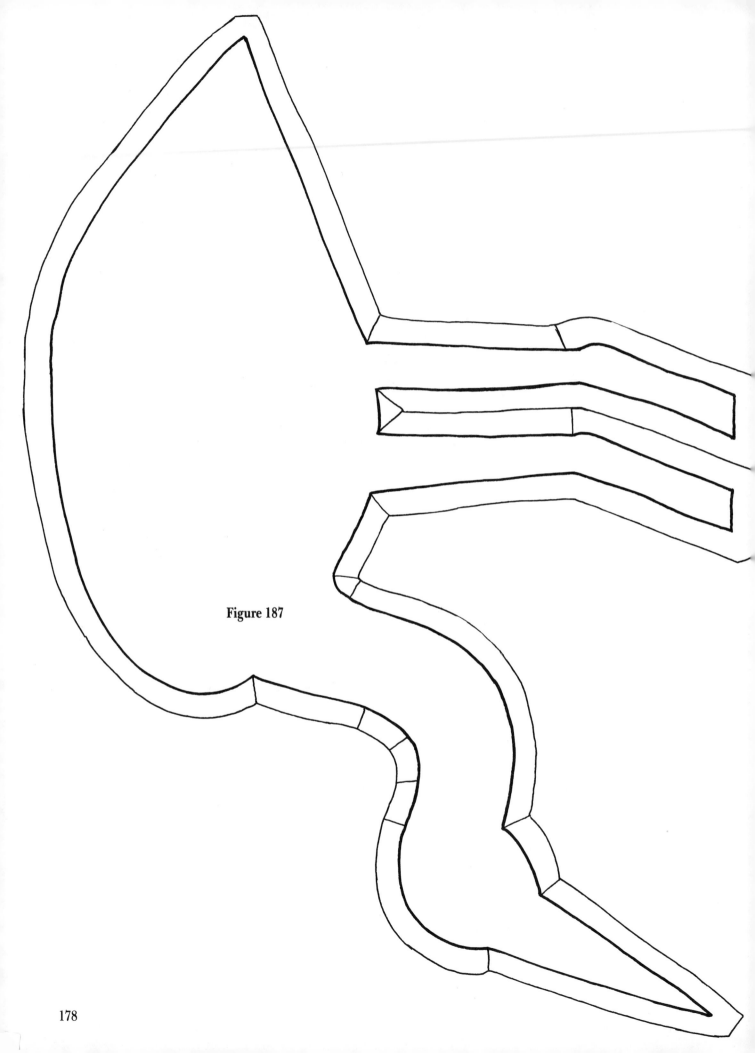

Figure 187

Figure 188

179

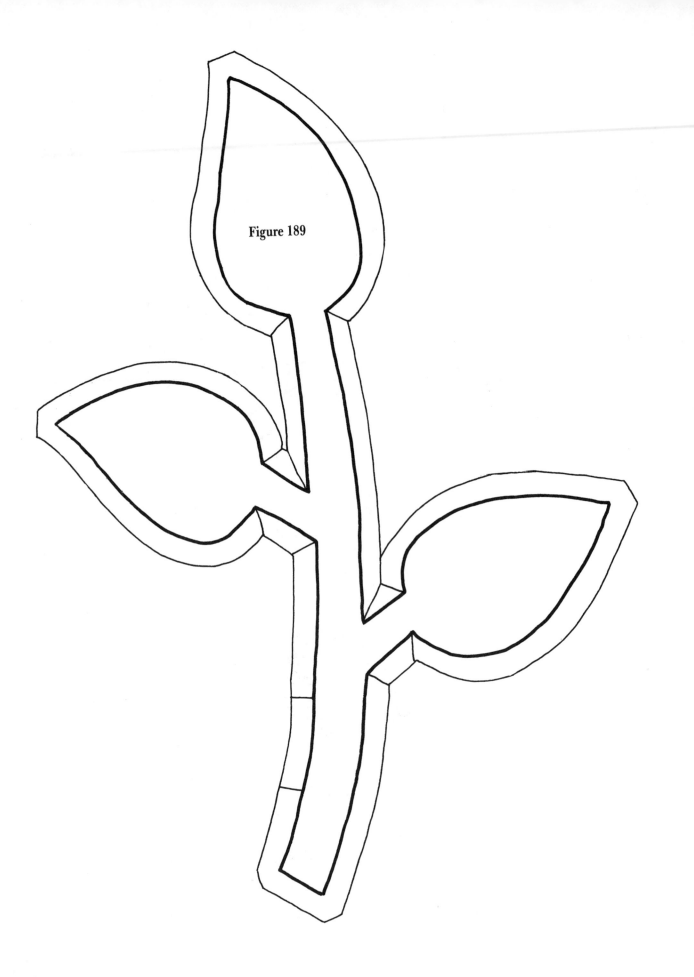

Figure 189

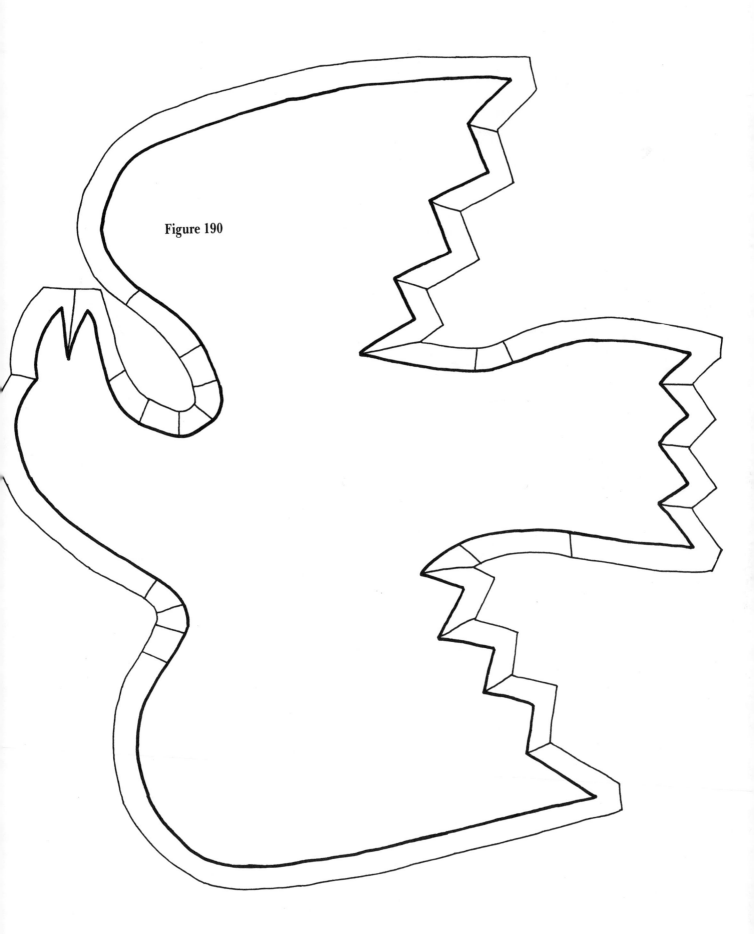

Figure 190

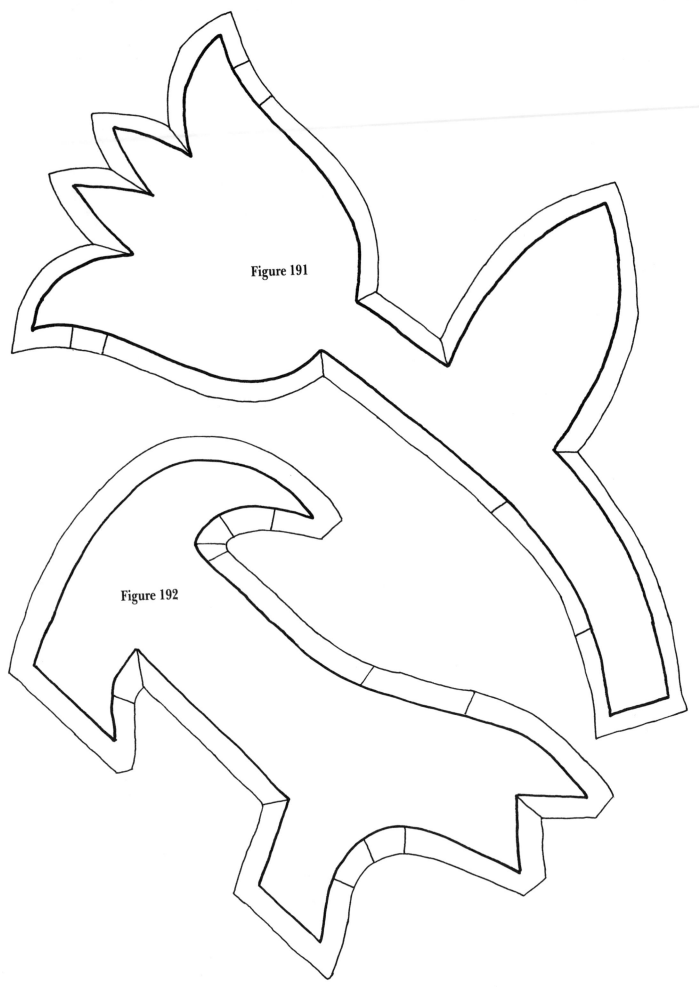

Figure 191

Figure 192

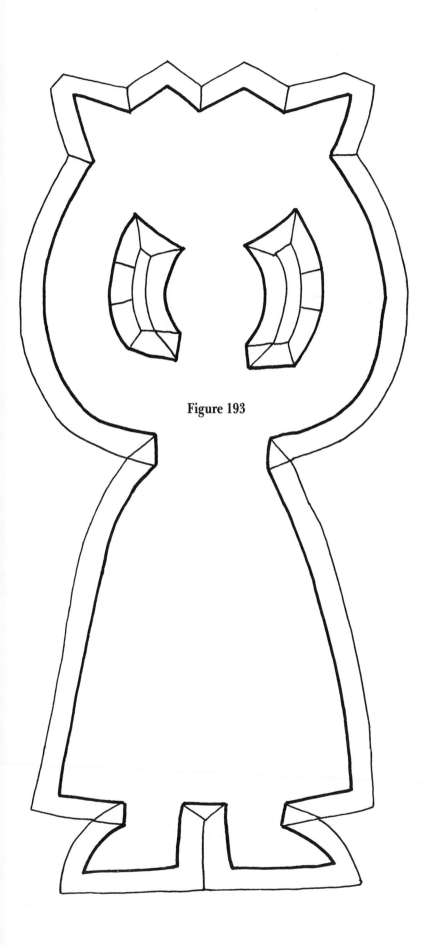

Figure 193

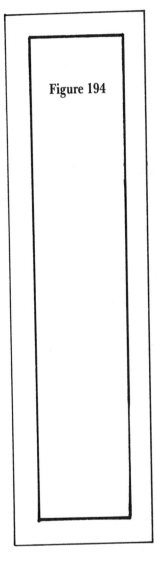

Figure 194

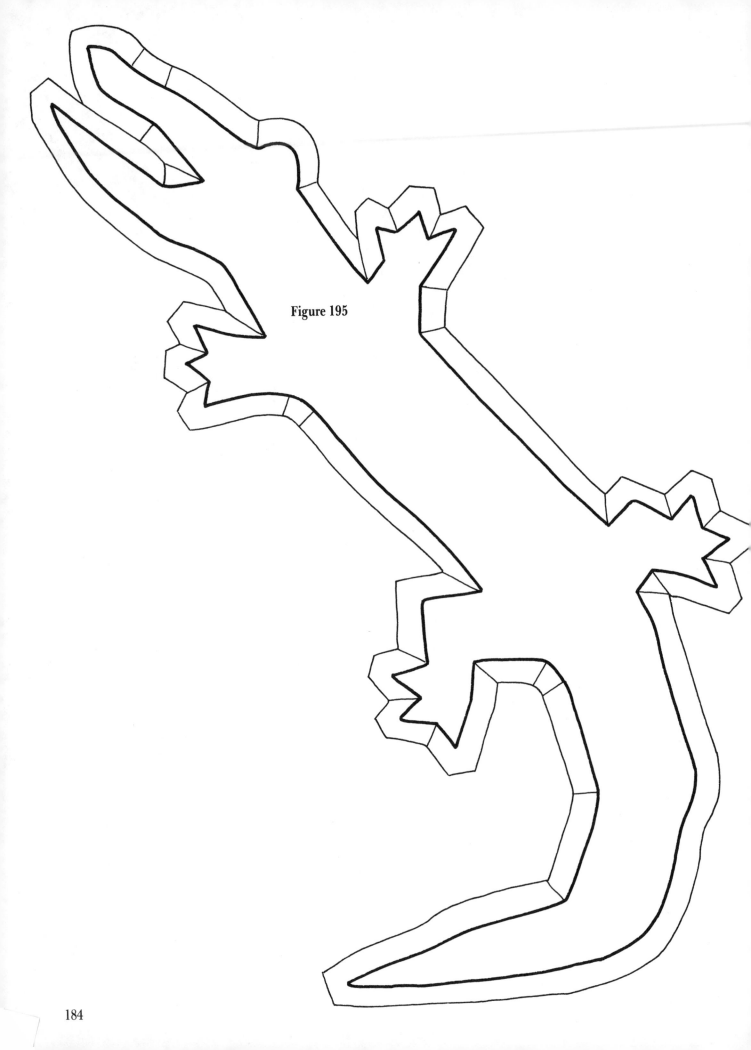

Figure 195

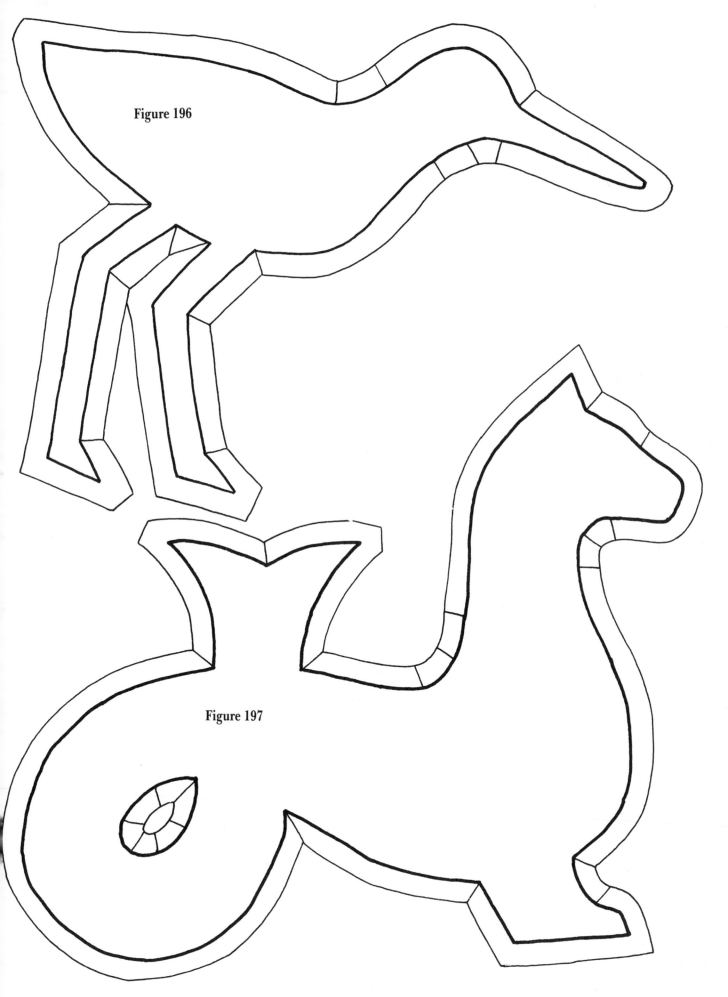

Figure 196

Figure 197

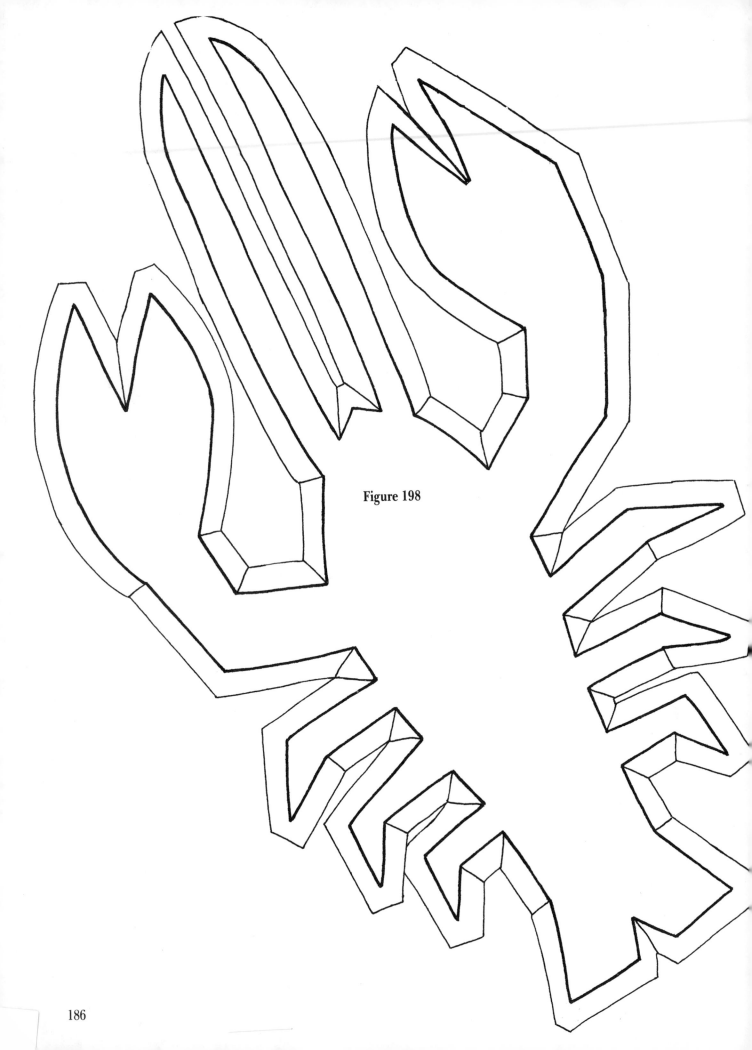

Figure 198

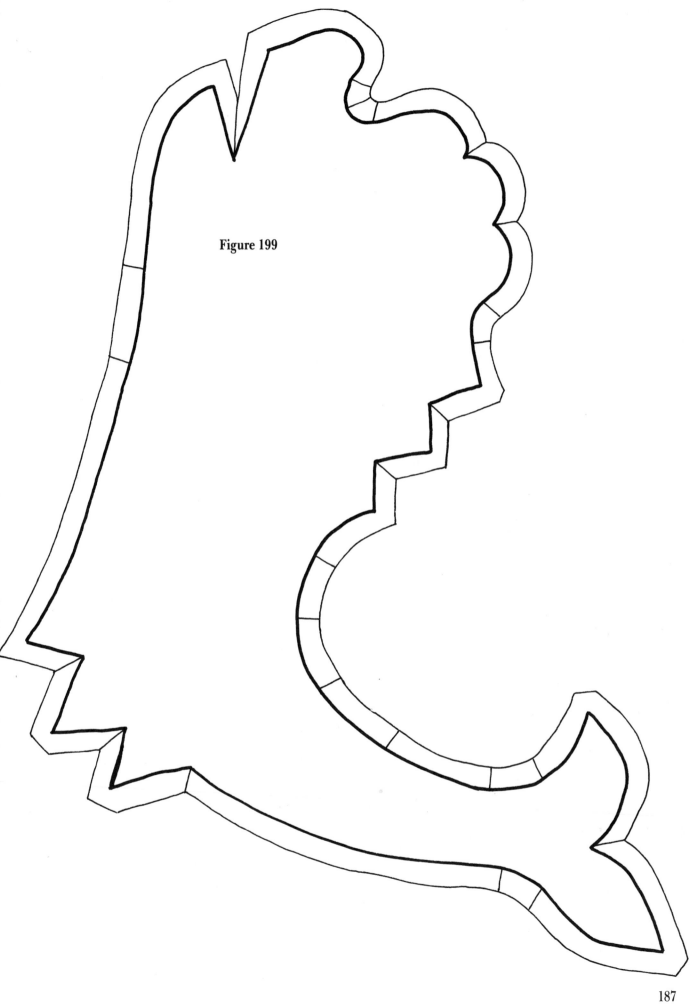

Figure 199

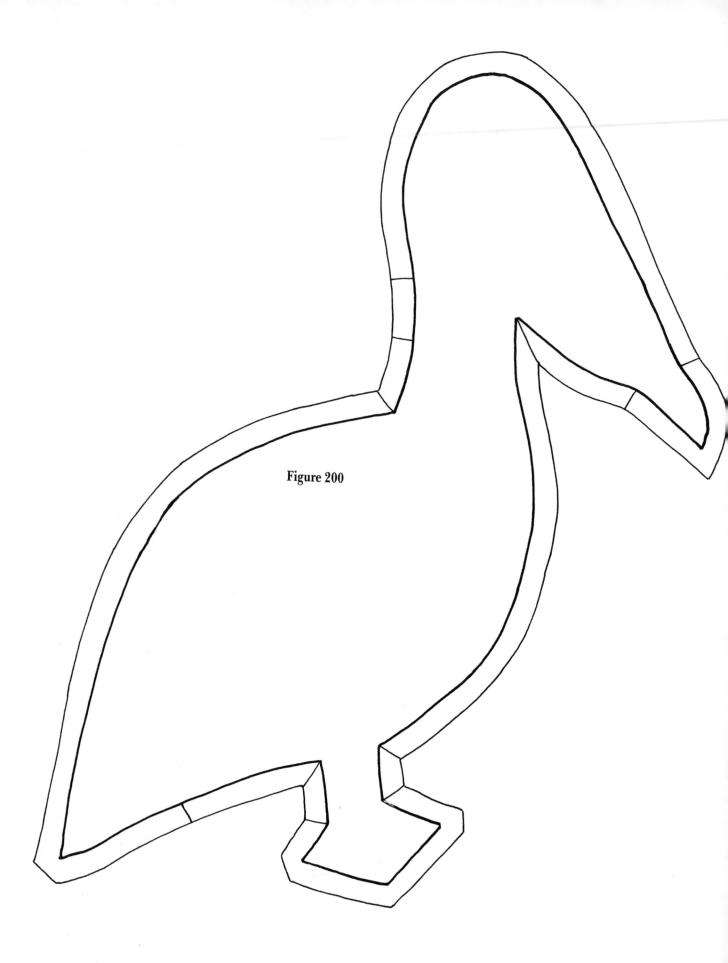

Figure 200

Readings and Sources

About Animal Quilts

Adams, Dr. Monni. "Harriet Powers' Bible Quilts." *The Clarion,* Spring 1982.

Bacon, Lenice Ingram. **American Patchwork Quilts.** New York: William Morrow and Co., 1973.

Bank, Mirra. **Anonymous Was a Woman.** New York: St. Martin's Press, 1979.

Binney, Edwin, 3rd, and Gail Binney-Winslow. **Homage to Amanda.** San Francisco: R K Press, 1984.

Bishop, Robert. **New Discoveries in American Quilts.** New York: Dutton and Co., 1975.

Carlisle, Lilian Baker. **Quilts at Shelburne Museum.** Shelburne, Vermont: Shelburne Museum Publications, 1957.

Johnson, Bruce. **The American Cat-alogue: The Cat in American Folk Art.** New York: Avon Books, 1976.

Kiracofe, Roderick, and Michael Kile, eds. **The Quilt Digest,** vols. 1, 2, and 3. San Francisco: Kiracofe and Kile, 1983, 1984, 1985.

McMorris, Penny. **Crazy Quilts.** New York: E. P. Dutton, 1984.

Nelson, Cyril I. **The Quilt Engagement Calendar,** vol. 1975–1985. New York: E. P. Dutton.

Nelson, Cyril I., and Carter Houck. **Treasury of American Quilts.** New York: Greenwich House, 1982.

Orlovsky, Patsy, and Myron Orlovsky. **Quilts in America.** New York: McGraw-Hill Co., 1974.

Safford, Carleton L., and Robert Bishop. **America's Quilts and Coverlets.** New York: Weathervane Books, 1974.

Weissman, Dr. Judith Reiter. "Anonymous Beauty: Quilts, Coverlets and Bedcovers Shown at the Museum of American Folk Art." *The Clarion,* Spring/Summer 1981.

Woodard, Thomas K., and Blanche Greenstein. **Crib Quilts and Other Small Wonders.** New York: Dutton and Co., 1981.

About Folk Art and Design Sources

Bishop, Robert. **American Folk Sculpture.** New York: Dutton and Co., 1974.

—, and Patricia Coblentz. **A Gallery of American Weathervanes and Whirligigs.** New York: Dutton and Co., 1981.

Carrick, Alice. **Shades of Our Ancestors.** Boston: Little, Brown and Co., 1928.

Christensen, Erwin O. **Index of American Design.** New York: Macmillan, 1950.

Cowart, Jack, and Jack D. Flam, Dominique Fourcade, and John Hallmark Neff. **Henri Matisse Paper Cut-Outs.** St. Louis, Missouri: The St. Louis Art Museum and the Detroit Institute of the Arts, 1977.

Dewhurst, C. Kurt, and Betty and Marsha MacDowell. **Artists in Aprons, Folk Art by American Women.** New York: Dutton and Co., 1979.

Elderfield, John. **The Cut-Outs of Henri Matisse.** New York: George Braziller, 1978.

Emmerling, Mary Ellisor. **American Country, a Style and Source Book.** New York: C. N. Potter, 1980.

Fjelstul, Alice Bancroft, and Patricia Brown Shad. **Early American Wall Stencils in Color.** New York: E. P. Dutton, 1982.

Gowing, Lawrence. **Matisse.** New York: Oxford University Press, 1979.

Graften, Carol Belanger. **Silhouettes.** New York: Dover Publications, 1979.

—. **More Silhouettes.** New York: Dover Publications, 1981.

Hopf, Claudia. **Scherenschnitte, Traditional Papercutting.** Lebanon, Pennsylvania: Applied Arts Publishers, 1982.

Horwitz, Elinor Lander. **Contemporary American Folk Artists.** Philadelphia and New York: J. B. Lippincott Co., 1975.

Kauffman, Henry J. **Pennsylvania Dutch American Folk Art.** New York: Dover Publications, Inc., 1964.

Kayne, Myrna. **Yankee Weathervanes.** New York: Dutton and Co., 1975.

Lasansky, Jeannette. **To Cut, Piece and Solder.** Lewisburg, Pennsylvania: An Oral Traditions Project of the Union County Historical Society, 1982.

Lichten, Frances. **Folk Art of Rural Pennsylvania.** New York: Charles Scribner's Sons, Inc., 1946.

Lipman, Jean. **American Folk Art in Wood, Metal and Stone.** New York: Dover Publications, Inc., 1972.

—, and Alice Winchester. **The Flowering of American Folk Art. New York: Viking Press, 1974.

Lord, Pricilla Sawyer, and Daniel J. Foley. **The Folk Arts and Crafts of New England.** New York: Chilton Books, Inc., 1975.

Marshall, Jo. **Kitchenware.** Radnor, Pennsylvania: Chilton Book Co., 1976.

McClinton, Katharine Morrison. **Antique Cats for Collectors.** Guildford and London: Lutterworth Press, 1973.

Modley, Rudolf, with William R. Myers. **Handbook of Pictorial Symbols.** New York: Dover Publications, Inc., 1976.

Riecken, Susan. **A Baker's Dozen: A Sampler of Early American Cookie Cut-Outs.** Cambridge, Massachusetts: Steam Press, 1982.

Russell, John. **The World of Matisse.** New York: Time-Life Books, 1969.

Swan, Susan Burrows. **Plain and Fancy: American Women and Their Needlework, 1700–1850.** New York: Holt, Rinehart and Winston, 1977.

— . **A Winterthur Guide to American Needlework.** New York: Crown Publishers, 1976.

Thuro, Catherine. **Primitives and Folk Art: Our Handmade Heritage.** Paducah, Kentucky: Collector Books, Inc., 1979.

Westervelt, A. B., and W. T. Westervelt. **American Antique Weathervanes: The Complete Illustrated Westervelt Catalog of 1883.** New York: Dover Publications, 1982.

Wheeler, Monroe. **The Last Works of Henri Matisse: Large Cut Gouaches.** New York: The Museum of Modern Art, 1961.

About Quiltmaking

Carroll, Amy, ed. **The Pattern Library: Patchwork and Applique.** New York: Ballantine Books, 1981.

Colby, Averil. **Patchwork.** London: B. T. Batsford, Ltd., 1973.

Houck, Carter, and Myron Miller. **American Quilts and How to Make Them.** New York: Charles Scribner's Sons, 1975.

Ickis, Marguerite. **The Standard Book of Quilt Making and Collecting.** New York: Dover Publications, Inc., 1959.

Lane, Rose Wilder. **Woman's Day Book of American Needlework.** New York: Simon and Schuster, 1963.

Laury, Jean Ray. **Quilts and Coverlets: A Contemporary Approach.** New York: Van Nostrand Reinhold, 1970.

Newman, Thelma R. **Quilting, Patchwork, Applique and Trapunto.** New York: Crown Publishers, 1974.

Pellman, Rachel T. **Amish Quilt Patterns.** Intercourse, Pennsylvania: Good Books, 1984.

— . **Small Amish Quilt Patterns.** Intercourse, Pennsylvania: Good Books, 1985.

Pellman, Rachel, and Kenneth Pellman. **Amish Crib Quilts.** Intercourse, Pennsylvania: Good Books, 1985.

— . **The World of Amish Quilts.** Intercourse, Pennsylvania: Good Books, 1984.

Tomlonson, Judy Schroeder. **Mennonite Quilts and Pieces.** Intercourse, Pennsylvania: Good Books, 1985.

Women, Quilts and History

Cooper, Patricia, and Norma Bradley Buferd. **The Quilters, Women and Domestic Art.** New York: Doubleday, 1977.

Earle, Alice Morse. **Customs and Fashions in Old New England.** Rutland, Vermont: Charles E. Tuttle Co., 1973.

Finley, Ruth. **Old Patchwork Quilts and the Women Who Made Them.** Newton Center, Massachusetts: Charles T. Branford, 1971.

Stratton, Joanna L. **Pioneer Women.** New York: Simon and Schuster, 1981.

Index

African Plains Scene, 59
Album Tree, 28
"American country," 8, 10, 14
American Eagle, 73
American Revolution, 9, 13
Angell, George, 10
ANIMAL ALPHABET, 62
Animal Alphabet Quilt, 63
ANIMALS AT OUR HOUSE, 60
Animals' Christmas Tree, 33
Animals Down Under, 59
ANIMAL TOWN, 34
ANIMAL TREE, THE, 26
Animal welfare movement, 10
Applique—basic techniques, 20
Applique (by hand), 21
Applique (by machine), 21
Appliqued border, 21
Appliques (for clothing), 80
At the Seashore, 36

Baby Ducks, 72
Batting, 22
Bear in the Woods, 53
Bergh, Henry, 10
Binding, 24–25
Block quilts, 16, 32, 61, 62, 63, 64, 65, 66
Blocks, setting, 22
Book Cover, 80
Borders, 21
Broderie Perse, 9
Brown, William Henry, 12

Canadian Geese, 69
CATS AND MICE, 66
Cats and Mice Pillow, 67
Cats and Mice Quilt, 67
Choosing fabric, 20
Cider Time, 50
Cohoon, Hannah, 30
Color fastness, 20
Contour quilting, 23
Contrast, 17–18, 22
Cookie cutters, 14, 15
Crazy quilts, 6, 10
Creating designs, 16
Crib quilts, 6, 10, 29, 32, 54, 56, 61, 62, 63

Depression, The, 10
Design sources, 11, 12, 13, 14, 15, 16
DOWN ON THE FARM, 49
Ducks in the Marsh, 45

Eighteenth century, 9, 12, 13
Elephants on the Move, 59
Enlarging templates, 25
Estimating fabric, 20
Estimating size, 20
European Style Folk Design, 61

Fabric, choosing, 20

Fabric, estimating, 20
Fabric pictures, 17, 18
Fairy Tale Castle, 53
Farming/farms, 8, 9, 14
Florida Shore, 77
Flower Tree, 32
FLYING GEESE, 68
Folk art, American, 8, 10, 11
FOLK TREE, THE, 30
FOX AND GEESE, 64
Fox and Geese or Goose Tracks Pillow, 65
Fox and Geese or Goose Tracks Quilt, 65
Fruit Tree, 31

Goose Tracks, 65
Graphic symbols, 15
GULLS ON THE WATER, 42

Hen, Rooster and Chicks, 51
Heron in the Pond, 72
House Block Crib Quilt, 61
Hummingbird and Butterflies, 41
HUMMINGBIRD AND FLOWERS, 40

"Iconic" (pictorial) symbols, 16
Irregular block quilt, 70, 72, 73, 74, 76, 77

Jefferson, Thomas, 8
Jungle Twin Bed Quilt, 59

LA PALOMA, 74

Making templates, 20
Mather, Cotton, 8
Matisse cutouts, 16, 20
Matisse, Henri, 12, 16
Mitering corners, 25
Mothers and Babies, 51

NIGHT IN THE FOREST, 52
Night Scene, 45
Nineteenth century, 6, 8, 9, 13
NOAH'S ARK, 54
Noah's Ark Border Quilt, 56
Noah's Ark with Removable Toy Animals, 56

OUT OF AFRICA, 57
Outline quilting, 24

Papyrotamia (paper-cutting), 12
Partridge in a Pear Tree, 29
Patchwork, 17, 21–22
Pelican on the Ocean, 44
Penguin Mother and Babies, 39
Pennsylvania German (PA Dutch), 12
Perspective, 18
Picasso, Pablo, 12, 14
Picture quilts, 6, 9, 10, 17
Pillows, 65, 67
Pioneer women, 6, 9
Placemats, 78

Planning designs, 19
POND, THE, 70
Porpoise Mother and Baby, 39
Potholders, 78

Quilt batting, 22
Quilt care, 22
Quilting, 22
Quilting by section, 24
Quilting, contour, 23
Quilting, expression of religious sentiment in, 10
Quilting frames, 23
Quilting hoops, 23
Quilting, outline, 24
Quilting patterns, 23
Quilting, significance to women of, 9
Quilting templates, 23

Riding Scene, 51

Scherenschnitte (scissors cuttings), 12
SEAL MOTHER AND BABY, 37
Setting blocks, 22
Sewing organizer, 79
Shawl, 79
SHORE, THE, 76
Shrinking templates, 25
Silhouettes, 12
Songbirds by the Pond, 72
Stencils, 13
Strip-pieced Tree, 33
Swans a-Swimming, 72

Teasing the Cows, 51
Templates, making, 20
Templates, quilting, 23
Theorems/theorem painting—see "Stencils"
Tote bag, 79
Toys, 15
Tracing patterns, 20, 25
Transfer-grid process, 19
Transferring designs (onto fabric), 20
Tree Full of Birds, 28
Two-dimension vs. three-dimension, 12, 18

Under Sahara Stars, 48

Valentines, 13
Victorian Era, 10

Weather vanes, 14
Wild Animals in Town, 36
Wolves and Crescent Moon, 48
WOLVES AND THE RISING MOON, 46

Yardage requirements, 11

UPPER CASE = project name
italic = project variation name

About the Author

Willow Ann Soltow is a writer and quiltmaker from Ithaca, New York. A former editor for The Humane Society of the United States, her interest in animals and in animal welfare grew out of her childhood experiences, living in a family that included a variety of rescued and adopted stray animals. She continues to help animals through the auspices of her local Humane Society.

Willow shares an interest in quilts and folk art with her husband, Ted. A graduate of Brown University, she is the author of *The Not For Kids Only Quilt Book.* Her articles and stories have appeared in such magazines as *Quilt, The Best of Quilt, Quilt World, Children & Animals,* and *Highlights Magazine for Children.*